MW00681760

UNEQUAL PROTECTION

The State Response to Violent Crime on South African Farms

Human Rights Watch
New York • Washington • London • Brussels

ISBN: 1-56432-263-7
Library of Congress Control Number: 2001093393

Cover design by Rafael Jiménez

Addresses for Human Rights Watch:
350 Fifth Avenue, 34th Floor, New York, New York 10118-3299
Tel: +1 (212) 290-4700, Fax: +1 (212) 736-1300, E-mail: hrwnyc@hrw.org

1630 Connecticut Avenue, N.W., Suite 500, Washington, D.C. 20009
Tel: +1 (202) 612-4321, Fax: +1 (202) 612-4333, E-mail: hrwdc@hrw.org

33 Islington High Street, London N1 9LH, UK
Tel: +44 (20) 7713-1995, Fax: +44 (20) 7713-1800, E-mail: hrwuk@hrw.org

15 Rue Van Campenhout, Brussels 1000, Belgium
Tel:+32 (2) 732-2009, Fax: +32 (2) 732-0471, E-mail: hrweu@hrw.org

Web Site Address: http://www.hrw.org

Listserv address: To subscribe to the list, send an e-mail message to
majordomo@igc.apc.org with "subscribe hrw-news" in the body of the message
(leave the subject line blank).

Human Rights Watch is dedicated to
protecting the human rights of people around the world.

We stand with victims and activists to prevent
discrimination, to uphold political freedom, to protect people from
inhumane conduct in wartime, and to bring offenders to justice.

We investigate and expose
human rights violations and hold abusers accountable.

We challenge governments and those who hold power to end
abusive practices and respect international human rights law.

We enlist the public and the international
community to support the cause of human rights for all.

HUMAN RIGHTS WATCH

Human Rights Watch conducts regular, systematic investigations of human rights abuses in some seventy countries around the world. Our reputation for timely, reliable disclosures has made us an essential source of information for those concerned with human rights. We address the human rights practices of governments of all political stripes, of all geopolitical alignments, and of all ethnic and religious persuasions. Human Rights Watch defends freedom of thought and expression, due process and equal protection of the law, and a vigorous civil society; we document and denounce murders, disappearances, torture, arbitrary imprisonment, discrimination, and other abuses of internationally recognized human rights. Our goal is to hold governments accountable if they transgress the rights of their people.

Human Rights Watch began in 1978 with the founding of its Europe and Central Asia division (then known as Helsinki Watch). Today, it also includes divisions covering Africa, the Americas, Asia, and the Middle East. In addition, it includes three thematic divisions on arms, children's rights, and women's rights. It maintains offices in New York, Washington, Los Angeles, London, Brussels, Moscow, Dushanbe, and Bangkok. Human Rights Watch is an independent, nongovernmental organization, supported by contributions from private individuals and foundations worldwide. It accepts no government funds, directly or indirectly.

The staff includes Kenneth Roth, executive director; Michele Alexander, development director; Reed Brody, advocacy director; Carroll Bogert, communications director; Barbara Guglielmo, finance director; Jeri Laber special advisor; Lotte Leicht, Brussels office director; Michael McClintock, deputy program director; Patrick Minges, publications director; Maria Pignataro Nielsen, human resources director; Jemera Rone, counsel; Malcolm Smart, program director; Wilder Tayler, general counsel; and Joanna Weschler, United Nations representative. Jonathan Fanton is the chair of the board. Robert L. Bernstein is the founding chair.

The regional directors of Human Rights Watch are Peter Takirambudde, Africa; José Miguel Vivanco, Americas; Sidney Jones, Asia; Holly Cartner, Europe and Central Asia; and Hanny Megally, Middle East and North Africa. The thematic division directors are Joost R. Hiltermann, arms; Lois Whitman, children's; and Regan Ralph, women's.

The members of the board of directors are Jonathan Fanton, chair; Lisa Anderson, Robert L. Bernstein, David M. Brown, William Carmichael, Dorothy Cullman, Gina Despres, Irene Diamond, Adrian W. DeWind, Fiona Druckenmiller, Edith Everett, Michael E. Gellert, Vartan Gregorian, Alice H. Henkin, James F. Hoge, Stephen L. Kass, Marina Pinto Kaufman, Bruce Klatsky, Joanne Leedom-Ackerman, Josh Mailman, Yolanda T. Moses, Samuel K. Murumba, Andrew Nathan, Jane Olson, Peter Osnos, Kathleen Peratis, Bruce Rabb, Sigrid Rausing, Orville Schell, Sid Sheinberg, Gary G. Sick, Malcolm Smith, Domna Stanton, John J. Studzinski, and Maya Wiley. Robert L. Bernstein is the founding chair of Human Rights Watch.

ACKNOWLEDGEMENTS

This report was written by Bronwen Manby, senior researcher in the Africa Division of Human Rights Watch, and the sections on discrimination against women and sexual violence by Rumbi Mabuwa, researcher in the Women's Rights Division of Human Rights Watch, based on research carried out in South Africa in April and September 2000. The section on the situation in Ixopo was written by Cheryl Goodenough, as a consultant to Human Rights Watch, and edited by Bronwen Manby. The report was edited by Peter Takirambudde, executive director of the Africa Division; by Regan Ralph and LaShawn Jefferson, executive director and deputy director of the Women's Rights Division; by James Ross, senior legal adviser; and by Malcolm Smart, program director. Maria Burnett-Gaudiani, Whitney Bryant, and Amanda Alexander proofread final versions. Tejal Jesrani formatted the report and prepared it for production.

The report would not have been possible without the collaboration and able assistance of the staff of the National Land Committee and its affiliated organizations. Jan Nolan, Tom Lebert, and Andile Mngxitama of the National Land Committee were central to the devising and implementation of the research and completion of the report. Maureen Moleya of the NLC was unfailingly efficient and helpful for all the administrative arrangements that had to be made. We would also like to thank in particular: Marc Wegerif, James Abhane and Shirhami Shirinda of the Nkuzi Development Association (Pietersburg); Musa Zwane of the Association for Rural Advancement (Pietermaritzburg); Alfred Ngomane of the Rural Action Committee (Nelspruit; now with Nkuzi); and Abdus Isaacs of the Surplus People Project (Cape Town). Other organizations also provided valuable assistance, including the Women on Farms Project, Lawyers for Human Rights, and the Centre for Rural Legal Studies (all in Stellenbosch). We would like to thank all those from the National Land Committee and other organizations who participated in a September 2000 workshop on the draft findings and recommendations of the report and gave their valuable insights. In particular, we acknowledge with respect and sadness the contribution of Alida van der Merwe, former director of the Centre for Rural Legal Studies and advocate for the rights of farmworkers, who died tragically in a car accident in June 2001.

We are also grateful for the assistance of the Transvaal Agricultural Union, the KwaZulu-Natal Agricultural Union, and Mike de Lange for setting up meetings with the owners of farms and smallholdings who have been victims of violent crime.

Many people gave their time to supply useful commentary and other information for the report, including in particular Jonny Steinberg, who generously shared the insights of his independent research, and also: Theunis Roux of the University of the Witwatersrand Faculty of Law; Bronwyn Page-Shipp of the Centre for Rural Legal Studies; Mary de Haas of the University of Natal Durban Department of Social Anthropology; Mark Shaw of the South African Institute of International Affairs; and Tom Karis and Stephen Ellmann of the Advisory Committee of the Africa Division of Human Rights Watch.

Human Rights Watch would like to thank the Ford Foundation and the Netherlands Organisation for International Development Cooperation (NOVIB) for their support for this report.

Last but not least, we would like to thank all those who gave their time to talk to us in the course of preparing this report, in particular both farm residents and farm owners who have been victims of violence.

South Africa

TABLE OF CONTENTS

SUMMARY

Violent crime on South Africa's farms has recently become a high profile media and political issue. Some of this attention has focused on assaults on farm residents by white farm owners, but the heightened interest has been driven mostly by a rise in violent crime against white farm owners. Since the early 1990s, there has been a marked increase in assaults and murders of the owners and managers of commercial farms and their families, disproportionate to general crime trends in South Africa. Several hundred white farmers have been murdered, mostly by strangers to their property. In the context of government-endorsed land invasions in neighboring Zimbabwe, some white farm owners have perceived this escalation in violent crime to be part of an organized conspiracy to drive them from the land, perhaps masterminded by elements within the government. The term "farm attacks," used by farm owners, police, and others to describe these crimes, has tended to reinforce this interpretation, by suggesting a terrorist or military purpose. Yet the available research shows that most crime against white farmers is criminally motivated, the perpetrators seeking firearms, money, or vehicles, and that the violence used is instrumental to these purposes. Farms, remote and scattered, are seen as easy targets. In a small number of cases, the motive may be revenge for eviction or past ill-treatment.

The new vulnerability of a group relatively protected from crime during the apartheid era, as well as the perceived political motivation for "farm attacks," led organizations representing commercial farmers to demand that the new African National Congress (ANC)-led government installed in 1994 take stronger action. These protests resulted first in the implementation of a "rural protection plan" in October 1997, and then in a "rural safety summit" in October 1998 called by then President Nelson Mandela. The rural safety summit endorsed the rural protection plan as the basis of a strategy to combat violent crime affecting farming communities, and called for a comprehensive policy framework to be developed to ensure long term safety. The rural protection plan coordinates the activities of the South African Police Service (SAPS), South African National Defence Force (SANDF), and farmers themselves in combating rural crime, and provides for regular police patrols of commercial farming areas. In many areas, white farm owners are also linked together by radio in security cells, often known as the "farmwatch" system. In some parts of South Africa, farmwatches are supported by commando units, a system of army reserve units made up largely of civilians who serve part-time in the security forces. In parallel with the implementation of the rural protection plan, the police began to distribute questionnaires to police stations in farming areas in order to collect statistics relating to "farm attacks"; that is, crime committed on farms by outsiders to the property.

1

The rural protection plan was presented as a comprehensive initiative aimed at addressing the concerns of all residents of commercial farming areas in relation to violent crime. In practice, however, the plan has significantly increased insecurity for black residents of and vistors to commercial farming areas, as they have become the targets of sometimes indiscriminate "anti-crime" initiatives. Members of the commandos, police reservists, full-time soldiers and police, and others participating in the rural protection plan have committed serious abuses against farmworkers and other farm residents. There are reports of abuses, ranging from the staging of illegal roadblocks to murder, by commando units in several areas, especially those operating in southern Mpumalanga and northern KwaZulu-Natal. Members of the Wakkerstroom commando, one of several commando units controlled by local farmers in this border region, are accused of assault, torture, forced and illegal evictions, and murder of farm residents.

In addition, the rural protection plan has largely failed to respond to crime committed against black farm residents, in particular crime committed by white farm owners. Yet farmworkers and residents on commercial farms in South Africa are frequently subjected to physical abuse by their employers and their agents. This abuse ranges from casual blows with fists for alleged mistakes in work or impertinence, to serious physical violence, including murder. While there are no reliable statistics relating to the number of assaults on farmworkers by their employers, and there has been no effort to collect such information similar to that in the case of "farm attacks," the problem is clearly widespread. Racial insults are routine. Rape of women employees by white farmers remains an unquantified problem. Rape and sexual assault of black women farmworkers or residents by other farmworkers or residents is common. A great deal of violence against farmworkers and residents takes place in the context of attempts to evict people from commercial farms in violation of new laws giving farm residents a degree of security of tenure—virtually all evictions are carried out under the actual or implied threat of force. Violence against farmworkers and residents is perpetrated not only by farm owners and managers, with whom they are in daily contact, but also by private security companies and vigilante groups hired by farm owners. Those seeking to uphold farmworkers' interests have also been harassed and assaulted when they have sought access to farms.

This report seeks to examine the state's response to violence on farms in comparative perspective, looking both at the response to violent crime against farm owners and at the response to violent crime against farm workers and other residents committed by farm owners. Assaults on black farm residents by other farm residents are also commonly reported, and in many farming areas these are among the crimes most frequently handled by the police. However, Human Rights

Watch focuses here on assaults by farm owners or managers against farm residents or workers both because of the particular significance attached to such assaults by farm residents themselves, and because the problems that farm residents have in accessing the criminal justice system are particularly acute in such cases. Although farm residents generally reported an inadequate response from the criminal justice system when they reported assaults, these problems were much worse when they attempted to report assaults carried out by (white) farm owners or managers.

Farmworkers and residents face great problems if they wish to report assaults by farm owners or managers, starting from a fear of retaliation should they speak out. The police are frequently unresponsive, sometimes hostile, and may even refuse to open a file. It is a common practice for a farmer accused of assault to file a "counter charge" such as theft, and for the police to hold the two to cancel each other out—even though this contravenes proper police practice. Police investigations of assaults on farmworkers or residents are often dilatory and inadequate; many prosecutors, who have the power to refer files back to the police for reinvestigation, seem prepared to accept substandard police investigations and all too easily to decline to prosecute. Often, where prosecutions have been sucessful, sentences applied have failed to reflect the seriousness of the offense. A crisis in the legal aid system, established to provide legal assistance for the indigent, has prevented many victims of assault or people facing eviction from obtaining legal representation to enforce their rights. As a consequence, farm owners and managers, private security company personnel, and police or army reservists who commit violence against black farmworkers and residents do so largely with impunity.

The state response to violent crime against farm owners is much more determined and effective—even if resource and other constraints mean that police response times are often too slow and police detective work inadequate, and that the state has therefore also relied on self-help initiatives from the farm owners. The police in commercial farming areas have been mobilized to treat crime against farm owners as a particular priority. The government has also endorsed the farmwatch system and the use of the commandos, which have in some cases played an important role in helping to protect farm owners and managers from violent crime and in catching those who have committed crimes against farm owners or managers. Indeed, the arrest rate in cases of violent crime against farm owners and managers is higher than in the case of most crimes committed in South Africa. As with other cases in the criminal justice system, too many of those arrested are not brought to trial despite a *prima facie* case against them; but, nonetheless, charges are more diligently pursued and investigated when the victim is a white farmer or farm manager than when the victim is a black farm resident, even where the crime committed is equally serious. Most of those convicted of violent crime against farm owners have been sentenced to long terms of imprisonment. Even so, white farm owners express dissatisfaction with the rural protection plan, which, as murders of farm owners continue, they see as inadequate.

Violent crime is a major problem in South Africa, with reported murder and rape at among the highest rates in the world. Crime rates do not differ significantly between rural and urban areas. In some rural areas, especially in KwaZulu-Natal, the effects of the former apartheid state's deliberate promotion of violence among black communities are still felt in continued "faction violence" between well-armed gangs, whose predations have long been suffered by black residents of the same areas, but are now spilling over, it seems, to affect white farmers.

In the face of this violence, and in common with other countries undergoing transition from autocratic rule, South Africa's criminal justice system is under severe strain. Despite efforts to demilitarize policing and instill a commitment to community service and human rights, the government has yet to be able to create an effective force devoted to the ideals of the new constitution. Community policing forums (CPFs) set up since 1994, at which police and community representatives sit together to sort out problems, have had only limited success in improving the accountability of police officers to the communities where they work. Police brutality and corruption remain depressingly common. Moreover, the police have severe resource constraints. Similarly, the transition to a new order has also been difficult for the court system, and delays in the criminal justice process have led to a vast backlog of cases awaiting trial, despite efforts by the National Director of Public Prosecutions (NDPP) to clear them. There are a disturbing number of cases in which dockets (case files) go "missing," apparently as a result of corruption among police or court officials. In response to these deficiencies, vigilante violence has become an increasing problem, with groups such as Mapogo a Mathamaga, founded in the Northern Province, rapidly becoming as much of a problem to society as the criminals which they originally targeted.

But the state's response to violent crime on farms cannot be viewed only in the context of the generally high rate of violent crime in South Africa. It is clearly influenced by factors such as race, gender, and socio-economic status. Farm owners and managers continue mostly to be white and much wealthier than farmworkers and other residents, invariably black and poor. During the apartheid years, state policies accentuated this divide, reinforcing the wealth and land ownership of the white farmer minority at the expense of the poor black majority, which was rendered largely landless by government policy. Today, apartheid has gone, but its legacy of inequality remains deeply rooted. Working conditions on farms vary, but mostly are poor. According to the government statistical service, people employed in agriculture are worse off than those in every other major sector of the economy. For black workers on farms, wages are low, housing poor, access to education difficult or non-existent, and health indicators bad.

The situation of women on farms is more precarious than that of men. Discrimination against women in the workplace is often linked to violence against them either at the workplace or in the home. The acute power imbalance on farms between farm owners and farmworkers, and between men and women, work to the disadvantage of women. Despite a court ruling that a woman farmworker could not be evicted because her husband lost his job on the same farm, women farmworkers' access to housing is still dependent, in practice, on their relationship to a man who is employed on the farm. Women are more likely to be seasonal or temporary workers than men, and usually carry out the less well-paid jobs, such as planting or harvesting, while men occupy the relatively prestigious positions, such as foremen or tractor drivers. Women are also discriminated against by being paid lower wages than men doing the same type of work or work of equal value. Many women are also denied maternity leave, although they have the right to four months' leave under the law: some are allowed only the absolute minimum time to give birth; others who do get permission to take leave do not obtain the benefits they are due from the Unemployment Insurance Fund.

Women farm workers' experience of gender discrimination thus intersects with racism. Rape and sexual harassment of black women when perpetrated by farm owners and managers amounts to a type of "superexploitation" of women by those who have dominance over them in their homes or workplaces. Women's dependence on men for access to housing and employment renders them vulnerable to abuse within the workplace and home by their male co-workers and partners. Many women who are raped or sexually abused fear to report the crime. To do so could be to risk dismissal or eviction. But even when women do seek protection from the criminal justice system, they face bias and obstruction from officials; blame from their family and the community, and possible retaliation from the perpetrators. Many women are unaware of their rights; and they lack access to information and social support services.

Under the apartheid system, white farmers could rely on the support of the state, including the police and army, to ensure control over their labor. This historically close relationship to such state institutions is maintained today in many areas: because farm owners are economically much more powerful than their black neighbors, they continue to hold a privileged position. Even where black police officers have been promoted and appointed as station commissioners, the economic realities of rural life mean that taking action against locally powerful figures is potentially hazardous. For the same reason, white farm owners who complain of criminal activity that affects them usually receive priority attention, even from black police station commissioners. Thus, implementation of the rural protection plan still shows its origins as a response to the demands of white farm owners for action, rather than to the needs of the all those living in commercial farming areas for protection against violent crime. In only a very few areas have those implementing the plan developed it in a way that seeks to respond effectively to the concerns of all sectors of the community; and even in those cases, control of the system is largely by white farm owners and businessmen.

The rural protection plan needs to be comprehensively restructured to take account not only of the needs the commercial farming community but also those of farm residents and those living in the former homeland areas, the "tribal reserves," that adjoin commercial farmland. In particular, the inadequacies of the police service must be addressed. The answer, however, is not to allow one powerful group effectively to take over the functions of the police by setting up parallel, essentially unaccountable structures. The criminal justice system must operate for the protection of all South Africans, irrespective of race, gender, or economic status.

The most pressing need is for the government to improve the quality of policing and prosecution in response to violence on farms—all violence, not only violent crime against white farmers. This will require an injection of additional resources and training for the police and prosecutors. Among other immediate steps, civilians who serve part-time in the military or police must, as well as their full-time colleagues, be brought under proper discipline and control. All those involved in policing should be instructed and trained to respond to reports of violent crime without discrimination on grounds outlawed by the South African constitution and international law. Effective mechanisms must be put in place to ensure that complaints of abuse by commando members or police reservists are thoroughly and promptly investigated, and that those responsible for abuse are appropriately disciplined or prosecuted.

The state's ability to address violence on farms effectively is limited by a lack of relevant data and statistics. There are no statistics relating to assaults on farmworkers by farm owners or managers or other farmworkers. The statistics about violent crime against farm owners do not distinguish between crimes affecting remote commercial farms and crimes affecting smallholdings, small properties whose owners do not derive their main income from farming, usually located near to cities and thus in a very different crime environment. They also tend to emphasize crime against farm owners and managers by recording only crimes committed by strangers. These problems have helped to produce distorted perceptions of the relative incidence of violence affecting farm owners, farmworkers, and other farm residents. Fuller and more accurate statistics should be compiled to document the nature and extent of all violence on farms. The figures for farms and smallholdings should be separately reported.

The government should examine whether it would improve police accountability to merge the structures of the rural protection plan with the community policing forums in commercial farming areas. Under the current system, there are supposed to be parallel sets of monthly meetings, but both are poorly attended, while the rural protection plan is often seen as being for the farm owners, and the CPFs for the black community. The new "community safety forums" being piloted in the Western Cape, which involve all government sectors in efforts to combat crime, not only the security forces, may form a useful model.

Human Rights Watch believes that other than in exceptional circumstances, such as a national emergency declared according to the proper procedures under the constitution and legislation, police and not soldiers should carry out policing duties. Accordingly, the commando units made up of army reservists should not be involved in policing. Civilians who wish to be involved in policing on a part time basis should be police reservists, and should receive training in policing skills and instruction on the laws of South Africa and respect for human rights, rather than army-style boot camp. Where soldiers are deployed for policing duties, they should not have full police powers, but only those that are required to fill a support role. For example, police should carry out duties such as house searches, even if soldiers are deployed to establish a cordon around the house.

Those in charge of implementing the rural protection plan should take urgent steps to implement a transition from military to civilian policing. In the interim, before this switch can be carried out, it should be required that commando units carrying out policing duties be accompanied by a full time police officer, preferably of middle or senior rank, not a reservist, who should be in command as regards all policing duties. The SANDF should urgently develop an effective internal mechanism for handling public complaints in order that persons who allege abuses by military personnel can obtain redress. In addition, the Independent Complaints Directorate (ICD), the body responsible for investigating complaints against the police, should be empowered to investigate or oversee the investigation of complaints against any state agent deployed for policing purposes.

Stricter controls should also be enforced against private security initiatives, including farmwatch and similar private schemes, to ensure that they do not act as vigilante groups. Government should introduce legislation to regulate such schemes, and work with representatives of commercial farmers and other interested parties to develop a code of conduct for those who participate in them. Private security companies and farmwatch structures should be permitted only to carry out preventive patrols and "citizen's arrests" of persons actually found in the course of committing a crime. It should be made clear that such security service providers have no policing or other authority beyond that of private citizens, and are to be held to account for crimes in the same way as private citizens. They should be required to hand individuals arrested to the police without delay, and they should be prohibited from taking the initiative in conducting house searches for illegal weapons or similar activities, but required rather to pass relevant information to the police. Laws regulating the private security industry should provide for the police and courts to be required to report to the regulatory authority alleged crimes, charges, and convictions involving security service providers.

Since 1994, the ANC-led government has taken important steps to reverse the existing racial inequalities affecting access to land that were enforced by the former colonial and apartheid governments. It has passed laws for the restitution of some land, redistributed other land through state purchases from private owners, and provided some degree of security of tenure for black farm residents. South African labor law has been completely overhauled, and its application, including the right to organize, extended to farmworkers. The government has also attempted to overcome the deficiencies of the criminal justice system, particularly in relation to violence against women.

Yet the legacy of apartheid and institutionalized racial segregation and discrimination remains potent, and continues to undermine the criminal justice system. Most criminal laws are now race-neutral on their face (by contrast with apartheid era laws criminalizing a variety of activities when undertaken by blacks). But in practice, law enforcement continues to be discriminatory, with adverse impacts on blacks and women.

The South African government has an obligation under international law to provide equal treatment under the law to all persons, irrespective of their race, gender, or other distinguishing characteristics. Yet, currently, it is failing in this obligation. In particular, the criminal justice system fails to ensure that police and court officials investigate, prosecute, and punish murder, rape, and other serious crimes against black South Africans with the same vigor as when these crimes are committed against whites. While the government has made great progress in promulgating laws that prohibit such discrimination, it has failed to ensure that such laws are then systematically enforced. Positive steps must be taken to ensure that all South Africans, regardless of race or gender, receive equal protection of the law.

Farm owners and farm residents have a mutual interest in mobilizing pressure on the government to provide effective law enforcement and in participating in the structures of the rural protection plan. There are many issues that could provide the focus for a common agenda, if all sides believed their concerns were being addressed; though joint action can only be very difficult to develop in the context of South Africa's deeply divided society. Ultimately, in law enforcement as in other areas, much will depend on a reduction in the stark economic inequalities so obvious in the South African countryside.

**

The information contained in this report is based on interviews conducted by Human Rights Watch researchers from the Africa and Women's Rights Divisions in South Africa in April and September 2000. We conducted the research in conjunction with fieldworkers from organizations affiliated to the National Land Committee, a South Africa-based land rights organization. These research findings are primarily based on interviews conducted on farms located in five provinces of South Africa: Northern Province, KwaZulu-Natal, Mpumalanga, Western Cape, and Gauteng. We interviewed dozens of current and former farm residents, male and female, as well as farm owners, police, members of commando units and private security companies, prosecutors, district surgeons, magistrates, and others in the criminal justice system. We spoke to representatives of farm owners, and to advocates for land reform and improved conditions for farm residents. We also interviewed former farmworkers now living in Johannesburg, Pietersburg, Pietermaritzburg, Cape Town, and other urban areas, following an eviction or voluntary termination of their residence on white-owned farms. Research in Ixopo was conducted for Human Rights Watch by a consultant. We also benefitted from research undertaken by the police, academics, and nongovernmental organizations (NGOs).

Human Rights Watch conducted a workshop in Johannesburg in September 2000, together with our partner organization on this project, the National Land Committee (NLC). The thirty participants included representatives of the NLC and its affiliated organizations, as well as of women's rights organizations working with farmworkers in South Africa, farmworkers' unions, and of the South African Human Rights Commission and the Commission on Gender Equality. The participants at the workshop discussed the preliminary research findings and made a key contribution to the recommendations on ways to combat violence on farms in South Africa.

RECOMMENDATIONS

To the South African Government:

- The government must ensure that the criminal justice system responds effectively and promptly to any reported serious crime, whoever the victim or the alleged perpetrator, and that all victims have equal access to the protection of the law, without discrimination in law or practice.

- The government should ensure that all allegations of human rights abuses by any state agent are promptly and thoroughly investigated by those responsible within the criminal justice system, and that perpetrators of abuse are disciplined or brought to justice. Security services should ensure proper screening and effective disciplinary oversight of reserve, as well as of full-time, members.

Commandos

- The government should establish a special investigation into the activities of the commando units operating in southern Mpumalanga and northern KwaZulu-Natal (the Piet Retief, Volksrust, Vryheid area), with a view to bringing to justice all those identified by the investigations as having committed human rights abuses.

- Commando units, made up of army reservists, should not be deployed for policing purposes. Civilians who wish to be involved in policing on a part-time basis should be police reservists, and should receive training in policing skills and instruction on the laws of South Africa and respect for human rights.

- The army should only be deployed for policing duties in exceptional circumstances, such as a national emergency declared according to the constitutional and legislative procedures. In any circumstances where soldiers or reservists are deployed for policing duties, they should not have full police powers, but only those that are required to fill a support role, and military personnel should be clearly and continuously under the command of civilian police structures.

- The army should put in place procedures and designate authorities at all group headquarters to receive, investigate, and act promptly on public complaints against any soldier, whether full time or a reservist. The

11

mandate of the Independent Complaints Directorate (ICD) should be expanded to include the investigation of complaints of human rights abuse by all state agents deployed for policing duties.

Farmwatches

• Legislation should be introduced to regulate private non-profit security networks such as the farmwatch units. In particular, members of private farmwatch structures should be restricted to activities aimed at the prevention of crime, and at immediate response to crime in accordance only with the powers of ordinary citizens. Farmwatch structures should not act on information such as reports of the possession of illegal weapons, but rather pass such reports to the police to take appropriate action.

Regulation of Private Security

• The Security Industry Regulation Bill should be passed into law and brought into force as a matter of urgency. As currently proposed, the act should provide for: an independent regulatory body, not linked to the industry; an effective system for screening out individuals with criminal records before an individual or company is registered; and a strict and legally binding code of conduct. The act should also provide for compulsory reporting by the police and courts to the new Security Industry Regulatory Authority of alleged crimes, charges, and convictions involving private security providers. It should be made clear that private security providers have no policing or other authority beyond that of private citizens, and are liable to prosecution for crimes to the same extent as other private citizens.

• The laws forbidding the use of military-style uniform (including camouflage) for those who are not members of the army should be enforced. The Security Industry Regulation Act should specifically prohibit the use by private security providers of uniforms that could reasonably be mistaken for those of a state law enforcement agency.

Police

• The government should institute a review of the collection of statistics in connection with violence on farms. The police should consider the creation of specific crime codes appropriate to distinguish between different types of crime: for example, for murders or assaults on farm owners or managers, murders or assaults on farmworkers or residents (including sexual assaults in all cases), and for illegal evictions. In collecting these statistics, the figures for "farms" and "smallholdings" should be disaggregated, and all statistics should allow for disaggregation by gender. A parallel effort to ensure that all reported incidents are correctly recorded by police will be necessary. The statistics collected should be made publicly available on a regular basis.

- The government should evaluate the needs of rural police stations for staff and equipment, and ensure that rural as well as urban police stations have the human and material resources necessary to combat crime effectively and on a nondiscriminatory basis in their areas.

- All reserve security force members, like full time members, should receive training that focuses on human rights within the criminal justice system, as protected by the South African constitution and international standards, including standards governing the use of firearms and force, as well as on South Africa's laws protecting farm residents from eviction. Emphasis should be placed on training to overcome racism and sexism and on nondiscrimination in responding to reported crime.

- All police should be trained to respond effectively to rape and other physical attacks against women, including women on farms, to ensure that women receive a sensitive response to their complaints and are protected against possible retaliation. Rural police stations (like urban police stations) should be staffed with detective officers who have received full training on how to investigate cases of sexual violence, including training on collecting forensic evidence and the importance of medical evidence in rape trials.

- The government should introduce a constitutional amendment to restore the Independent Complaints Directorate to the status it held under the interim constitution as one of the State Institutions Supporting Constitutional Democracy established under Chapter 9. As such, the ICD should report to parliament rather than the minister for safety and security. In addition, new legislation should be introduced, separate from the Police Act, to regulate the ICD and strengthen its powers. In particular, the ICD should have the duty and power to investigate criminal offenses and misconduct by members of the commandos when they are undertaking policing duties, including to investigate deaths in custody or as a result of action taken by the commandos. The army should be placed under an obligation to report such deaths promptly to the ICD, as well as to local police stations. The government should ensure that the powers and resources given to the ICD are sufficient to enable it to fulfill its statutory duties satisfactorily, including the investigation of systematic failures by the police to conduct proper investigations into abuses by commando units and private security companies.

Courts
- The National Directorate of Public Prosecutions (NDPP) should monitor prosecutions involving violence on farms, whether directed against farm residents or farm owners, and assess the backlog of cases in these categories, with a view to taking steps to ensure that any backlog is cleared. The NDPP should conduct exemplary prosecutions in especially egregious cases.

- The Department of Justice should monitor the handling of cases involving violence on farms by prosecutors, magistrates, and judges, with a view to ensuring that there is no race- or gender-based discrimination in the management of such cases.

- Rural magistrates courts (like urban courts) should be staffed with prosecutors who have received proper training in how to respond appropriately to cases of alleged sexual violence.

Evictions
- Police officers should receive training in and instructions to enforce section 23 of the Extension of Security of Tenure Act, which makes it an offence for any person to be evicted except on the authority of an order of court, or for any person to obstruct or interfere with a state official or a mediator in the performance of his or her duties under the act.

- The NDPP should conduct exemplary prosecutions in particularly egregious illegal eviction cases, and should issue directives to all magistrates courts giving guidance on how to conduct prosecutions in cases of illegal eviction.

Legal Aid

- The establishment of legal aid centers in commercial farming areas, providing assistance in civil as well as criminal cases, should be a matter of priority, to ensure effective access by all to the protection of the law. Pending the establishment of such centers, the Legal Aid Board should urgently consider resuming payments to legal practitioners under the existing "judicare" system in cases of alleged illegal eviction.

Protection of those Assisting Farmworkers

- The Extension of Security of Tenure Act should be amended in order to ensure that farmworkers' rights to organize and access legal protection are effectively protected. Lawyers, fieldworkers from NGOs working on land rights issues, union officials, and others with a legal right to consult with clients living on farms must be able to do so. Farm owners' legitimate concerns about security in relation to access by strangers to their farms could be addressed by, for example, the development of a system for the accreditation of NGO fieldworkers, in particular, with the Department of Land Affairs (DLA).

- The South African Law Commission should be instructed to institute a review of the law of trespass, with a view to ensuring that it cannot be used to prevent legitimate access to farms.

Racial and Gender Discrimination and Working Conditions

- The Department of Labour should ensure compliance on farms with international labor standards set out by the International Labour Organization (ILO) and with the provisions of national legislation. The government should ratify relevant ILO treaties, where it has not yet done so, including the Maternity Protection Convention, No. 183 of 2000, and the Protection of Wages Convention, No. 95 of 1949. The government should strengthen the labor inspectorate and increase the number of trained inspectors to ensure that it can carry out its mandate effectively.

- Existing mechanisms responsible for resolving labor relations disputes, such as the Commission for Conciliation Mediation and Arbitration (CCMA), the Land Claims Court, and the Labor Court, should be strengthened and given financial support and staffing to enable them to fulfill their mandates. Staff should, in particular, be trained in women's

rights and all existing legislation guaranteeing equality and equal
protection of the law to women in the agricultural labor force.

• The government should strengthen the capacity of the South African
Human Rights Commission, the Commission on Gender Equality, and the
Independent Complaints Directorate to operate branch offices in all
provinces with enough financial resources to carry out proper
investigation of cases reported to them within their mandates and to
identify and act in response to patterns of abuse.

Restructuring of the Rural Protection Plan
• The government should convene a forum of the relevant parties to
evaluate the operation of the rural protection plan, with a view to
restructuring it to ensure equal protection of the law to all those resident
in commercial farming areas. In addition, the government should
commission an independent study of the effectiveness of the rural
protection plan, and monitor the plan's operation on an ongoing basis.

• Each government structure involved in implementing the rural protection
plan, at national, provincial, and local level, should conduct an evaluation
of all violent crime reported in the area for which it is responsible, with
a view to identifying which crimes are of particular concern to different
sections of the community, including violent crimes against farm workers
and residents and women and children on farms. The results of this
evaluation should be used to ensure that structures created to combat
crime respond effectively to the needs of all sections of the community.

• The government should consider merging the local and area coordinating
committees for the rural protection plan with the community policing
forums, and establishing new structures chaired by local government and
involving all relevant government agencies, as well as representatives of
farmworkers and farm owners, to ensure effective coordination of efforts
to combat crime.

• The government should commission a thorough and independent study of
the extent of and reasons for violence on farms, including violence against
women, based on interviews with farm owners, workers and residents in
all nine provinces, as well as members of the police, army, and court
officials.

To the Human Rights and Gender Equality Commissions:

- As currently planned, the South African Human Rights Commission (SAHRC) should hold comprehensive hearings on the issue of conditions on farms in different provinces in South Africa, with the aim of establishing the patterns of violence and abuse, as well as the extent of racial bias in the handling of cases by the criminal justice system, and making recommendations to government for these issues to be redressed.

- The Commission on Gender Equality (CGE) should, in partnership with groups involved in programs for women on farms and in coordination with the SAHRC, conduct a detailed study of the situation of women farm workers and residents: in particular, it should document cases of rape by farm owners, managers, or other farm residents, and make recommendations to government to ensure that discrimination and violence against women farmworkers is ended.

To All Those Working for Rural Safety and Security:

- Politicians, representatives of commercial agriculture, farmworkers' unions, nongovernmental organizations (NGOs) concerned with land or farmworkers' rights, and other interested parties, should consistently, unambiguously, and evenhandedly condemn all forms of violence on farms in South Africa, whether committed against farm workers and residents or against farm owners. Organizations should take steps to make clear to their members their opposition to violence, and should put in place procedures to respond to allegations that an employee or member has committed or incited a violent crime.

BACKGROUND

History of Land Expropriation in South Africa[1]

An entire history of colonial conquest and dispossession, of cheap labor and systematic exploitation, and of segregation, apartheid and white supremacy has created a society in which 60,000 capitalist farmers own 12 times as much land as over 14 million rural poor. Fundamental to the construction of an unjust, inequitable, repressive and brutal social order is an unjust, punitive and untenable allocation of land and rights to land.[2]

Unequal access to land, enforced by law, underpinned white control of power in South Africa during both the colonial and apartheid eras. From the date of the first European settlement at the Cape, founded by Jan van Riebeeck in 1652, the indigenous peoples of South Africa—the Khoi and the San (the Bushmen) and

---

[1] There is a large literature on land expropriation in South Africa from which this summary is put together. Among the important works are: Sol Plaatje, *Native Life in South Africa* (Johannesburg: Ravan Press, 1982); Francis Wilson, A. Kooy and D. Hendrie (eds.), *Farm Labor in South Africa* (Johannesburg: South African Labor and Development Research Unit (SALDRU) and David Philip, 1977); Colin Bundy, *The Rise and Fall of the South African Peasantry* (London: Heinemann, 1979); Belinda Bozzoli (ed.), *Town and Countryside in the Transvaal* (Johannesburg: Ravan Press, 1983); Laurine Platzky and Cherryl Walker, *The Surplus People: Forced Removals in South Africa* (Johannesburg: Ravan Press, 1985); Helen Bradford, *A Taste of Freedom: The ICU in Rural South Africa 1924-1930* (New Haven: Yale University Press, 1987); Christina Murray and Catherine O'Regan, (eds.), *No Place to Rest: Forced Removals and the Law in South Africa* (Oxford: Oxford University Press, 1989); Wendy Davies, *We Cry for Our Land: Farm Workers in South Africa* (Oxford: Oxfam, 1990); Michael Lipton, Frank Ellis and Merle Lipton (eds.) *Land, Labor and Livelihoods in Southern Africa* (1996); Shamim Meer, (ed.), *Women, Land and Authority: Perspectives from South Africa* (Oxford and Cape Town: Oxfam and David Philip, 1997); Alan Jeeves and Jonathan Crush (eds.), *White Farms, Black Labor: The State and Agrarian Change in Southern Africa 1910-50* (Pietermaritzburg, Portsmouth, NH, and Oxford: University of Natal Press, Heinemann, and James Currey, 1997). For a detailed and compelling history of the effect of South Africa's land laws on one man and his family, see Charles van Onselen, *The Seed is Mine: The Life of Kas Maine, a South African Sharecropper 1894-1985* (Oxford: James Currey, 1996).

[2] Colin Bundy, "Land, Law and Power: Forced Removals in Historical Context," in Murray and O'Regan, (eds.), *No Place to Rest*, p.11.

subsequently the Bantu language-speaking peoples to the north and east of the Cape—were, at first gradually, and later more comprehensively, driven from the land from which they had previously derived their livelihoods. Although the dispossession of peasant producers is a process common to many modernizing societies, South Africa saw a particularly extreme and violent version of this process. Land was acquired by force of arms, a cash economy and cash taxation system forced peasant producers into debt and alienation of their land, and laws were passed to benefit the property-owning classes.

In the British Cape Colony, the nineteenth century saw a series of wars between settlers and different African chiefdoms which opened up most land west of the Kei river to white settlement by the 1880s. Several small reserves for Africans who had supported the whites in the wars were created amongst the white farms, but most Africans had no choice but to live on white-owned farms as full-time workers—and were integrated into the structures of settler society far earlier and more extensively than elsewhere in southern Africa. From the 1870s, land east of the Kei was annexed and brought under British rule as African reserves. In Natal, from the 1840s the British administrators created a series of small reserves from land deemed undesirable by settlers. When the Zulu kingdom was annexed by the British in 1887, a similar system of reserves was applied there, with the remaining land opened up for white settlement or declared to be state land. By contrast, the early settlements of whites in what became the Boer republics of the Transvaal and Orange Free State (now Mpumalanga, Northern, North-West, Gauteng, and Free State Provinces), were established with the permission of the chiefs. But, following the first British occupation of the Transvaal (1877-1881), the Transvaal government launched a series of wars of conquest against the independent chiefdoms on the still ill-defined borders of the republic. Little land was designated as "reserves" for the African population, because of the resistance of white farmers, for whom land was the only major economic resource available. In the Orange Free State, an even smaller proportion of the land was left under African control.

By the end of the nineteenth century, the process of conquest was almost complete. Yet in many areas blacks continued to farm on white land through systems of land tenure that allowed some independent African production. These systems included cash tenancy; labor tenancy, by which people secured access to land in return for the labor of some of the members of the family for an agreed proportion of their time; and sharecropping, pejoratively known by whites as "kaffir farming," by which Africans obtained the right to farm with their own implements and livestock, on condition they gave a share of their crop to the white owners of the land. Some Africans succeeded in accumulating sufficient cash to purchase land from whites; these areas of African freehold came in later years to be called "black spots" by the National Party government which took power in 1948. Together, these developments produced a small but growing class of African smallholders and market farmers—peasants—who supplied the small towns of South Africa with much of their food and provided a growing economic challenge to white producers.

The mineral discoveries of the late nineteenth century and the development of the gold mining industry in the Transvaal in the 1880s brought major economic changes, and with them political restructuring. Tensions between the Transvaal Boer republic and the British-dominated mining and industrial companies over control of the wealth of the Witwatersrand led to the outbreak of the Anglo-Boer, or South African, War in 1899. The eventual military victory of the British led in turn to the creation of the Union of South Africa, incorporating what were by then the four British colonies south of the Limpopo, in 1910. The rapid growth of an urban population with these developments encouraged white commercial farming, and white farmers used their political strength to bring pressure on the independent black producers, and force them into working on white farms. As early as 1885, the Orange Free State government passed a law designed to limit the number of rent-paying or sharecropping African families allowed on each white-owned farm; and taxes, rents and other fees were generally raised. At the same time, the mining industry was anxious to force Africans into wage employment, favoring a migrant labor system where Africans had their primary homes in tribal reserves, and the young men entering the wage economy could be paid low wages on the basis that their families could make a living off land in the reserves. Farmers, on the other hand, disliked the reserves, which preserved the possibility of independent African agricultural production. The mining and industrial revolution also stimulated new political organizations among the black population: in 1912, the African National Congress (ANC) was formed by members of the small mission-educated African elite.

The South Africa Party, which formed the first government of the Union in 1910, adopted a "native policy" designed to promote a stable labor supply for industry, and at the same time to benefit farmers by ending independent African agricultural production. The 1913 Natives Land Act (later renamed the Black Land Act) was the result. The act was one of the most important pieces of legislation of the new government, providing the statutory basis for territorial segregation in South Africa. It divided the rural parts of the country into areas where Africans could own land (the reserves)—thus ensuring that Africans would not become a totally landless group and preserving the migrant labor system—and the rest, where Africans were prohibited from "purchase, hire, or other acquisition of land or of any right thereto."[3] The schedule to the act listed land already set aside as reserves by the four provinces prior to the Union, approximately nine million hectares or less than 8 percent of South Africa's land, mostly in the Cape and Natal. In recognition that this land was inadequate to house all Africans, there were also provisions to allow the increase of the reserves to 13 percent of the land. The 1913 land act intended to end the more independent forms of tenure which until then had allowed Africans to live and work on land that was technically owned by whites, especially sharecropping and cash tenancy, and turn all Africans on white farms into wage laborers, or, as a second best, labor tenants. Tens of thousands of black tenants (increasingly referred to as "squatters") and sharecroppers were forced off the land they had been farming and onto the roads in search of white farmers who were prepared to defy the law and enter into tenant or sharecropping arrangements with them. In his classic work *Native Life in South Africa*, written in 1916, ANC leader Sol Plaatje described how, "Awakening on Friday morning, June 20, [1913] the South African native found himself not actually a slave but a pariah in the land of his birth."[4]

As a result of the 1913 land act, the most common form of farm labor and of black independent production in the northern parts of South Africa, especially in the Transvaal and northern Natal, came to be the labor tenant system, by which people secured access to land by working for the landowner. In the Western Cape, in particular, farming moved much more quickly to a system of cash labor in a capitalist market. The relationship of labor tenancy is essentially between the family and the farm owner, rather than the individual worker and the farm owner as employer; traditionally, the extended family could live on the farm and grow their own crops or graze livestock on land designated for the purpose, so long as one or more members provided their labor in accordance with the agreed terms. The head of the household, the father, as well as the farmer, was thus involved in the extraction of labor from his wives and children, creating the potential for severe inter-generational and gender conflict within the tenant household. If any one of the family members broke the contract, then the whole family was liable to eviction. In its original form, no cash wages were paid for the labor provided, which was on the basis of a number of days a week the year round, and the tenant used his own livestock and implements on his own and the landowner's land. By the 1920s, however, most labor tenants were contracted to work full-time for part of the year (usually anything from three to nine months), many received cash

[3] Africans continued to have the right to hold freehold land in urban areas—a right they had acquired in the mid-nineteenth century—until the 1950s.
[4] As quoted in Platzky and Walker, *The Surplus People*, p.85.

wages to supplement the right to use the land, and they increasingly used the landlord's implements and animals rather than their own. Nevertheless, labor tenants' continued relative independence and their sense that the land was theirs, not the legal landowner's, made them often unreliable workers for the farm owner, and notorious among whites for letting their cattle roam all over the farm, helping themselves to wood, and other misdemeanors. The system persisted—as did sharecropping, though to a lesser extent, despite its banning—because South African agriculture was profoundly unprofitable and white farmers could not otherwise secure the labor they needed, given their inability to pay competitive wages. For some black families the independence from increasingly autocratic chiefly control in the tribal reserves was also appealing. Finally, whites could usually depend on the state to give the backing of law and force to their demands on their black tenants.

By the 1920s, the longer term effects of the 1913 land act were becoming clear, and generated broad demands among the African population for the right to hold land and end white control. These demands were led by the Industrial and Commercial Workers Union (the ICU), the first black political organization to make the transition to a mass movement. At least partly in response to the threat posed by this mobilization, and the fear of communism it engendered among the increasing numbers of white farmers,[5] the Natives Administration Act (No. 38 of 1927; later renamed the Black Administration Act) granted the government extensive new powers. The act criminalized the fomenting of racial hatred between "natives and Europeans," set the framework for a uniform system of administration for black people in South Africa (strengthening the powers of chiefs to control dissident elements and moving away from the greater integration tolerated in the Cape), and created the power of forced removal of blacks from "white" land. In its original form, section 5(1)(b) of the Native Administration Act provided for the government to "order the removal of any tribe or portion thereof or any Native from any place to any other place... upon such conditions as he may determine," if he deemed it "expedient in the general public interest." Over the years before its repeal in 1986, the law was strengthened in various ways, including to allow a removal "without prior notice." This was the primary legal provision used during

---

[5] The number of white-occupied farms rose by 23 percent from 1918 to 1928, reaching some 94,000 holdings. Bradford, *A Taste of Freedom*, p.23. The number of white farmers peaked in the 1950s, at 116,848 in 1950, and by 1985 had reduced to 59,088 (the average farm size doubled in the same period). David Copper, *Working the Land: A review of agriculture in South Africa* (Johannesburg: Environment and Development Agency, 1988), p.19.

the apartheid years for the forcible removal of many thousands of people living in "black spots" in "white" South Africa.

At the same time, the need for more land to be set aside for the reserves, in accordance with the commitment of the 1913 land act, eventually became sufficiently urgent to overcome white farmers' resistance. The 1936 Development Trust and Land Act (No. 18 of 1936) identified land to be "released" for African occupation, thus expanding the reserve areas defined ("scheduled") in 1913. Part of this land was already owned by the state; other areas had to be purchased by the state from private owners, a process that continued over the next fifty years. (By the end of 1987, the "quotas" set in 1936 for land that might be acquired under this process had been exceeded by about 10 percent, with the result that the ten homelands together constituted about 13.8 percent of South Africa's surface area.[6]) The 1936 land act also established an elaborate system for the compulsory registration and control of labor tenants. Any "native" unlawfully on land, including those who had the consent of the landowner but were in excess of a number set down by the labor tenants control board, could be summarily ejected by the police, using force if necessary. Even those farmers who wished for good relations with their black tenants were therefore pushed into confrontation. These drastic measures provided the basis for most farm removals that were to follow, though they were not widely enforced until the 1950s.

By the 1940s, the African reserves were reaching levels of immiseration that threatened the very existence of the migrant labor system. People who could no longer scrape any living from the land were moving in increasing numbers to the urban areas. The years of the Second World War also saw increasingly rapid industrialization, which brought with it a massive housing crisis for the black population, labor unrest, rising black expectations and political consciousness, as well as demands from manufacturing industry for a more stable and skilled African workforce. At the same time, the profits of the mines rested on cheap, unskilled, migrant labor, and white workers feared competition from skilled blacks; while white farmers had been hard hit during the depression of the 1930s and by the war, and faced a chronic shortage of labor they blamed on "unfair" higher wages available in the towns and the "soft" policy of the previous government on African urbanization and the reserves. Organized white agriculture, in the form of the

---

[6] Michael Robertson, "Dividing the Land: An Introduction to Apartheid Land Law," in Murray and O'Regan, (eds.), *No Place to Rest*, p.128.

South African Agricultural Union (SAAU), and its constituent elements, especially the Transvaal Agricultural Union (TAU), formed a powerful political lobby.[7]

The National Party was the party of the white worker and the white farmer. It was elected in 1948 on a platform promising *apartheid*, or (euphemistically) "separate development." The party's aims were to keep blacks out of urban areas as much as possible and to crush the ever more vocal demands from the ANC and its allies for greater political freedom and for an end to racial and economic discrimination. Its policies included the expansion of controls on the movement of African workers and the toughening of security legislation. By the 1960s and 1970s, its program also included the creation of "homelands," or "bantustans," for each major African ethnic group. The government also embarked on a program to eliminate persistent black "squatting" on white land and transform the "wasteful" (because part-time) system of labor tenancy into one of full-time, wage-paid, farm labor. Commercial farmers received generous subsidies for agricultural production, as well as tariff protections, marketing controls protecting them from price fluctuations, cheap credit, and other benefits. Black prison labor was extensively deployed on farms: at the height of the scheme in 1957 to 1958, some 200,000 convicts were hired out to white farmers annually, at the rate of a few pence per day.[8] The use of prison labor in this way was only formally ended in 1987 (though there were reports of its continued availability as late as 1989). The government also engaged in some efforts to improve the situation in the reserves, through so-called betterment planning, the first aspects of which had been introduced in the 1930s, including fencing, erosion controls, culling of cattle, and the separation of residential and farm land.

In 1950, the first Group Areas Act was passed (Act No. 41 of 1950), providing for the legal, rather than informal and *de facto*, designation of separate (and unequal) living spaces for four major population groups: whites, natives (meaning people of African ancestry), Indians, and "Induna [headman] " (those of mixed race); the Population Registration Act of 1959 provided the legal framework

---

[7] The SAAU was formed in 1904 as an umbrella organization bringing together agricultural unions representing white farm owners in areas that would become the four provinces of the Union and then Republic of South Africa (Cape Province, Natal, Transvaal and the Orange Free State); TAU was formed in 1897. Henk van de Graaf and Chris L. Jordaan (eds.), *Property Rights in South Africa* (Pretoria: Transvaal Agricultural Union, 1999), Preface.

[8] Bundy, *Rise and Fall of the South African Peasantry*, "Aftermath and Conclusions," p.234.

to designate the racial category of every person.[9] The Group Areas Act superseded rather than repealed the provision of the 1913 land act prohibiting Africans from owning land outside the areas set aside for them, and applied everywhere except in the reserves, black urban townships, national parks, and other less significant areas. Although actual group areas were only ever declared for a small proportion of the land falling under the act, its effect was felt everywhere, in particular through the requirement that the occupier of land be of the same racial group as the owner. In the white-owned rural areas especially, this provision meant that it was unnecessary to invoke the full extent of the act to prevent cross-racial tenancy contracts. The first large scale forced removals, mostly from urban areas, took place under this act (and other location-specific legislation) from the mid-1950s.[10]

The Prevention of Illegal Squatting Act, No. 52 of 1951 (amended and strengthened as late as 1988), provided legal powers aimed at reducing the informal settlements that had mushroomed around the urban centers. The key provision of the act provided for it to be a criminal offense for any person to "enter upon or into ... or remain on or in any land or building" without "lawful reason" or the permission of the "lawful occupier" (a clause that touched even the casual trespasser who had no intention of remaining permanently on the land). The act also empowered a land owner to demolish any buildings on his land without the need to obtain a court order, and gave a magistrate administrative powers to order the removal of persons from land or to demolish structures in the interests of "the health and safety of the public generally." Laws were also introduced making it compulsory for all Africans over the age of sixteen to carry a "pass," a personal identity document, at all times, and restricting the right of Africans to leave white farms and enter urban areas except to provide labor needed by white families and industries. Once a person got a "farmworker only" stamp in his pass book, it

---

[9] In this report, Human Rights Watch will use "black" to refer to all three subcategories of those not previously designated as "white," including those of African or Indian ancestry and those of mixed race. Where it is necessary for the context, we will use the subcategories (using "African" for those of African ancestry), since their previous racial classification remains relevant to the socio-economic circumstances of all South Africans today and, as this report demonstrates, to the response of the state machinery to their attempts to obtain official assistance.

[10] In 1954 the Natives Resettlement Act provided for the removal of all Africans from the "western areas" of Johannesburg (including Sophiatown, Martindale, Newclare, and Pageview) to Soweto. See David Welsh, "The Growth of Towns," in Monica Wilson and Leonard Thompson (eds.) *The Oxford History of South Africa* (Oxford: Oxford University Press, 1971), vol. 2, pp.142-243 at pp.238-241.

became virtually impossible for him to work legally in any other capacity. Tens of thousands of people were jailed for infringement of the pass laws over the following years.

The Trespass Act, No. 6 of 1959, which is still in force, was also widely used in conjunction with other measures to secure the removal of people from land when their presence became inconvenient to the "lawful occupier." The four-section act makes it an offense—in terms very similar to the Prevention of Illegal Squatting Act—to enter into or be upon any land or building without permission or "lawful reason." Although the act contains no provisions empowering the courts to order the eviction of anyone convicted of trespass, the practical effect of arrest and conviction has often been to drive those convicted off the land—without the need to institute civil proceedings. Despite its apparent character as an ordinary criminal statute, the act is closely linked to other historical legislation created to advance racially-based ownership of land.

Under these laws, the process of evicting farm residents was simple. When he decided that their presence was no longer wanted, the white farmer would usually give a tenant or farmworker family a "trekpas," a letter stating that the worker or labor tenant, his family, and all their livestock must vacate the farm by a certain date. If the family had not left by that date, the farmer would report the matter to the police and lay a charge of trespass or illegal squatting. The head of the family would then be arrested and brought to court. In most cases, the only basis for challenging the eviction would be the unreasonableness of the circumstances of eviction and the shortness of the notice period, generally not more than two weeks or a month. The law could be invoked even if the family had been living on the farm for decades and there was no breach of the contract from the tenant side—only, perhaps, a refusal to shift the terms of the contract to that of wage-paid labor from labor tenancy. The farmer was not compelled to give any reason for ordering a worker and his family to move, and had no responsibility for finding alternative accommodation nor to compensate evicted tenants or workers for houses they had built.

Despite these draconian laws, there was continued agitation from the agricultural associations representing white farmers, and in parliament, for the complete ending of labor tenancy and the substitution of wage labor. The 1936 land act was repeatedly amended to achieve this purpose. In 1961, the Nel Committee of Inquiry into the Labor Tenant System recommended the complete abolition of labor tenancy within seven years, a recommendation given effect in 1964. The Bantu Laws Amendment Act, No. 42 of 1964, which substantially amended the 1936 land act as it applied to labor tenancy, increased the costs of registration, limited the numbers of contracts allowed, and provided for the prohibition of labor tenant contracts district by district. The labor tenancy system was finally formally abolished throughout South Africa in 1981 (under a proclamation gazetted in 1980). It became an offense to enter into a labor tenant contract, and any such contract was null and void. The result of this legislation was the forced removal of hundreds of thousands of labor tenants from farms in the 1960s and 1970s—a process hastened by the increasing mechanization of agriculture, which reduced the demand for labor. Of the perhaps one million people living on farms as labor tenants in 1936, the government announced in 1973 that only 16,000 such contracts remained, and were due to be phased out.[11] (Nevertheless, labor tenancy continued to survive in southern Transvaal and northern Natal, under a hybrid system by which families were allowed access to much less land for cultivation or grazing, but were also paid minimal wages for the labor supplied, thus passing as wage-paid laborers.)

At least 3.5 million people were forcibly removed from their land and homes through the use of these laws, the majority of them in the 1960s and 1970s; approximately 1,129,000 of these people had lived on white-owned farms, the largest single category.[12] The proportion of Africans living in urban areas fell from 29.6 to 26.7 percent of the total population from 1960 to 1980; the proportion of the African population living on white-owned farmland fell from nearly a third of the total to one fifth (though, with population growth, the absolute numbers still grew, and the ratio of blacks to whites in farm areas increased, even though the number employed in agriculture fell[13]), and the reserve-based population grew from under 40 to nearly 53 percent, a total rising to over 60 percent if migrant laborers absent for work were included.[14] The removals coincided with an economic boom

---

[11] Bundy, *Rise and Fall of the South African Peasantry*, "Aftermath and Conclusions," p.235.

[12] The other categories were: "black spots" and homeland consolidation (614,000); urban areas (730,000); informal settlements (112,000); Group Area relocations (860,400); infrastructural and strategic developments (103,500). Platzky and Walker, *The Surplus People*, p.10 and pp.372-3. At the time the book was published, in 1985, government policy still threatened a further two million people with removal.

[13] One study found that between 1951 and 1980, the absolute number of black people living in rural areas outside the reserves grew by two million. Aninka Claassens, "Rural Land Struggles in the Transvaal in the 1980s," in Murray and O'Regan (eds.), *No Place to Rest*, p.44, citing C. Simkins, *Four Essays on the Past, Present and Possible Future of the Distribution of the Black Population of South Africa* (Cape Town: SALDRU, 1983).

[14] Bundy, "Land, Law and Power," p.10.

for whites. As one author opined: "At some point around 1970, white South Africans overtook Californians as the single most affluent group in the world."[15]

In order to accommodate all those removed from "white" South Africa, the National Party government elaborated and extended the reserve system, by the passing of legislation to provide for black "self-government" in the reserve areas, intended to become ethnically (as well as racially) segregated "homelands" for each of South Africa's African "tribes," units to be defined by the white government. The Bantu Authorities Act, No.68 of 1951, provided for the establishment of tribal, regional, and territorial authorities in the reserves, and in 1954 the Tomlinson Commission was appointed to investigate the future of the tribal areas, making several radical proposals. The Promotion of Bantu Self-Government Act (No. 46 of 1959) formalized the political transformation of the reserves, and removed the last traces of black representation in white political institutions. With the creation of the bantustans, the removal of "black spots" in "white" South Africa became a government priority, blighting as they did the propaganda picture that all Africans naturally belonged in their own ethnic homelands. Consolidation of the scattered scraps of reserves into more coherent units, through the purchase of white farmland if necessary, was also accepted as a policy. The Bantu Homelands Citizenship Act, No. 26 of 1970, by which all African South Africans automatically became citizens of one or other of the homelands, and the Bantu Homelands Constitution Act, No. 21 of 1971, completed the legislative framework. Eventually, ten homelands were created, of which four (Transkei, Bophuthatswana, Venda, and Ciskei) were declared "independent" by the South African government.

In 1985, in the face of growing national and international pressure to end these policies, the government announced that it was suspending the policy of forced removals, though "voluntary" removals would continue. The next year, the Abolition of Influx Control Act (No. 68 of 1986) repealed the provisions of the 1936 land act relating to labor tenancy, along with the pass laws and other apartheid provisions restricting freedom of movement of blacks in white rural areas. Labor tenant contracts once again became legal, subject to the common law surrounding such arrangements. At around the same period, the government introduced token political reforms, adopting a new constitution in 1983 that created a tricameral parliament in which Indians and Coloureds (but not Africans) would have representation in separate chambers. This lifting of control was short-lived. The suspension of forced removals was reversed in 1986, when political challenge to the government from the United Democratic Front (UDF) and unions led to the

---

[15] R.W. Johnson, *How Long Will South Africa Survive?* (London: Macmillan, 1977), as quoted in Bundy, "Land, Law and Power," p.9.

declaration of a second state of emergency in as many years. However, subsequent removals of whole communities were carried out largely in urban areas (for example, at Crossroads, near Cape Town), though the process of forced "incorporation" of rural communities into the homelands continued, involving not the physical removal of people, but the redrawing of homeland boundaries to include their land. In 1988, the Prevention of Illegal Squatting Amendment Act (No. 104 of 1988, promulgated in February 1989) reintroduced many of the controls abolished in 1986, by providing for the removal of persons living on land but not employed by the owner or occupier of the land, even where they were present with the consent of the owner or occupier. This provision was apparently designed to reintroduce a clause of the 1936 land act, repealed in 1986, allowing unemployed residents of white farms to be easily and forcibly removed. The South African Agricultural Union issued a memorandum to its members in November 1988, suggesting that they compile lists of all those living but not employed on their farms, with a view to invoking the new amendment.[16]

On February 2, 1990, President F.W. de Klerk announced the unbanning of the ANC and other black political organizations, the imminent release of Nelson Mandela and other political prisoners, the lifting of the state of emergency in most parts of the country, and the beginning of a process of open dialogue that ultimately resulted in the nonracial elections of 1994 and the installation of South Africa's first democratically chosen government. In 1991, the Abolition of Racially Based Land Measures Act (No. 108 of 1991) repealed the 1913 and 1936 land acts, the Group Areas Act, and other laws.[17] A white paper on land reform was published, proposing very limited land redistribution and rejecting the notion of restitution; the ANC published its own land policy in 1992, and a policy on farmworkers in 1993. It was left to the new government of national unity, elected in 1994 and led by the ANC, to institute a comprehensive program to redress the injustices of past land expropriations and provide a measure of security of tenure.

---

[16] Catherine O'Regan, "The Prevention of Illegal Squatting Act," in Murray and O'Regan (eds.), *No Place to Rest*, p.171.

[17] Other laws passed during this transition period improved black access to land, including the Upgrading of Land Tenure Rights Act (No. 112 of 1991), the Distribution and Transfer of Certain State Land Act (No. 119 of 1993), and the Provision of Land and Assistance Act (No. 126 of 1993).

Land Reform Since 1994

The land shall be divided among those who work it.[18]

The reality of South Africa's negotiated transition has meant that the ANC's historic pledge to redistribute land, made in the Freedom Charter adopted at Kliptown in 1955, has not been honored. Nevertheless, the ANC in government has made significant commitments to redress the racially-based land allocations of South Africa's colonial and apartheid past, and has ensured that those commitments are enshrined in the constitution.

Section 25 of the South African constitution, relating to property rights, includes the following provisions:

> (5) The state must take reasonable legislative and other measures, within its available resources, to foster conditions that enable citizens to gain access to land on an equitable basis.
>
> (6) A person or community whose tenure of land is legally insecure as a result of past racially discriminatory laws or practices is entitled, to the extent provided by an Act of Parliament, either to tenure which is legally secure, or to comparable redress.
>
> (7) A person or community dispossessed of property after 19 June 1913 as a result of past racially discriminatory laws or practices is entitled, to the extent provided by an Act of Parliament, either to restitution of that property, or to equitable redress.
>
> (8) No provision of this section may impede the state from taking legislative and other measures to achieve land, water and related reform, in order to redress the results of past racial discrimination, provided that any departure from the provisions of this section is in accordance with the provisions of section 36(1).[19]

---

[18] *The Freedom Charter*, adopted at the Congress of the People, Kliptown, June 26, 1955.
[19] Constitution of the Republic of South Africa, 1996 (Act 108 of 1996). Section 36(1) governs the limitation of rights, providing that "The rights in the Bill of Rights may be limited only in terms of law of general application to the extent that the limitation is reasonable and justifiable in an open and democratic society based on human dignity, equality and freedom, taking into account all relevant factors, including:S (a) the nature of

Section 25 also provides that "No one may be deprived of property except in terms of law of general application, and no law may permit arbitrary deprivation of property," that land may be expropriated only for a public purpose or in the public interest, and that "just and equitable" compensation shall be paid if property is expropriated, taking into account "all the relevant circumstances."[20]

Four laws provide the framework for the main elements of the government's land reform program: the Provision of Land and Assistance Act (No. 126 of 1993); the Restitution of Land Rights Act (No. 22 of 1994), the Land Reform (Labour Tenants) Act (No. 3 of 1996), known as the Labour Tenants Act, and the Extension of Security of Tenure Act (No. 62 of 1997), known as ESTA.[21] The Labour Relations Act (No. 66 of 1995) and the Basic Conditions of Employment Act (No. 75 of 1997) also afford farmworkers protection under the law.

Restitution

The Restitution of Land Rights Act 1994 was enacted in accordance with provisions of the interim constitution in force between April 1994 and February 1997. It aimed to restore rights in land of which people were dispossessed under apartheid laws since 1913 and promote the protection and advancement of

---

the right; (b) the importance of the purpose of the limitation; (c) the nature and extent of the limitation; (d) the relation between the limitation and its purpose; and (e) less restrictive means to achieve the purpose."

[20] Constitution of the Republic of South Africa, 1996, sections 25(1), (2), and (3). Section 25(3) provides in full: "The amount of compensation and the time and manner of payment must be just and equitable, reflecting an equitable balance between the public interest and the interests of those affected, having regard to all relevant circumstances, including:- (a) the current use of the property; (b) the history of the acquisition and use of the property; (c) the market value of the property; (d) the extent of direct state investment and subsidy in the acquisition and beneficial capital improvement of the property; and (e) the purpose of the expropriation." Section 25(4)(a) provides that "the public interest includes the nation's commitment to reform and to reforms to bring about equitable access to South Africa's natural resources."

[21] Other relevant statutes include the Land Administration Act (No. 2 of 1995), the Development Facilitation Act (No. 67 of 1995), the Communal Property Associations Act (No. 28 of 1996), the Interim Protection of Informal Land Rights Act (No. 31 of 1996), and the Prevention of Illegal Eviction from and Unlawful Occupation of Land Act (No. 19 of 1998).

individuals or groups who were disadvantaged by unfair discrimination.[22] Restitution can take the form of restoration of the land from which claimants were dispossessed, provision of alternative land, payment of compensation, or priority access to government housing and development programmes.[23] The process of restitution is administered by a Commission on Restitution of Land Rights and a Land Claims Court established under the act. The Communal Property Associations Act (No. 28 of 1996) provides a framework for group ownership of land, following the restitution or redistribution of land under one of the government programs.

All claims for restitution had to be lodged by December 31, 1998.[24] Once a claim was lodged, the commission was obliged to publish a notice and contact all involved parties. The commission investigates the claim and attempts to mediate a settlement.[25] If a settlement is not possible, the commission refers the claim to the court in any event, which then decides what restitution is appropriate.[26] The Department of Land Affairs (DLA) assists the commission in preparing claims, is involved in negotiations for the transfer of land and payment of compensation, and can release additional resources to claimants. In 1997, an amendment to the act allowed claims to be submitted directly to the court to streamline the processing of restitution claims, though this process is not being utilized in practice.[27] By the deadline of December 31, 1998, 63,455 claims had been lodged with the commission, most of them relating to urban land.[28] A major complaint about the

---

[22] Restitution of Land Rights Act, 1994, preamble and section 2. The date of 1913 is significant since it means that land taken by conquest before the codification of ownership patterns by the 1913 Natives Land Act is not covered by the restitution process. Section 121 of the interim constitution (Constitution of the Republic of South Africa Act, No. 200 of 1993), which was negotiated by different political parties (effectively the ANC and the National Party) prior to the 1994 elections, required that an act of parliament should provide for restitution of land rights for people or communities dispossessed of land under racially discriminatory laws.

[23] Department of Land Affairs, *White Paper on South African Land Policy* (Pretoria: April 1997), Executive Summary.

[24] Commission on Restitution of Land Rights, *Annual Report* (April 1999-March 2000), p.4. This deadline was extended from April 30, 1998 to allow for the filing of claims in the wake of an awareness campaign.

[25] Restitution of Land Rights Act, 1994, sections 10-14.

[26] Restitution of Land Rights Act, 1994, sections 14 and 22-38.

[27] Land Restitution and Reform Laws Amendment Act, No. 63 of 1997, section 29, inserting sections 38A to 38E into the original act.

[28] Department of Land Affairs *Annual Report 1999*, p.93.

restitution process has been the backlog in dealing with claims, leading to a ministerial review in 1998 which developed recommendations to speed up the restitution process.[29] Since mid-1999 the process has quickened. While only forty-one claims had been settled by the end of March 1999, as of April 3, 2000, 3,916 claims had been settled (13,608 claimant households and 80,889 beneficiaries at a cost to the state of R178.6 million (U.S.$ 23.5 m));[30] by November 2000, the Department of Land Affairs reported to parliament that 6,535 claims had been settled.[31] Most of the claims settled have been awards of monetary compensation to urban claimants, rather than land restitution to rural claimants, though only three hundred thousand people stand to benefit from urban claims, as against 3.6 million people from the settlement of rural claims.[32] By May 2001, the number of claims settled had almost doubled again, to 12,150, involving more than 27,600 families and 164,000 individuals, with R198 million ($26.1 m) spent in the 2000/2001 financial year.[33] R464.7 million ($63.8 m) had been spent on the program since 1995, of which R182.3 million ($24 m) was spent on buying land for restitution, R260.6 million ($34.4 m) to pay financial compensation.

Secure Tenure

The government's tenure reform program has sought to provide security of tenure by recognizing *de facto* systems of vested rights existing on the ground, based on the principle that established occupation should not be jeopardized unless viable and acceptable alternatives are available for tenants to move elsewhere.[34] The Land Reform (Labour Tenants) Act 1996 and the Extension of Security of Tenure Act 1997 were passed "to protect farm workers and labor tenants from

---

[29] Department of Land Affairs, *Annual Report 1999*, Director-General's Review,

[30] Vuyo Mvoko, "Govt moves to avoid land crisis," *Business Day* July 5, 2000. Unless otherwise noted, all currency amounts have been converted to dollars at the rate of 7.585 rands to one dollar, the rate prevailing at the end of 2000.

[31] "Land Restitution increases, but more can be done: Mgoqi," South African Press Association (SAPA), November 7, 2000.

[32] Land rights activists have argued that the program has therefore failed to address the primary purpose of land reform: the restoration of land to those from whom it was unjustly taken. "Land claimants demand meeting Mbeki on 'lack of delivery,'" *Business Day* June 7, 2000; Siyabulela Qoza, "Land Reform a slow but sure process," *Financial Mail* April 28, 2000.

[33] Minister of Agriculture and Land Affairs Budget Vote Speech, Ministry for Agriculture and Land Affairs, May 15, 2001.

[34] Department of Land Affairs, *White Paper on South African Land Policy* (April 1997), section 4.16.

arbitrary evictions and to provide mechanisms for the acquisition of long term tenure security."[35]

The Labour Tenants Act defines a labor tenant, a person who exchanges labor for a right of access to land, as a person:

> (a) who is residing or has the right to reside on a farm;
> (b) who has or has had the right to use cropping or grazing land on the farm referred to in paragraph (a), or another farm of the owner, and in consideration of such right provides or has provided labor to the owner or lessee; and
> (c) whose parent or grandparent resided or resides on a farm and had the use of cropping or grazing land on such farm or another farm of the owner, and in consideration of such right provided or provides labor to the owner or lessee of such or such other farm, including a person who has been appointed a successor to a labor tenant ... but excluding a farmworker.[36]

A labor tenant can only be evicted for specified reasons, which must be "just and equitable," and on the basis of an order of the Land Claims Court.[37] Labor tenants aged over sixty-five who can no longer work cannot be evicted, and the family of a labor tenant who dies must be given twelve months notice prior to eviction.[38]

---

[35] Department of Land Affairs, *Annual Report 1999*, under heading "Land Rights," p.35. See also Donna Hornby, *"All we need is a piece of land": A National Land Committee Investigation into the Current Status of Labour Tenancy* (Johannesburg: National Land Committee, March 1988).

[36] Land Reform (Labor Tenants) Act, 3 of 1996, section 1(xi). The legislation does not specify how long the parents or grandparents need to have resided on the farm, but the inclusion of criterion (c) means that many who are first generation labor tenants are excluded from the act. Section 1(ix) defines a farmworker as "a person who is employed on a farm in terms of contract of employment which provides that (a) in return for the labor which he or she provides to the owner or lessee of the farm, he or she shall be paid predominantly in cash or in some other form of remuneration, and not predominantly in the right to occupy and use land; and (b) he or she is obliged to perform his or her services personally."

[37] These reasons include a breach of the relationship between owner and labor tenant and failure of the labor tenant to provide the agreed upon labor. Land Reform (Labor Tenants) Act, 3 of 1996, section 7(2).

[38] Land Reform (Labor Tenants) Act, 3 of 1996, section 9.

An amendment passed in 1997 shifted the onus to the farm owner to prove that an individual is not a labor tenant, inhibiting farmers from easily claiming that the labor tenant is not protected by the law because he or she is really a farmworker, and therefore not covered under the statute. The amended act requires that labor tenant cases be transferred to the Land Claims Court.[39]

In addition to providing security of tenure, the Labour Tenants Act also seeks to enable labor tenants to acquire title to land in which they historically have had usage rights.[40] Claims for land rights under this statute must be filed by March 31, 2001.[41] The owners of land affected by the statute are entitled to "just and equitable" compensation, as determined by the Land Claims Court, for land given over to labor tenants.[42] Upon application for ownership rights under the legislation, the labor tenant may be eligible for government grants to pay the owner compensation or to develop the land.[43]

The Extension of Security of Tenure Act aims to protect rural occupiers of land other than labor tenants against arbitrary eviction, by regulating the circumstances under which they may be evicted, and to ensure basic rights, such as the right to allow access to visitors and the right to visit family graves on land belonging to another person.[44] (The act does not give the right to carry out new burials on such land, even if the deceased person was legally resident there and the relatives are still resident. Land rights organizations see this as a major weakness of the act.[45]) Under ESTA an occupier's right of residence may be terminated on

---

[39] Land Restitution and Reform Laws Amendment Act (No. 63 of 1997).

[40] Land Reform (Labor Tenants) Act, 3 of 1996, chapter III.

[41] Land Affairs General Amendment Act (No. 11 of 2000), section 7. This deadline was set so as to provide some certainty to land owners regarding the status of their land.

[42] Land Reform (Labor Tenants) Act, 1996, section 23.

[43] Land Reform (Labor Tenants) Act, 1996, section 26.

[44] An occupier is defined under the act as "a person residing on land which belongs to another person and who has ... consent or another right in law to do so," but excluding labor tenants, a person using the land for mining purposes, or a person with an income over a prescribed limit. Extension of Security of Tenure Act 1997, section 1(1)(x).

[45] In August 1999, the Pretoria High Court ruled that the Extension of Security of Tenure Act could not be read as implying a right to bury the bodies of those who had lived on land they did not own, even if they were residing there legally. "High Court refuses woman right to bury son on farm," SAPA, August 31, 1999; *Bührmann vs. Nkosi and Another*, 2000 (1) SA 1145 (T); [1999] 4 All SA 337 (T). See also the judgment of the Land Claims Court in *Serole and another vs. Pienaar* LCC 9/99 (February 5, 1999). Both farm residents and farm owners see the right to bury the dead as symbolizing a connection with the land, and hence the issue has achieved a significance that is political as well as emotional: where permission

"any lawful ground, provided that such termination is just and equitable" on the basis of factors set out in the act.[46] An occupier who has been resident on the land in question for ten years, and is over sixty years of age or is a former employee of the owner who is disabled or otherwise unable to work, has further protections. A person may be evicted only in terms of an order of a magistrates' court: once a right to occupy the land is terminated by the owner, the court will consider whether the termination is in accordance with the law, considering various factors, and may then grant an order for eviction, but only "if it is satisfied that suitable alternative accommodation is available."[47] It is a criminal offence, punishable by up to two years imprisonment and a fine, to evict a person other than in accordance with an order of court.[48] In a landmark April 1999 ruling, in the case of *Conradie vs. Hanekom*, the Land Claims Court ruled that a woman farmworker could not be evicted from the farm where she worked following the dismissal of her husband and that the right to family life gave the woman the right to allow her husband to continue living in her home on the farm.[49]

All eviction orders granted by magistrates' courts are required to be referred to the Land Claims Court for review: the Land Claims Court reportedly overturns perhaps more than half of the eviction orders that reach it, for non-

---

might previously have been granted, farmers are now reluctant to concede this right.

[46] Extension of Security of Tenure Act 1997, section 8(1).

[47] Extension of Security of Tenure Act 1997, section 10(2). Both magistrates courts and the Land Claims Court have jurisdiction over the act.

[48] Section 23 of the Extension of Security of Tenure Act provides that:

> (1) No person shall evict an occupier except on the authority of an order of a competent court.
>
> (2) No person shall wilfully obstruct or interfere with an official in the employ of the State or a mediator in the performance of his or her duties under this Act.
>
> (3) Any person who contravenes a provision of subsection (1) or (2) shall be guilty of an offence and liable on conviction to a fine, or to imprisonment for a period not exceeding two years, or to both such fine and such imprisonment.
>
> (4) Any person whose rights or interests have been prejudiced by a contravention of subsection (1) shall have the right to institute a private prosecution of the alleged offender.

[49] *Conradie vs. Hanekom* (LCC8R/99). See also Lawyers For Human Rights, *Newsletter for the Human Rights Security of Farm Workers*, vol. 1, no. 1, March/April 1999. The court ruled that the right to family life conferred by section 6 of ESTA afforded Mrs. Hanekom the right to allow her husband—who had been dismissed from his employment on the farm—to continue living in her home on the farm.

compliance with the terms of the act.[50] Although the act provides that cases are to be referred to the LCC it sets no precise time limit for this to be done; the LCC rules provide for the referral to be "forthwith," but there are still delays. In some cases the file only reaches the Land Claims Court six months after the initial decision, and "what is the review worth if the guy has gone from the land and maybe can't even be traced when we overturn the order."[51] In order to address this problem, the government amended the act to provide for magistrates' court orders for eviction to be suspended pending review by the Land Claims Court. Despite this change, there are still cases in which removals in terms of a magistrate's order are carried out before the Land Claims Court has reviewed and approved the decision.

Redistribution
The stated goal of the government's land redistribution program is "to provide the wider majority of South Africans with access to land for residential and productive use in order to improve their livelihoods, with particular emphasis on the poor, labor tenants, farm workers, women and emergent farmers."[52] According to one survey, about 68 percent of South Africa's black rural households desire farmland, most of them small amounts.[53] The government initially decided to provide the landless poor with a "settlement and land acquisition grant," set at R15,000 (U.S.$2,000), to purchase land from willing sellers and make other capital investment.[54] In 1999, the grant system was revised following a ministerial

---

[50] Email communication from Theunis Roux, University of the Witwatersrand Law School, to Human Rights Watch, March 5, 2001.

[51] Human Rights Watch interview with Judge Justice Moloto, Land Claims Court, Randburg, September 18, 2000.

[52] *White Paper on South African Land Policy* (April 1997), section 4.3; Department of Land Affairs, *Annual Report 1999*, Director-General's Review.

[53] T. Marcus, C. Eales, and A. Wildschut, *Down to Earth: Land Demand in the New South Africa* (Durban: Land and Agricultural Policy Centre and Indicator Press, 1996), cited in Julian May (ed.) *Poverty and Inequality in South Africa: Meeting the Challenge* (Cape Town and London: David Philip and Zed Press, 2000), p.241. Forty-eight percent of those wanting farmland desired one hectare or less, and the mean demand for thirteen hectares was skewed by a few people wanting large amounts of land.

[54] Under the Provision of Land and Assistance Act (No. 126 of 1993, as amended in 1998, when its name was also changed from the Provision of Certain Land for Settlement Act). See also *White Paper on South African Land Policy* (April 1997), section 4.7; Samantha Hargreaves, "A piece of land to call their own," *Reconstruct* April 23, 2000. To be eligible for the program claimants must be legal, permanent residents of South Africa, have a

review, to award grants of various amounts, depending on the total cost of the proposed project. Small, medium, and large projects would respectively receive grants of 70 percent, 40 percent, and 20 percent of the total cost of the project. The settlement and land acquisition grant was replaced by a "land reform grant" distributed according to different criteria, which would distinguish between land for residential settlement and land for market-based agriculture. In May 1999, a Land Reform Credit Facility was launched to provide wholesale loans to assist in the creation of commercially viable land reform projects.[55] The government's aim is to transfer ownership of fifteen million hectares of land by 2005, and 30 percent of South Africa's arable land within fifteen years.[56] To date, the government has been unwilling to use its power under section 25 of the constitution to expropriate land, preferring to adhere to a willing-seller, willing-buyer model.[57]

---

monthly household income of not over R1,500 (U.S.$200), and have secure access to less than one hectare of arable land.

[55] Department of Land Affairs, *Annual Report 1999*, Director-General's Review; summary of section on "Delivering Land Reform."

[56] "The Minister and the Land Affairs Programme: Briefing," *Minutes of the Agriculture and Land Affairs Portfolio Committee*, June 20, 2000. Parliamentary minutes are available on the website of the Parliamentary Monitoring Group, <www.pmg.org.za>. The government intends to dispose of 669,000 hectares of state land for land redistribution purposes in 2001-2002, according to the May 15, 2001, budget vote speech of the Minister of Agriculture and Land Affairs, available on the Ministry for Agriculture and Land Affairs website, <land.pwv.gov.za>, accessed June 12, 2001.

[57] *White Paper on South African Land Policy* (April 1997) Executive Summary. At a conference in October 2000, agricultural minister Thoko Didiza stated that the powers of the government under the Expropriation Act 1975 could be used to resolve some of the problems facing land reform; she later reiterated that a willing buyer-willing seller would be the norm in acquiring land for redistribution and that expropriation would be used only as "a last resort" to carry through land reform. Barry Streek, "Farmland expropriation threat denounced," *Mail and Guardian*, October 20, 2000; "No reason for panic about land reform: Didiza," SAPA, October 25, 2000. In February 2001, the government threatened to use its powers of expropriation to take land for the first time (in order to satisfy a claim for restitution relating to a farm near Lydenburg in Mpumalanga; the farmer had agreed to sell but there was a dispute over the price), but later stated that it would attempt to revive negotiations for the sale of the land. A settlement was reached in May, by which the farm was sold to the government for a compromise price. "Lydenburg farmer faces expropriation for land restitution," SAPA, February 12, 2001; Jane Stanley, "SA farmer wins land reprieve," at the BBC website, <www.bbc.co.uk> March 21, 2001; "Agri-SA welcomes Boomplats settlement," SAPA, June 1, 2001; "Letter from the President," in *ANC Today*, vol.1, no.9, June 1-7, 2001.

Implementation

Implementation of land reform has been impeded by a lack of financial and other resources. The DLA receives only 0.4 percent of the national budget, of which only about half is allocated for land acquisition.[58] Although the state has huge landholdings in South Africa, little of it is in practice available to the redistribution program.[59] Because of staff shortages and other problems, processing of a claim by the DLA can take years, and implementation problems have meant that the department has in fact had difficulties spending its budget for redistribution. The restitution program has been plagued by structural problems in the relationship between the DLA and the land claims commission, a lack of effective cooperation between agencies, logistical problems, difficulties in identifying beneficiaries, and a lack of trained and effective staff.[60]

The slowness of delivery in the land reform program has caused significant tension on the ground. Organizations working with farm residents are becoming increasingly frustrated.[61] As one lawyer working on eviction cases put it to Human Rights Watch, "The temperature is rising. It is a major problem that land reform is not happening. I don't want to blame the Department of Land Affairs, but they are under-resourced, under-capacitated, and they can't cope. And people are becoming very frustrated; in the rural areas they say they are no better off than they were before. The consequences could be problematic."[62] Another

---

[58] Ben Cousins, "Zim crisis: our wake-up call," *Mail andGuardian* May 5-11, 2000.

[59] Responding to a question in the National Council of Provinces in July 2000, Minister of Agriculture and Land Affairs Thoko Didiza provided figures indicating that the state owned at least 20 percent of land in South Africa (24.3 million hectares), excluding land owned by parastatals and the 2.9 million hectares owned by the Ingonyama Trust in KwaZulu-Natal (the former KwaZulu homeland). Only between 5 and 7 percent of state land was available for redistribution, since the rest was in use for other purposes. "The Minister and the Land Affairs Programme: Briefing," *Minutes of the Agriculture and Land Affairs Portfolio Committee*, June 20, 2000; Barry Streek, "State owns 20% of SA land—Didiza," *Mail and Guardian*, August 2, 2000.

[60] Marj Brown, Justin Erasmus, Rosalie Kingwill, Colin Murray, and Monty Roodt, *Land Restitution in South Africa: A Long Way Home* (Cape Town: IDASA, 1998); see also "Land Redistribution for Agricultural Development," Executive Summary, December 19, 2000, available on the Department of Land Affairs website, <land.pwv.gov.za>, accessed April 12, 2001.

[61] See *Farm Tenure: Media Guide—A National Land Committee Resource on Farm Workers and Labour Tenants*, June 2000.

[62] Human Rights Watch interview with Peter Rutsch, attorney, by telephone, October 4, 2000.

commented, "The biggest problem at this point is the department. The legal issues have been decided in the Land Claims Court and Appellate Division, but the difficulty is implementing agreements between landowners and farm residents, to see to it that there is an actual transfer of land, for which the department must be involved. Everything is stuck, we just get no reply to letters, or proposals for discussions. Because of the delays, there is no transformation in practice, and so people are beginning to have doubts about the good faith of the government."[63]

Farm owners and their representatives agree with this assessment, in particular that the failure to deliver on land reform is likely to exacerbate tensions between farm owners and their workers or tenants. Some farm owners believe that the problems in delivering land reform reflect a politically-motivated hidden agenda rather than simple bureaucratic delays: "Land Affairs is a big problem. It seems that it is a political organization. For example, there are three farmers in this area with 7,000 hectares they are willing to sell, but they are battling now for three or four years to get the sale through. Land Affairs are not willing to help people, but then they are instigating people on the ground to think that it is the farmers' fault, not the Department of Land Affairs."[64] A representative of organized agriculture commented to Human Rights Watch "The land claims process is not a transparent system; often the farmer does not know a claim has been lodged until he sees it in the Government Gazette."[65] When considering promises made for future speeding up of the land redistribution program, farm owners are even more concerned: "The government says that 30 percent of commercial farmland must be redistributed, but there is no money set aside; and what is going to happen when it doesn't take place? The farmers will be sitting with the problem."[66] Farm owners' assessments are based on the premise, challenged by land rights organizations, that land ownership as it currently exists is fundamentally legitimate, even if some redistribution is justified: "There are problems because promises were made that have not been kept, and nobody's bothered to tell the tribal community that it's not their land."[67]

---

[63] Human Rights Watch interview with Christo Loots, attorney, Pietermaritzburg, September 11, 2000.

[64] Human Rights Watch interview with farmers, Vryheid, September 14, 2000.

[65] Human Rights Watch interview with Jack Loggenberg, Transvaal Agricultural Union, April 17, 2000.

[66] Human Rights Watch interview with Mike de Lange, formerly KwaZulu-Natal Agricultural Union (KWANALU) security desk, September 14, 2000.

[67] Human Rights Watch interview with Mike de Lange, formerly KWANALU security desk, September 14, 2000.

The land invasions promoted by the government of Zimbabwe have concentrated the minds of government, farmers, and farmworkers on the land issue in South Africa. President Mbeki has been criticized for being slow to speak out against President Robert Mugabe's policies, including both land invasions and the violence visited on opposition candidates in the country's 2000 elections. Nevertheless, in its formal statements the South African government has repeatedly stated that land redistribution in South Africa will only take place within the context of the law, and that invasions along the lines of those taking place in Zimbabwe will not be tolerated—even though some comments have been interpreted by the media to express support for Zimbabwe's policies.[68] While there have been no organized land invasions along the lines of those in Zimbabwe, many farm owners reported to Human Rights Watch that, especially in areas adjoining the overcrowded former homelands, there has been a "creeping" invasion of individual farms through methods such as the breaking down of fences in order to graze stock, or a rapid increase in the number of people living on a farm without the permission of the landowner.

In October 2000, the National Land Committee and the Centre for Applied Legal Studies, University of the Witwatersrand, held a joint media briefing at which they warned that there could be a serious breakdown of law and order in the rural areas, as had happened in Zimbabwe, if the government did not speed up land reform.[69] In May 2001, the government condemned a threat to invade farms made by the Mpumalanga Labour Tenants Committee, and said that land invaders would

---

[68] For example, remarks made by Deputy President Jacob Zuma at a Southern African Development Community summit in Namibia were interpreted to indicate support for President Mugabe. The South African government later issued a statement reporting that Zuma had given an assurance "that the situation in Zimbabwe would not happen in South Africa. His view is that there are constitutional guarantees and a strong adherence to the rule of law in South Africa to guard against this." Statement issued by the Office of the Presidency, "Reported comment by Deputy President Zuma on the Zimbabwe situation," September 11, 2000. *Business Day* (Johannesburg) editorialized on October 13, 2000, that Zuma's comments "by no stretch of the imagination could be construed as supporting Zimbabwean style land invasions." In May 2000, Mbeki stated in parliament that any land invasions in South Africa would be "contrary to policy and contrary to the law. Therefore the government would take all necessary steps to ensure that the breaking of the law comes to an end. That is not a problem, that is not an issue." "Government won't tolerate farm invasions in SA: Mbeki," SAPA, May 10, 2000.
[69] "Land reform essential to end rural 'war,'" SAPA, October 18, 2000.

be dealt with severely in terms of the law.[70] In June, the government ordered the removal of people who invaded a farm from which their families had been forcibly removed during the apartheid era, near Kuruman in the Northern Cape.[71]

Labor Rights

Only very recently, since the transition to democratic government began, has the protection of employment law been extended to farmworkers. The 1983 Basic Conditions of Employment Act (BCEA) was amended with effect from May 1, 1993, to provide farmworkers for the first time with rights to maximum working hours, overtime pay, sick leave, lunch hours, and other basic protections.[72] The 1993 Agricultural Labor Act (No. 147 of 1993) further formalized these rights, and in particular gave farmworkers for the first time a right to organize. The 1966 Unemployment Insurance Act, extended to the agricultural sector in 1994, entitles workers to receive unemployment insurance funds should they be laid off.[73] However, seasonal or temporary workers employed for four months or less each year, were still largely excluded from these newly introduced protections.

After the ANC-led government took office in 1994, the new constitution included provision for comprehensive protection for labor rights.[74] The Labor

---

[70] "Labour tenants committee threatens Mpuma land invasion," SAPA, May 27, 2001; "Press statement on reported threats to invade farms in Mpumalanga," Department of Land Affairs, May 28, 2001.

[71] "Land invaders to be ejected: Land Affairs," SAPA, June 22, 2001.

[72] The Basic Conditions of Employment Amendment Act (No. 137 of 1993), amended the Basic Conditions of Employment Amendment Act (No. 3 of 1983) to extend provisions relating to maximum daily and weekly hours, Sunday work, overtime, etc., to farmworkers, defined as employees "employed mainly in or in connection with farming activities, and includes an employee who wholly or mainly performs domestic work on dwelling premises on a farm." (Section 1(d)). These legal protections were at the same time extended to domestic workers.

[73] Unemployment Insurance Act, No. 30 of 1966, as amended. Every employee is entitled to an Unemployment Insurance Card (UIF card, also known as a "blue card"), which serves to prove his or her entitlement to UIF benefits in the event of retrenchment. It is the employer's responsibility to apply to the Department of Labor for their employees' UIF cards.

[74] Section 27 of the interim constitution (Constitution of the Republic of South Africa Act No. 200 of 1993), which was in force between April 27, 1994 and February 4, 1997, provided that "(1) Every person shall have the right to fair labor practices. (2) Workers shall have the right to form and join trade unions...." Section 23 of the final constitution (Constitution of the Republic of South Africa Act No.108 of 1996) sets out more

Relations Act (No. 66 of 1995) then provided a new framework for the regulation of relations between all employers and employees in South Africa, including the commercial farming sector. The act also established the Commission for Conciliation, Mediation, and Arbitration (CCMA), an independent government-funded dispute resolution mechanism, whose governing body is formed of representatives of government, organized labor, and organized business. A new version of the Basic Conditions of Employment Act was passed in 1997 (No. 75 of 1997), which further extended the rights accorded to farmworkers, so that in most regards they now have the same rights as all other workers in South Africa. In particular, the new BCEA extended employment benefits to all employees working for twenty-four hours or more a month, on a *pro-rata* basis, thereby giving greater protection to seasonal and temporary workers. Domestic workers are still excluded from the act.

The 1998 Employment Equity Act brings into statutory effect the protections against discrimination included in the constitutional bill of rights, and similar provisions under international law,[75] and provides that no employer may unfairly discriminate against an employee on a comprehensive list of grounds, including race, gender, sex, pregnancy, marital status, family responsibility, ethnic or social origin, color, sexual orientation, age, disability, religion, or HIV status.[76] The act defines harassment of an employee as a form of unfair discrimination.[77]

---

comprehensive provisions, including that "(1) Everyone has the right to fair labor practices. (2) Every worker has the right (a) to form and join a trade union; (b) to participate in the activities and programmes of a trade union; and (c) to strike." Other subsections relate to the right to collective bargaining.

[75] Race- or sex-based discrimination is prohibited under the International Labour Organization's Discrimination (Employment and Occupation) Convention No. 111, adopted in 1958. The convention includes provisions relating to equal remuneration for work of equal value; hours of work; rest periods; and occupational health, as well as social security measures and welfare facilities and benefits provided in connection with employment. In 1952, the ILO adopted the Equal Remuneration Convention No.100. Article 2 of Convention No.100 provides that, "Each member shall, by means appropriate to the methods in operation for determining rates of remuneration... ensure the application to all workers of the principle of equal remuneration for men and women workers for work of equal value." South Africa ratified ILO Convention No. 111 on March 5, 1997, and Convention No. 100 on March 30, 2000.

[76] Section 6 (1) of the Employment Equity Act, No. 55 of 1998.

[77] Section 6 (3) of the Employment Equity Act provides, "Harassment of an employee is a form of unfair discrimination and is prohibited on any one, or a combination of grounds of unfair discrimination listed in Subsection (1)." See also Lisa Vetten, "Paper Promises,

Farmers (and other businesses) with more than fifty workers or a turnover of more than R2 million (U.S.$264,000) a year are required to submit "employment equity plans" to the government aimed at eliminating discrimination in the workplace. In the Free State, for example, about 700 of 7,000 commercial farmers fall in this bracket, and stated they would submit their plans in December 2000.[78] The Promotion of Equality and Prevention of Unfair Discrimination Act of 2000 strengthened the Employment Equity Act in its intended aim to prohibit unfair discrimination. This legislation provides that "No person may subject any person to harassment," defined as "unwanted conduct which is persistent or serious and demeans, humiliates or creates a hostile environment or is calculated to induce submission by actual or threatened adverse consequences and which is related to sex, gender, or sexual orientation."[79]

Women farmworkers have a right to four months of maternity leave, beginning at any time from one month before the expected date of birth, under the 1997 Basic Conditions of Employment Act.[80] The payment of benefits during maternity leave is determined under the Unemployment Insurance Act, which restricts these rights to women who are employed for more than four months a year.[81] While her employer is not obliged to pay her normal wages while she is on maternity leave, a woman can claim a percentage of the wages from the Unemployment Insurance Fund (UIF), through the Department of Labor.[82] The

---

Protests and Petitions: South African State and Civil Society Responses to Violence Against Women," in Yoon Jung Park, Joanne Fedler, and Zubeda Dangor (eds.), *Reclaiming Women's Spaces: New Perspectives on Violence Against Women and Sheltering in South Africa* (Johannesburg: Nisaa Institute for Women's Development, 2000), pp.83-120, p.85.

[78] "Free State farmers prepare employment equity plans," SAPA, December 8, 2000.

[79] Section 11 and Section 1(xiii) of the Promotion of Equality and Unfair Discrimination Act, No. 4 of 2000.

[80] The Basic Conditions of Employment Act, No. 75 of 1997, section 25.

[81] Unemployment Insurance Act, No. 30 of 1966, as amended, section 37(5).

[82] In June 2000, the ILO adopted the Maternity Protection Convention No. 183, relating to protection before and after child birth of the rights of women wage earners. In terms of the convention, women wage-earners in agriculture are entitled to a period of maternity leave "of not less than fourteen weeks," including "compulsory leave for a period of six week after child birth" in order to ensure protection of the health of the mother and that of the child. Further, the Maternity Protection Convention provides that women in agriculture are entitled to receive "cash benefits" during maternity leave. Where a woman does not meet the conditions to qualify for a cash benefit under national laws and regulations, she should receive adequate benefits either out of the public funds or by means of a system of insurance, subject to the means test required for such assistance. At the time of this writing,

UIF is financed by contributions from workers and employers, and to be eligible for UIF payments during maternity leave, an employee must have made contributions.[83] Domestic workers (including domestic workers on farms) are still excluded from the protections of the Unemployment Insurance Act, although proposed reforms to the act may bring them within its ambit.[84]

The Department of Labour is responsible for the enforcement of labor legislation, particularly the provisions of the BCEA, through its labor inspectorate. However, there is a shortage of inspectors, meaning that farms are seldom inspected in practice. The CCMA has responsibilities in relation to dismissals and other matters under the Labour Relations Act.

Although organization of agricultural labor has been legal since 1993, only between 12 and 14 percent of farmworkers are unionized.[85] As in other countries, the agricultural sector is difficult to organize, given low pay and problems of access and communication with workers who are geographically isolated and seldom have access to telephones or private vehicles. Where agricultural workers are successfully unionized, it tends to be among the employees of the big agri-businesses using factory-like methods, such as the poultry industry, especially those that are easily accessible to urban areas.

The two main unions representing farmworkers are the South African Agricultural, Plantation, and Allied Workers' Union (SAAPAWU) and the Food and Allied Workers' Union (FAWU), both of them affiliated to the ANC-aligned

---

June 2001, this convention had not yet come into force. The convention revises and replaces a previous convention of 1952.

[83] While a person is employed, his/her employer is supposed to pay two percent of the full wages to the Unemployment Insurance Fund. One percent of the contributions comes from the employee's wages and the employer must pay the other one percent. See Centre For Rural Legal Studies *Rights for Women Farm Workers* (Stellenbosch: Centre for Rural Legal Studies, 2000), p.7.

[84] A draft Unemployment Insurance Bill was published by the Department of Labour in 2000, which will repeal the existing act and introduce important reforms, among other things de-linking maternity benefits from unemployment benefits. The original draft of the bill excluded both farmworkers and domestic workers, but the parliamentary labor committee recommended that both should be included, a debate that is still ongoing. See "Report on Rural Women's Workshop, Report on Unemployment Insurance Bill, Budget Hearings Strategy," *Minutes of the Joint Monitoring Committee on the Improvement of Quality of Life and the Status of Women*, May 9, 2001.

[85] According to then Minister of Agriculture and Land Affairs Derek Hanekom in a written reply to a parliamentary question put by the National Party. Clive Sawyer, "Farm unions struggling to recruit members: Hanekom," *Cape Argus* August 21, 1998.

trades union umbrella body, the Congress of South African Trades Unions (COSATU). There are also a host of smaller unions in different parts of the country, some affiliated with the Pan Africanist Congress-aligned National Council of Trades Unions (NACTU), others independent. Even the better established unions have not much capacity, even on the most urgent matters affecting their members. Howard Mbana of SAAPAWU, for example, noted to Human Rights Watch that the union had adopted a resolution at its annual meeting to monitor violence on farms with the aim of gaining greater exposure of the issue, but that the union's financial and organizational weakness had prevented this from being implemented effectively.[86]

The Response of Farm Owners to Government Reforms

> *What is not realised is that commercial farmers have been subject to more change in the past ten years than any other group in this country. In addition to adapting to the changes all other South Africans have made, they have also lost all government support in the shape of tariffs, subsidies, cheap loans and the like. They have also had to start making unemployment fund payments; they have had to get used to trade union membership among their workers; and they have had to adapt to the huge problems caused by [the] new land laws.[87]*

Among employment sectors, the 1994 change of government has had perhaps the most profound effect on the working environment of the commercial farmer in South Africa. While those speaking for farmworkers and residents see far too little change in practice, farm owners and managers have had to adapt from a situation in which they received privileged treatment from government, including hefty subsidies and protective tariffs, to one in which subsidies and cheap finance have been largely ended, labor legislation extended to the agricultural sector, and trade tariffs progressively cut. At the same time, the protection of state security forces and the use of state violence to check challenges to white control of the land has been exchanged for a government commitment to land redistribution and laws protecting farm residents from arbitrary eviction. The depth of the change in

---

[86] Human Rights Watch interview with Howard Mbana, SAAPAWU, March 24, 2000.

[87] Interview with Graham McIntosh, (then) president of the KwaZulu-Natal Agricultural Union, published in *Briefing* 12, (Johannesburg: Helen Suzman Foundation, September 1998).

attitude that has been required is illustrated by the results of a referendum conducted by the Transvaal Agricultural Union (TAU) in 1990, in which 94.52 percent of the 11,895 farmers who participated voted "yes" to the question: "Are you in favor of farmland being preserved for white ownership?"[88]

Following the transition to democratic government, organized agriculture also debated its new role. There were, and remain, differences in how to respond to the new dispensation, with divisions in particular between those who oppose the new government on almost all fronts, and those who favor engagement with the policy process and expansion of the representation of organized agriculture to include "emerging" black farmers. In 1999, the South African Agricultural Union, the umbrella body for the white farmers' associations (known as agricultural unions) in the four old provinces of South Africa, renamed itself Agri-SA, which now represents at national level its affiliated agricultural unions in the nine new provinces. The KwaZulu-Natal Agricultural Union (KWANALU), an affiliate of Agri-SA and traditionally more liberal, has merged with structures representing black farmers in the province and now represents 33,000 small scale black farmers as well as 3,700 farmers paying the full subscription to the organization (mostly white commercial farmers). KWANALU estimates it represents 60 to 80 percent of all commercial farmers, and probably 90 percent of the larger farms.[89] The Transvaal Agricultural Union, however, rejected this process, choosing to continue to organize its membership according to the old provincial boundaries and to resist, even if not explicitly, the process of racial integration. In May 2000, Agri-SA formally ended the affiliation of TAU with the umbrella body, on the grounds that TAU had failed to comply with the terms of Agri-SA's constitution since it was adopted in October 1998, and had not paid membership dues.[90] TAU claims that its members include 50 percent of all commercial farmers in the four northern provinces that make up the former Transvaal, approximately 6,000 farmers in all. Since March 2000, TAU has begun recruiting new members nationwide.[91]

As several government officials acknowledged to Human Rights Watch, the split in organized agriculture between Agri-SA and TAU, and the fact that many farmers are not members of either association, makes it difficult to

---

[88] Cited in Lauren Segal, *A Brutal Harvest: The Roots and Legitimation of Violence on Farms in South Africa* (Johannesburg: Project for the Study of Violence and Black Sash, 1991), p.16.

[89] Email to Human Rights Watch from KWANALU, August 7, 2000.

[90] "Transvaal Agric Union scrapped from Agri-SA," SAPA, May 11, 2000.

[91] Human Rights Watch interview with Jack Loggenberg and Boela Niemann, TAU, Pretoria, September 19, 2000.

communicate government policy and to find solutions to the problems of unequal land distribution. "Not all farmers are in the agricultural union, and we have a problem in reaching those who are not.... The people we speak to are more moderate, the real right wingers exclude themselves."[92] The threat posed by the "real right wingers" to the South African polity has faded since 1994, when at some points it seemed as though right wing violence might prevent the transition to majority rule from going ahead; nevertheless, right wing opposition to government policy remains a serious concern in some cases.

The Transvaal Agricultural Union now voices the concerns of the more conservative farmers who choose to engage with organized agriculture. Their view is that:

> South Africa's white farmers are also under attack from a government in thrall to millions of landless voters, many of whom say—as do their Zimbabwean brothers—that whites 'stole' their land. This is of course a ludicrous assertion. When whites came to southern Africa, there was little if any systematic cultivation and certainly no agricultural industry to speak of. Western farming methods allowed South Africa to become one of the world's six food-exporting countries. Yet under the new government, assaults on farmers, and their property rights and their very future are increasing.[93]

Noting President Mbeki's failure openly to condemn land seizures in Zimbabwe, TAU asserts that "What happened illegally in Zimbabwe has become a legal process in South Africa. People now making demands for land are protected by South African legislation."[94] Speaking to Human Rights Watch, TAU representatives reinforced this view: "We need to change direction or there will be conflict on the ground, and the government seems simply not to care."[95] Reflecting

---

[92] Human Rights Watch interview with Dion Pelser, Director of Support Services, Northern Province Department of Safety and Security, Pietersburg, March 29, 2000.

[93] "South Africa's White Farming Industry: How its destruction will affect the United State," on the Transvaal Agricultural Union website, <www.rights2property.com/>, accessed October 6, 2000.

[94] "Liberation of the land, known as LAND REFORM," on the Transvaal Agricultural Union website, <www.rights2property.com/background.htm>, accessed October 6, 2000.

[95] Human Rights Watch interview with Jack Loggenberg and Boela Niemann, TAU, Pretoria, September 19, 2000.

this general approach, individual farmers have expressed their opposition to government legislation to Human Rights Watch and others: "The whole attitude in northern KwaZulu-Natal is that the farms belong to them [labor tenants]. A farm is something you bought with your own money but that is not actually yours. They talk of apartheid—this is apartheid at its best."[96]

More moderate representatives of commercial agriculture accept that land reform and labor legislation is necessary, though many still question the government's approach, believing that land redistribution should focus on creating new black commercial farmers. A survey commissioned by Agri-SA among commercial farmers in early 2001, found that 63 percent of those who responded thought that land reform was indispensable for peaceful coexistence in South Africa, and that 79 percent thought that commercial farmers are anxious to assist emerging black farmers.[97] Many perceive that current government policy is, however, to take land from the richest and give it to the poorest, who, they believe, will not use it profitably. "The land reform program needs clarity and realism. The government must not create expectations that are unrealistic in a global context."[98] Many farmers argue that land reform legislation has been misused in practice; and that the process of land restitution and redistribution has created uncertainty and contributed to a worsening of labor relations. "The land redistribution acts have played a major part in upsetting relations on farms, with the role of the NGOs and the Department of Land Affairs in creating a perception that land will be redistributed, an expectation among the people living on the land and in the townships that they will get land. The long process frustrates people on the ground, and then what happens is that the project of Land Affairs to get people to apply for land is creating tension on the farms."[99]

---

[96] Wessel Potgieter, the defendant in a prominent case of eviction brought before the Land Claims Court, speaking to a representative of the Helen Suzman Foundation, Cheryl Goodenough, "This land is ours," *KwaZulu-Natal Briefing* no. 11 (Johannesburg: Helen Suzman Foundation, June 1998).

[97] Summary of March 2001 Markinor survey commissioned by *Landbouweekblad*, the magazine of Agri-SA, among 405 randomly selected readers of the magazine. The percentages reflected the number of respondents "agreeing" or "wholeheartedly agreeing" to these statements. See also, "Letter from the President," *ANC Today*, vol.1, no.19, June 1-7, 2001.

[98] Human Rights Watch interview with Jack Raath, Agri-SA, March 23, 2000.

[99] Human Rights Watch interview with Lourie Bosman, Mpumalanga Agricultural Union, Ermelo, April 12, 2000.

In direct opposition to the close connection to the land expressed by many black farm residents, many farm owners who spoke to Human Rights Watch see the relationship of a farm owner with those who live on his land and work for him as no different from the relationship of any other employer to his or her workforce. Many assert that a farm owner without further need for labor need not have any continuing relationship or obligation to those he formerly employed who have been resident on his land (sometimes for decades, or their families for generations). Yet at the same time, they note with dismay that their black tenants are increasingly asserting such an obligation. "Farmers with labor tenants find that they are just getting more and more cattle and overgrazing the land, and at the same time they are refusing to work any more for the farmer. And though the farmer can't let them stay on the farm if they are not working—if you don't work you should leave—there is no way except at high legal cost that you can evict them. It is a great frustration to the farmers."[100]

The agricultural unions blame the current government for what they see as a deterioration of the relations between farm owners and their workers—based, it seems, on a somewhat unrealistic evaluation of the relationship during the apartheid years. A representative of TAU commented to Human Rights Watch: "After 1994 it slowly started to happen that the good relations between laborers and farm owners were disturbed by all the legislation coming in with protection for the laborers. The cracks were starting to show. The farmer must protect himself financially and also he is seeing murders taking place so he is making other plans, for example to mechanize more. The laborer is becoming a burden and a threat, and there is now starting to be mistrust."[101] Accordingly, many farmers point out that the new legislation has reinforced rather than halted a trend among farmers to move away from employing individuals from families resident on and with a connection to the farm towards the use of labor hired from among people with no historic link to the land: "The law is the law, though people are unhappy about the way it is being implemented, and it is affecting the number of people employed, since farmers are doing away with labor because of all the changes. Farmers are moving to contract labor."[102]

---

[100] Human Rights Watch interview with Theo van Rooyen, farmer, Utrecht, September 15, 2000.

[101] Human Rights Watch interview with Jack Loggenberg, Transvaal Agricultural Union, Pretoria, April 17, 2000.

[102] Human Rights Watch interview with Mike de Lange, formerly KWANALU security desk, September 14, 2000.

There has been little structured dialogue between the agricultural unions representing farm owners and organizations representing farmworkers. Individual farm owners also often prefer to use consultants specializing in labor relations to manage interaction with farmworker unions or NGOs. The farm owners' unions tend to have hostile attitudes towards these groups: "These NGOs are fading now, but they represent the dregs of the old Marxist way of looking at everything.... It is their sort of irresponsible radicalism and encouragement to people to stage land invasions and the like which seeps down to such young people [those who carry out farm attacks]."[103] Land rights groups are accused of giving farm residents false information about their rights, and leading them to sign documents that they do not understand, "one of the main factors giving rise to conflicts."[104]

In May 2001, however, in an encouraging development, Minister of Labor Membathisi Shepherd Mdladlana announced an agreement brokered by the government among SAAPAWU, FAWU, the National African Farmers' Union, and Agri-SA, setting out a "vision for labor relations in agriculture." All parties agreed to the aim of ensuring that labor relations in the agricultural sector respect fundamental human rights and promote sound labor relations practices, skills development, compliance with health and safety standards, productivity improvements, and the effective management of HIV/AIDS on farms. Minister Mdladlana commended Agri-SA for its commitment to improving the conditions of workers on farms.[105]

Government subsidies to agriculture have been greatly decreased in recent years, and are now among the lowest in world; a weak currency boosts exports but makes input costs higher.[106] Severe flooding and an outbreak of foot and mouth disease in 2000 added to the pressures on commercial farmers—and even in 1988 it was estimated that only a third of white-owned units were financially viable, the rest marginal.[107] When natural disasters are added to the changes brought about by

---

[103] Interview with Graham McIntosh, (then) president of the KwaZulu-Natal Agricultural Union, published in *Briefing* 12, (Johannesburg: Helen Suzman Foundation, September 1998).

[104] Human Rights Watch interview with Lourie Bosman, Mpumalanga Agricultural Union, April 12, 2000.

[105] "Statement by Honourable Minister of Labour, Mr Membathisi Mphumzi Shepherd Mdladlana, at the signing of a historic agreement between AgriSA, SAAPAWU, FAWU and NAFU, Pretoria, May 29, 2001," Ministry of Labour, May 29, 2001.

[106] "Crisis in SA agriculture as competition hits," SAPA, November 3, 2000, reporting on a conference on the agricultural sector.

[107] Copper, *Working the Land.*

government policy reform, many farm owners feel themselves under siege. At the annual congress of Agri-SA in 2000, the outgoing president of the farmers' union called on government to "just leave us alone.... The camel's back is breaking. Most politicians are so involved in populist politics that they don't realise a cornerstone of the economy is crumbling because of government action."[108]

Conditions on Farms Today

> *The mutual dependence and common environment that they*
> *share suggest a sense of community and intimacy on the farm.*
> *Yet this is a community which is highly divided and stratified;*
> *the dimensions of apparently common interest are ultimately*
> *shattered by the farmers' ownership of the land and the*
> *underlying relationships of domination and subordination. The*
> *relationship is ultimately a relationship between a master and a*
> *servant, between a white 'baas' and a black worker.*[109]

There are in the region of 60,000 farms in the commercial sector in South Africa, whose average size is around 1.3 thousand hectares, much the same as it was in 1988; by comparison, in the former homelands, 50 percent of households cultivate an area of less than one hectare, and only 1 percent have ten hectares or more under cultivation.[110] Livestock farms raising cattle for meat occupy about 80

---

[108] "State drives farmers to the wall," *ZA Now* (on the *Mail and Guardian* website <www.mg.co.za>), October 5, 2000; "State policies driving farmers to bankruptcy: Agri-SA," SAPA, October 4, 2000. Agri-SA president Chris Du Toit stated that agricultural input costs had increased by 43.7 percent since 1995, while product prices had only increased by 16 percent.

[109] Segal, *A Brutal Harvest.*

[110] *Employment Trends in Agriculture in South Africa* (Pretoria: Stats SA and National Department of Agriculture, 2000), pp.22-23. The question of how many commercial farms there are is, however, complicated, given the new membership of some small-scale farmers from the former homeland areas in the structures representing commercial agriculture. In August 1999, Agri-SA referred to "85,000 commercial and small scale farmers," in connection with the launch of a fund to provide security. "Farmers' union raising money for rural security," *ZA Now*, August 11, 1999. Less than a year later, however, commercial agriculture was quoted as stating that there are 40,000 commercial farmers and 32,000 small scale farmers. "MPs express concern about SA farm attacks," SAPA, May 10, 2000. Statistics relating to farmworkers also remain unreliable, because of a lack of consistent collection of uniform and disaggregated data and an increase in temporary employment in

percent of South Africa, though most are marginal in economic terms; dairy cattle and sheep raised for wool (in the Karoo) are also important; maize and wheat are grown in a number of areas, the most important being the "highveld" of the Free State and parts of Northern, North Western, and Mpumalanga Provinces; plantation agriculture raising sub-tropical fruit, cotton, and other crops has expanded over the last decade or so, especially in the "lowveld" of Mpumalanga and Northern Province; sugar is extensively grown in coastal KwaZulu-Natal; forestry for the paper industry is increasingly important in areas marginal for other crops; in the Western Cape, some of South Africa's best land, fruit and wine production dominates. Agriculture is a major earner of foreign exchange for South Africa, but today contributes less than 5 percent of gross domestic product.[111]

Formal employment in agriculture in South Africa is declining, though it still provides more than 10 percent of formal employment opportunities. Annual surveys of the commercial agricultural sector carried out by Stats SA, the government statistics office, indicate that the number of people employed in regular work on commercial farms declined by 15.7 percent, from 724,000 to 610,000, during the period 1988 to 1996. Other research suggests that employment of regular workers declined by a further 7.6 percent during the period 1994/95 to 1998/99, while employment of contract labor increased from 18.8 percent to 24.2 percent of the agricultural labor force over the same period. The total number of people employed fell by 25 percent (from 1.2 million to 914,000) during the 1988 to 1996 period, reflecting a greater absolute decline among those engaged in casual or seasonal work.[112] The position of farmworkers is especially precarious given the high unemployment rate in South Africa generally: "One morning when we were reporting to work the farmer said 'why do you look angry? The gate is open, there are plenty of other people who are looking for a job.' So we just said nothing and carried on."[113]

The 1996 census revealed that nine out of every ten Africans or coloreds working in the commercial agriculture sector were employees, but two in every

the farming sector which makes it difficult to maintain accurate statistics.
[111] Nick Vink (ed.), "The Determination of Employment Conditions in South African Agriculture: A Report to the Department of Labour," Centre for Rural Legal Studies, Stellenbosch, and National Institute of Economic Policy, Johannesburg, March 2001, Part I "The Livelihoods of Farm Workers in South Africa," section 5.
[112] *Employment Trends in Agriculture*, Summary of Findings and pp.21, 32, 35, and 37.
[113] Human Rights Watch interview with farm resident, Northern Province, March 30, 2000. Translated from Pedi.

five whites were employers.[114] Reflecting this division, 41 percent of Africans had no schooling at all and 60 percent had not completed primary education, whereas 77 percent of whites had obtained matric (school leaving certificate) or higher qualifications.[115] Among those working in agriculture, including in the former homelands, 79 percent of Africans, compared to 10 percent of whites, had monthly incomes of R500 (U.S.$66) or less. The average remuneration of employees in the commercial farming sector rose from R142 per month in 1988 ($40) to R524 in 1996 ($143); nevertheless, in 1996 the amount paid to Africans was on average 12 percent of that received by white employees and some were paid substantially less than the average, only a few tens of rand a month. "In-kind" payments formed a larger proportion of the remuneration paid to Africans (25 percent) than of any other population group, and a lower proportion of total remuneration in those provinces where average remuneration was highest.[116] A separate 1998 study of farmworkers in KwaZulu-Natal found that they earned an average R709.27 a month ($120), before deductions (R447.40 ($76) cash after deductions), plus the use of roughly eight hectares of land for grazing or cultivation.[117] Only in private households (which include domestic workers) is the distribution of occupations more inequitable than in the agricultural sector, in the sense that low-skilled, low-paid, work forms a high proportion (58 percent) of all jobs in agriculture.[118]

Farm workers fall into different categories. The most common category includes men and women living and working in permanent or temporary positions on farms. A second category consists of men and women employed on farms but living off-farm. Seasonal workers constitute yet a third category of farmworkers. Seasonal workers are mostly women and a few men recruited every year from rural areas, townships, or squatter camps to work on farms during the planting and harvesting seasons. They are often housed in farm compounds during the time of

---

[114] *Employment Trends in Agriculture*, p.43.

[115] Ibid., p.26. As a proportion of all those employed in agriculture, 32 percent have no schooling, and 3 matric or higher qualifications. By comparison, among all employed people in the economy, only 10 percent have no schooling, and 13 percent have matric or higher. Ibid., p.86.

[116] Ibid., pp.51-56.

[117] R.W. Johnson and Lawrence Schlemmer, *Farmers and Farmworkers in KwaZulu-Natal: Employment conditions, labor tenancy, land reform, attitudes and relationships* (Johannesburg: Helen Suzman Foundation, 1998), p.51. All currency conversions at contemporary rates in this paragraph.

[118] *Employment Trends in Agriculture*, p.91.

their employment. The last, and probably most vulnerable, group are migrant farmworkers from neighboring countries.

Working conditions on farms vary considerably, but in general they are poor. Rounding up a survey of employment trends in agriculture, Stats SA concluded that "in terms of key socio-economic variables, the situation of people employed in the agricultural sector tends to be less favorable than every other major sector of the economy."[119] A survey of conditions for farmworkers carried out by the Farmworkers Research and Resource Project (FRRP) in 1996 found that a majority of farmworkers earned less than the "minimum living level" defined by the Labour Market Commission. On 27 percent of the 196 farms surveyed there were no toilet facilities.[120] 56 percent of farms had no electricity in farmworkers' dwellings, and only 34 percent had taps for running water in the dwellings. It is usual for deductions from wages to be made where these services are provided. Schools were on average within ten kilometers of the farm, but doctors and clinics were on average more than twenty kilometers from farms.[121] Farmworkers have the lowest levels of literacy in the country.[122]

Food rations form a substantial part of the payment of agricultural workers across South Africa. Despite attempts to end the system, and in violation of international norms, some wine farms of the Western Cape still issue part payment of wages to their workers in wine, contributing to the chronic alcoholism prevalent in the wine-producing areas.[123] Also, some farm owners sell wine on credit to their

---

[119] Ibid., p.93.

[120] One woman farmworker told Human Rights Watch that farm owners denied them permission to go to their compounds to use the toilets, telling the women to "just do the shit" in the field, meaning that women should relieve themselves in public within the sight of men working in the same fields. Human Rights Watch interview, group of women farmworkers, Western Cape, April 12, 2000.

[121] Stephen Greenberg, Meshack Hlongwane, David Shabangu, and Ellen Sigudla, *State of South African Farmworkers 1996* (Johannesburg: Farmworkers Research and Resource Project, 1997), Summary.

[122] Vink (ed.), "The Determination of Employment Conditions in South African Agriculture," Executive Summary.

[123] Articles 3 and 4 of ILO Protection of Wages Convention No. 95 (1949), allow partial payment of wages "in the form of allowances in kind," but expressly forbid payment of wages in the form of liquor in any circumstances. This convention came into force in 1952 and was partially revised in 1992 by ILO Convention No. 173. South Africa has not ratified ILO Convention No 95.

farmworkers, promoting a cycle of debt for farmworkers who return a percentage of their wages to their employers as payment for the wine debt.[124]

Although farmworkers are now protected by labor legislation, Human Rights Watch repeatedly heard accounts of farmers flouting the rules relating to working hours, paid holidays or maternity leave, health and safety, or the right to organize. Health and safety regulations are often poorly observed during the use of agricultural chemicals: while Human Rights Watch did not systematically investigate this aspect of conditions on farms, many farmworkers reported that they were not trained in how to use pesticides and herbicides, nor given protective clothing. At one farm on the East Rand, Gauteng, for example, a woman farmworker reported, "Sometimes we have to run away because of the smell. People have been sick, especially the men, who are doing the spraying using the pesticides the most. One has died, one is coughing very badly. We have never seen anyone from the government to check health and safety; when the health inspector comes they just give him vegetables and he goes back. It is only when the police come to harass us for identity documents that we see any government person."[125]

During 2000, the Department of Labour held public hearings in all nine provinces and conducted other investigations for the purposes of making a "sectoral determination" under the Basic Conditions of Employment Act in relation to the commercial agricultural sector. A sectoral determination involves the setting of basic conditions of employment, in this case in the agricultural sector; in

---

[124] Perhaps up to 10 percent of farmers continue with the "dop" system of payment in alcohol. Human Rights Watch interviews, Jackie Sunde, Department of Sociology, University of Cape Town, April 14, 2000; legal officer, Centre for Rural Legal Studies, Stellenbosch, April 13, 2000. In April 2001, a green paper published by the Western Cape provincial government proposed the creation of an offence for an employer to supply liquor to an employee in lieu of wages or to deduct from wages sums owing for the purchase of liquor from the employer or from a third party. Barry Streek, "Tot system finally to be outlawed," *Mail and Guardian*, April 20, 2001.

[125] Human Rights Watch interviews with women farm workers, Boksburg, Gauteng, April 15, 2000. See also Stephanie Barrientos, Sharon McClenaghan, and Liz Orton, *Gender and Codes of Conduct: A Case Study from Horticulture in South Africa* (London: Christian Aid, August 1999; also on the web at <www.christian-aid.org.uk/indepth/9908grap/grapes2.htm, accessed February 6, 2001), a study that found that health and safety regulations in particular in relation to chemicals were poorly observed.

particular, the fixing of an agricultural minimum wage.[126] The announcement of
the sectoral determination was scheduled for mid-2001.[127]

Women

Most workers in commercial agriculture are male: according to
government statistics, for every one hundred men employed in the sector in 1996,
only forty-two women had jobs; that is, 70 percent of agricultural workers are male
(by contrast, twice as many women as men work in subsistence agriculture in the
former homeland areas).[128] However, accurate statistics on the number of women
farm workers are difficult to obtain, because of the seasonal and temporary nature
of the work done by most women. The situation of women on farms is more
precarious than that of men.[129] When asked by Human Rights Watch about their
terms and conditions of employment, common complaints from women
farmworkers included: lower wages for women compared to men; no independent
employment contracts for married women, whose security of employment and
housing therefore is dependent on husbands; no housing for single women; and no
paid maternity leave.[130]

The 1996 survey carried out by FRRP found that women received lower
wages than men, and the differential was greatest at the lowest pay levels.[131] The
tasks typically performed by women are regarded as less skilled, and women are
more often seasonal or temporary workers. The most common tasks for women
who work on farms include hoeing, weeding, picking fruits and vegetables,

---

[126] Human Rights Watch interview with Virgil Seafield, Deputy Director Minimum
Standards, Department of Labour, February 14, 2001.

[127] "Sectoral determination for farm, domestic workers soon," SAPA, May 29, 2001.

[128] *Employment Trends in Agriculture in South Africa*, p. 24.

[129] For more information on discrimination against women farmworkers, especially in the
Western Cape, where most research has been done, see Sandra Hill Lanz, *Women on Farms*
(Pretoria: Lawyers for Human Rights, 1994); Jackie Sunde and Karin Kleinbooi, *Promoting
Equitable and Sustainable Development for Women Farmworkers in the Western Cape*
(Stellenbosch, Centre for Rural Legal Studies, July 1999); Barrientos, McClenaghan, and
Orton, *Gender and Codes of Conduct* (Christian Aid); Linda Waldman, "'This house is a
dark room': Domestic violence on farms in the Western Cape," in Lorraine E. Glanz and
Andrew D. Spiegel (eds.) *Violence and Family Life in a Contemporary South Africa:
Research and Policy Issues* (Pretoria: Human Sciences Research Council, 1996), pp.103-
119; Davies, *We Cry for Our Land*.

[130] Human Rights Watch interviews, individual and groups of farmworkers, Northern
Province, KwaZulu-Natal, and Western Cape, South Africa, April and September 2000.

[131] Greenberg et al, *State of South African Farmworkers*, Summary.

packing, sticking of labels, pruning branches on fruit or orchard trees, drying fruit, and domestic work. Tasks mentioned by women that only men perform include driving tractors or forklift trucks, carrying heavy stones, building, and tieing the bales. When asked by Human Rights Watch why they would not do other work apart from farm work, women's responses were commonly that they lacked education and skills to do any other work; lacked opportunities for alternative jobs; feared to take the risk of leaving the farm; or could not think of leaving the farm because it was their home.[132] Women farmworkers, like their male counterparts, have low levels of literacy. In the Western Cape, the majority of women started working on farms when they were as young as sixteen years old and have acquired a very low level of formal education—the highest standard of education on average being standard four (four years of primary schooling).[133] Most women living on farms have not done any other work other than farm, domestic, or child care work, or work as shop sales assistants on farms.[134] Women may also be paid lower wages compared to their male counterparts even in situations where they are hired for the same type of work or work of equal value.[135] In some cases, women get half of what men are paid as wages.[136] A woman working at a farm in the Levubu area of Northern Province told Human Rights Watch, "After deductions for accommodation, food, electricity, and other charges, men are paid R325 (U.S.$43) per month, and women get R250 ($33) per month for the same type of work."[137]

Housing is a particular concern. The majority of women farm workers are married or living with a partner. Others are single and living with their relatives. Some women farm workers do not live on farms permanently, because they are hired on a temporary or seasonal basis; indeed, some employers define only men as permanent employees. In many cases farm owners will hire a male worker, and his wife then works as a domestic servant or is recruited to carry out various tasks on a temporary basis. A majority of married women farmworkers do not have

---

[132] Human Rights Watch interviews, group of women farm workers, Western Cape, April 12, 2000 and group of women farm workers, Northern province, March 28, 2000. See also Sunde and Kleinbooi, *Promoting Equitable and Sustainable Development*, pp.12-17.

[133] Sunde and Kleinbooi, *Promoting Equitable and Sustainable Development*, p.11.

[134] Sunde and Kleinbooi, *Promoting Equitable and Sustainable Development*, p.12.

[135] "Equal Pay for Work of Equal Value," Report researched by the Community Agency for Social Enquiry (Johannesburg) for the Commission on Gender Equality, undated draft (1999?).

[136] Human Rights Watch interview with teacher, Piketberg, Western Cape, April 11, 2000.

[137] Human Rights Watch interview with former farmworker, Louis Trichardt, March 29, 2000.

employment contracts in their own names, so that their jobs are dependent on those of their husbands. In addition, despite a Land Claims Court ruling that a woman working on a farm may not be evicted because her husband has lost his job,[138] in practice a woman farmworker's access to housing is still often determined by her relationship to a man.   The provision of housing constitutes part of the remuneration package provided to male farmworkers and their families; thus, if her husband is dismissed from employment or dies, the woman's contract is regarded as automatically terminated, as well as her right to live on the farm.

Women in the Western Cape complained to Human Rights Watch that in cases where a woman works on the farm and the husband is not working on the farm, the woman is not given housing, yet if a man is employed on the farm, his family gets a house.[139] One single mother told Human Rights Watch, "I have been working for this farm for several years, but [I have] no house of my own. We were told houses are for married people, but many single men have been allocated houses. We single women are forced to stay with our parents or other relations whether we like it or not."[140] Where women farmworkers are migrants, the compound or hostel is standard; sometimes women are segregated from men in these circumstances, sometimes not.[141] Where seasonal workers are provided with accommodation on farms, the actual wages may be very low, since rent for housing is usually deducted from wages.[142]

Another problem is the denial of maternity leave. Although the law gives women a right to four months' of maternity leave, some are literally forbidden to go on maternity leave by their employers, being allowed only the absolute minimum time to give birth; many others who are given permission to take leave fail to obtain the benefits they are due from the Unemployment Insurance Fund (UIF), either because their employers did not make the required contributions or simply because women are unfamiliar with the steps they should take to obtain UIF

---

[138] *Conradie vs. Hanekom* (LCC8R/99), April 1999.

[139] Human Rights Watch interview, group of women farmworkers, Grabouw, Western Cape, 2000.

[140] Human Rights Watch interview, Grabouw, Western Cape, 2000.

[141] Theresa Ulicki and Jonathan Crush, "Gender, Farmwork, and Women's Migration from Lesotho to the New South Africa," *Canadian Journal of African Studies* vol. 34, no. 1, 2000, pp.64-79, p.76.

[142] Human Rights Watch interview, group of National Land Committee affiliates field workers, Johannesburg, September 8, 2000.

payments.[143] A woman farmworker in the East Rand told Human Rights Watch, "if a person gets pregnant, she will be given a week off from work after delivering her baby. The following week, she has to be on the job."[144] Another woman told Human Rights Watch:

> There is no time for maternity leave here. You go from the field to the hospital when you are already experiencing labor pains. And you don't get paid for the day you are away from work delivering your baby. So the choice is to come back to work sooner, otherwise you lose your wages."[145]

Children

Children living on farms also face particular problems. Children living on commercial farms are more likely suffer from stunted growth and be underweight than any other children in South Africa, and only children in the former homeland areas have a higher likelihood of showing symptoms of wasting.[146] There are persistent reports of the continuing use of child labor for farm work, especially during school holidays,[147] and access to education is often difficult.

South Africa has signed a memorandum of understanding with the International Programme for the Elimination of Child Labor of the International Labor Organization to undertake a survey to compile comprehensive national statistics on child labor and has made significant efforts to bring national legislation into line with international labor standards. It ratified the ILO Convention on the Worst Forms of Child Labor (No. 182, adopted in 1999) in June 2000.

Farm schools are facing a difficult and slow transition. Originally established under the 1953 Bantu Education Act, they were explicitly designed to provide only the most basic education appropriate to unskilled farm labor. Farmers received a subsidy from the state for hosting and administering these schools. The 1996 South African Schools Act repealed the Bantu Education Act, and set out

---

[143] Human Rights Watch interview Alida van der Merwe, Director, Centre For Rural Legal Studies, Stellenbosch, April 19, 2000.

[144] Human Rights Watch interviews, legal officer, Centre for Rural Legal Studies, Stellenbosch, April 15, 2000; woman farmworker, East Rand, April 19, 2000.

[145] Human Rights Watch interview, woman farmworkers, East Rand, April 19, 2000.

[146] Vink (ed.), "The Determination of Employment Conditions in South African Agriculture," Executive Summary.

[147] See, in this regard, *Concluding Observations of the Committee on the Rights of the Child: South Africa*, U.N. Document CRC/C/15/Add.122, January 28, 2000.

rules for the management of public schools on private land, which required an agreement between government and the landowner setting out the responsibilities of each side. Yet, despite efforts by Minister for Education Kader Asmal to ensure that this process was completed by the end of 2000 and the cooperation of the agricultural unions, it was estimated that agreements had been concluded with only about 10 percent of the 4,500 farmers concerned by the year-end deadline. Meanwhile, farm schools in several provinces remain under threat of closure—in the Eastern Cape, for example, because of the failure of government to continue to pay subsidies to farmers—and school age children in rural areas face long distances to travel and poorly resourced schools when they reach their classrooms.[148]

Foreign Migrants

Many farmworkers are migrants from South Africa's neighboring countries, especially in Northern Province and Mpumalanga, where Zimbabweans and Mozambicans are often employed, and in the Free State, where Basotho play the same role. Unlike migrants in other sectors of the economy, in particular mining, many migrant farmworkers are women.[149] This pattern of migration has existed for many years, and some foreign farmworkers enter South Africa under bilateral agreements with their governments designed for the mining industry but also used by white farmers during the apartheid era.[150] However, many foreign migrant farmworkers enter or remain in South Africa without papers, and their status as "illegal aliens," or "prohibited persons," in the terms of South Africa's legislation, makes them a class of easily exploitable labor. There are numerous reports that undocumented migrant farmworkers are hired at a rate of just a few

---

[148] See Julia Grey, "From oppressive beginnings towards an uncertain future," *The Teacher/Mail and Guardian*, January 29, 2001; South African Schools Act, No. 84 of 1996, section 14.

[149] See Ulicki and Crush, "Gender, Farmwork, and Women's Migration."

[150] South Africa's major legislation regulating immigration, the Aliens Control Act (No. 96 of 1991, a consolidation of earlier statutes), provides for such agreements for contract workers to enter South Africa "in accordance with a scheme of recruitment and repatriation approved by the Minister of Home Affairs" (section 40(1)(d)). There is no bilateral agreement with Zimbabwe, a major supplier of labor, although employment of Zimbabweans is allowed in the far north of Northern Province under the terms of a special arrangement endorsed by both governments. See David Lincoln with Claude Makarike, "Southward Migrants in the Far North: Zimbabwean Farmworkers in Northern Province," in Jonathan Crush (ed.), *Borderline Farming: Foreign Migrants in South African Commercial Agriculture* (Cape Town: Southern African Migration Project, Migration Policy Series No. 16, 2000), pp.40-62.

rands a day plus their food, housed in atrocious conditions, or deported just before their pay is due at the end of the month.[151] Farm owners regularly confiscate migrant workers' travel documents for the duration of their contract, in order to hold workers on the farm.[152]

The South African government's stated policy is that foreign workers should only be employed when no South Africans are available. Farmers, however, say that foreign labor is essential: South Africans do not want poorly paid farm work, despite high domestic unemployment, and commercial farms would be unable to function without foreign labor, especially for the lowest paid and seasonal jobs, such as harvesting. Women migrants are preferred over men for the same reason: men will not work for the wages offered.[153] By definition, it is difficult to quantify the numbers of undocumented foreigners working on South Africa's farms, but a 1996 survey found at least some non-South Africans on 30 percent of the 196 farms in four provinces that were surveyed. A substantial proportion of these had been working in South Africa for many years, in some cases decades, though the findings suggested increased employment of non-South Africans after 1990.[154] Farms along the borders clearly use foreign migrant workers to a greater extent, and there are often informal understandings with local police in these areas allowing for "farm IDs" issued by the farmer to protect workers from arrest as illegal aliens; or, conversely, for the police to arrest and deport workers who are troublesome, or before they are due to be paid.

---

[151] See Human Rights Watch, *"Prohibited Persons": Abuse of Undocumented Migrants, Asylum Seekers, and Refugees in South Africa* (New York: Human Rights Watch, March 1998); and the articles in Crush (ed.), *Borderline Farming.*

[152] Ulicki and Crush, "Gender, Farmwork, and Women's Migration," p.76.

[153] Ulicki and Crush, "Gender, Farmwork, and Women's Migration," p.71.

[154] Greenberg et al, *State of South African Farmworkers.*

ASSAULTS AGAINST FARMWORKERS

Human rights are human rights, whatever the color, but the situation here is totally unacceptable. The farmers have the same color skin as Jesus in the pictures, but what they are doing is unchristian.[155]

The treatment of farmworkers is bad round here. There is a high level of basic abuse, and then some cases going to situations which result in death or permanent disablement. The people always have the police, but the local police are part of the problem in terms of not responding to what the farmer has done. So people say it's always been like this, there is no point in reporting anything, especially if they are illiterate, with the cost in taxis, and so forth. People are helpless. And instead of it getting better, the farmers are seeing no action taken against them. And those who are trying to mobilize the people are victims of the farmers' wrath, so we can't make sure that rights are respected. We have no go areas where there are 200 people on the farm and you can't visit, not even if you're from the same family.[156]

Statistics: How Many Assaults Are There?

There are no reliable statistics relating to assaults by farm owners against farmworkers; indeed, there are virtually no statistics of any kind. As in the case of violence in the home, it is in the nature of violence committed within the enclosed world of the farm, between people who have a long-term relationship to maintain and where power relations are very unequal, that it is likely often to be concealed from outside observers. Even if assaults by farm owners against farmworkers are reported to the police, there is no crime code identifying this particular category of assault; nor has there been an effort by the authorities similar to that made in relation to violent crime against farm owners to collect this type of information through the distribution of questionnaires to police station commissioners.

---

[155] Human Rights Watch interview with Mpumalanga Department of Land Affairs official, April 12, 2000.

[156] Human Rights Watch interview with community leader, near Lanseria, Gauteng, April 20, 2000.

Violence on South African farms is a longstanding problem. Although there are and have always been many farm owners who have good relations with their workers or those who live on their farms, the power imbalance based on the racial and economic disparities of the colonial and apartheid state meant that the use of violence was always an implied threat, even if mediated by a paternalistic ethic.[157] A 1991 report concluded that: "Assaults are part and parcel of the lives of farmworkers. Violence is resorted to at the slightest provocation, with little or no restraint being exercised on the part of the farmers. One wrong word uttered by the worker is sufficient to unleash the extreme violence of the farmer. In a rather bizarre twist, the farmer's abusive behavior often results in the assaultees then being kicked off the farm."[158] Eugene Roelofse, appointed "ombudsman" by the South African Council of Churches in 1976 with a wide brief to expose and fight injustice, noted that, among all the complaints that received his attention during the seven years he held the position before it closed down for lack of funds, "One of the most distressing problems was physical maltreatment of workers by farmers—often with the connivance, and sometimes with the active participation, of the police. Cover-ups, perjury, non-submission of hospital records to courts and even downright frauds by district surgeons, enabled many accused to escape justice."[159] As one white farmer acknowledged to Human Rights Watch, "I would not be surprised if most black South Africans hadn't at one time or another had some personal experience of violence on farms."[160]

Farm owners' representatives consistently state that they believe that the extent of assaults against farmworkers is exaggerated: "the bulk of farmworkers have good relations with farmers; less than 15 percent, if that, do not."[161] An independent study commissioned by the KwaZulu-Natal Agricultural Union (KWANALU) found that less than 7 percent of farmworkers characterized their

---

[157] See Martin J. Murray, "Factories in the Fields: Capitalist Farming in the Bethal District, c.1910-1950"; Robert Morrell, "'Synonymous with Gentlemen'? White Farmers, Schools and Labor in Natal, c.1880-1920"; and Charles van Onselen, "Paternalism and Violence on the Maize Farms of the South-Western Transvaal, 1900-1950," all in Jeeves and Crush (eds.), *White Farms, Black Labor.*

[158] Segal, *A Brutal Harvest*, p.10.

[159] Eugene Roelofse, "Of Serfs and Lords," *Sidelines* (Johannesburg), Winter 1998, p.22.

[160] Human Rights Watch interview with farmer, April 4, 2000.

[161] Human Rights Watch interview with Jack Raath, Agri-SA, March 23, 2000.

relationship with the farm owner as "fairly" or "very bad."[162] The survey was, however, criticized on methodological grounds, given that the farms surveyed would be those whose owners were prepared to cooperate with the report(and therefore not a random sample), that many farmworkers would have very low expectations of their relations with a white man, and that, despite assurances of confidentiality, farmworkers might have concluded that the reports of the survey would be reported to the owner of the farm where they lived.[163] Other research among migrant farmworkers in the Free State found that 74 percent of those surveyed reported that relations with their employer were good or satisfactory—but that no less than half of those who stated that labor relations on the farm were satisfactory still reported that they had been verbally abused, and 19 percent that they had been physically abused.[164] The expected standard of treatment is clearly low. Overall, 15 percent of respondents reported physical abuse (19 percent of men and 11 percent of women), and 32 percent reported verbal abuse (36 percent of men and 28 percent of women). Nearly 40 percent of farmworkers reported some kind of abusive treatment from farm owners, often as a response to perceived minor infractions such as incorrect operation of machinery.[165]

Commercial farmers' leaders maintain the "few bad apples" thesis: "The agricultural union is definitely not saying that violence on farms is not existing, but the situation is blown out of all proportion. If you look at relationships on farms, when you really go into the details you find that the vast majority of farmers are handling their workers in excellent conditions.... The few incidents that have

---

[162] Of a total 1,067 farmworkers living on farms owned by members of KWANALU, 24 percent described their relationship with the farm owner as "very good," 69 percent as "fairly good," 6 percent as "fairly bad," and less than 1 percent as "very bad." Of the 535 farmers questioned, 37 percent described their relationship with their workers as "very good," and another 59 percent as "fairly good," with 4 percent saying it was "very bad." Johnson and Schlemmer, *Farmers and Farmworkers in KwaZulu-Natal*, p.59 and 76.

[163] Brendan Pearce and David Husy, "Survey on farmers carries no weight," *Star* (Johannesburg), January 29, 1999.

[164] The research involved detailed interviews with 152 male and female migrant farmworkers in the eastern Free State. Sixty-one percent said that labor relations on the farm were good, 13 percent that they were satisfactory, 17 percent that they were poor, and 9 percent that there was no interaction with the farm owner. All the farmers said there were good labor relations on the farm. Theresa Ulicki and Jonathan Crush, "Poverty and Women's Migrancy: Lesotho Farmworkers in the Eastern Free State," in Crush (ed.), *Borderline Farming*, pp.63-101, p.82. (This article is a longer version of the article by the same authors published in the Canadian Journal of African Studies, cited above.)

[165] Ibid.

happened have been pulled totally out of context; and most have gone through the legal process."[166] Or again, TAU told Human Rights Watch that it was "on record requesting government ministers to give examples of assaults that we could address through the organization, but we have had not one bit of information from any of those departments, and that worries us. We're not saying there are no issues that require attention, but that they are nowhere near the magnitude that is alleged."[167] The Free State Agricultural Union has asserted that "isolated incidents are being blown out of all proportion, and are used to tarnish the entire sector.... Isolated cases should be treated on their merits and must not be made out as the modus operandi of the entire sector."[168]

The agricultural unions are on record condemning assaults on farmworkers. Agri-SA has called on its affiliated unions not to accept as members farmers who deliberately contravened labor and land reform legislation or who violated their workers' rights.[169] Speaking to the parliamentary portfolio committee on labor, Agri-SA called for the law to be fully applied against these "rotten apple" law breakers.[170] Similarly, the Mpumalanga Agricultural Union stated that "MAU strongly objects to mishandling of people and physical abuse. We tell our members that they must not do that kind of thing and the law must take its course. We condemn these actions."[171] The more conservative Transvaal Agricultural Union stated to Human Rights Watch that "We have a project to involve our laborers in the safety structures to defend the property and people on the farm, and we tell them that there is no way to get the laborers involved if they are not treating them well."[172] The agricultural unions have also condemned some specific incidents of reported ill treatment of farmworkers,[173] and the KwaZulu-Natal Agricultural

---

[166] Human Rights Watch interview with Lourie Bosman, Mpumalanga Agricultural Union, Ermelo, April 12, 2000.

[167] Human Rights Watch interview with Jack Loggenberg, TAU, April 17, 2000.

[168] "Free State farmers ask for a fair portrayal," SAPA, August 17, 2000.

[169] SAPA, June 22, 2000, quoting Agri-SA president Pieter Erasmus.

[170] "Act on farm brutality, urges Agri-SA," SAPA, September 26, 2000.

[171] Human Rights Watch interview with Lourie Bosman, Mpumalanga Agricultural Union, Ermelo, April 12, 2000.

[172] Human Rights Watch interview with Col. Boela Niemann, coordinator for safety, Transvaal Agricultural Union, Pretoria, April 17, 2000.

[173] For example, Agri-SA put out a press release condemning the action of the Potchefstroom farmer who had allegedly tried to drive forty-seven workers out of their homes with poisonous gas, and indicated that the organization had established that the farmer in question was not a member. "Agri-SA condemns ill-treatment of farm workers," Agri-SA press release, March 7, 2001.

Union, for example, states that it checks its membership lists to find out if a case of assault brought to its attention involves one of the union's members and investigates further through local farmers' associations. KWANALU's experience is that in general those accused of carrying out the assault are not its members, and that in some cases they are not "typical" farmers, but rather smallholders whose real income is earned elsewhere. If a crime is alleged, KWANALU lets the criminal process take its course without interference, and has "not yet had cause" to follow the route of disciplinary action.[174] The Transvaal Agricultural Union states that it leaves investigation of allegations of assault to the legal process and to the district agricultural unions that are its affiliates.[175]

It is certainly the case that many cases of assault by white farmers on farmworkers or residents do not reach the criminal justice system. Police and prosecutors in many different parts of the country were unable to recall such assaults that had been brought to their attention when interviewed by Human Rights Watch. But it is also true that when such assaults are reported, they may not assume the same importance in the minds of the police as crime against white farmers. In several police stations officers immediately assumed, when asked by Human Rights Watch about violence on farms, that the question must relate to crime against farm owners or managers, and only addressed assaults against farmworkers when their attention was specifically brought to the issue. A station commissioner of a small police station in rural KwaZulu-Natal, for example, was able to recollect by name the half dozen cases where farm owners had been assaulted or murdered in the region, or their homes broken into, but was unable to recollect a single case of assault by a farm owner on a farm resident or worker, even though farm residents reported to Human Rights Watch that several such cases had been referred to the police: "I don't think we have a problem with assaults on farmworkers so far, though there have been one or two. But there have been a couple of assaults on farmers, including a case of attempted murder when people living on a farm assaulted the farm owner when he tried to remove a structure that was obstructing his irrigation system."[176]

There are a number of obstacles to farmworkers reporting crime to the police, obstacles which are particularly severe in the case of assaults by farm owners against farmworkers. Communication with the authorities is difficult,

---

[174] Email from KWANALU to Human Rights Watch, August 7, 2000.
[175] Human Rights Watch interview with Jack Loggenberg and Boela Niemann, TAU, Pretoria, September 19, 2000.
[176] Human Rights Watch interview with Insp. De Klerk, station commissioner, Ingogo police station, April 7, 2000.

especially when many farms are in very isolated locations, many kilometers from the nearest police station: "It may be the case that cases of assaults by farm owners against workers are not reported because it is difficult for the farmworkers to contact us since the farm compounds don't have telephones. In most cases if there is an incident in a compound it is the farm owner himself who contacts us."[177] But the problems of communication are probably less important then the fear that farmworkers have of reprisal should they report an incident. One official in provincial government commented: "You must remember that for a farmworker to make a case of assault against his employer is a Catch 22 situation; I should think many cases are not reported."[178] The sister of a farmworker who had been assaulted and then arrested at the farm owner's instance, and assaulted again, confirmed this view, "He is not a guy with a criminal record, he is a good guy; he has never been arrested before. But if he tried to report the matter they might end up killing him. It is difficult to report anything that is happening here on the farm to the police, because the people here, we are afraid of the farmers. We don't have telephones and anyway if we report the farmer here the farmer will report us to all the other farmers that you are a troublemaker and you will never get work anywhere."[179] Another farmworker talking to the press was even more explicit in his accusation: "You report any incident to the police, and you're evicted the following day."[180] Migrant workers are particularly vulnerable: "Everybody is afraid of the farmer and no one can complain to him because if you do he will give you your passport and you will have to walk to Lesotho."[181] A group of former farmworkers now living in a tent encampment outside Greytown in KwaZulu-Natal after being evicted from the farm where they were living, reported regular assaults and threats from the owner of the farm to Human Rights Watch: "He used the gun to hit us, fists, and he was a good kicker. He beat women as well as men, and children too. He would threaten us with a gun and shoot into the ground where we

---

[177] Human Rights Watch interview Inspector Stuart Brodie, Mid-Illovo police station, KwaZulu-Natal, April 4, 2000.

[178] Human Rights Watch interview with Dion Pelser, Director of Support Services, Northern Province Department of Safety and Security, Pietersburg, March 29, 2000.

[179] Human Rights Watch interview with farm resident, near Naboomspruit, Northern Province, March 30, 2000. Translated from Pedi.

[180] Farmworker quoted in Phalane Motale, "Terror of nightly 'kaffir bashing,'" *City Press*, January 9, 2000.

[181] Ulicki and Crush, "Poverty and Women's Migrancy," p.85.

were standing. We never reported this to the police; it would just cause him to evict us."[182]

Many of those within government or the criminal justice system are aware that it is difficult for farmworkers to report abuse. But even where there is a recognition, it can be difficult for the police to act. As one black station commissioner noted, when asked about the response of the police to assaults on farmworkers: "They work because they have to, for their families; and there is a lack of jobs elsewhere. They fear victimization and expulsion if they complain of assaults.... If you talk to them they will try to give information, but their concern is that they must not be exposed: 'Hey, I am afraid, he is doing one, two, three, but you mustn't tell it in public.' So it is not something that the police can give attention to.... And we need assistance from the farmers, who play an influential role also in motivating their laborers for crime prevention. The moment we start investigating assaults the farmers are no longer going to cooperate."[183]

In other cases, as noted below in the section on the police response to violence against farmworkers and throughout this report, farmworkers attempt to report abuse, but the police refuse even to open a docket. "Three years ago the farm owner came when I was sleeping, around 5 am, and hit me on the chest and said I should leave the farm. About one week later he came back again early in the morning with the induna [headman], who held my feet, and he beat me with his fists. I was bleeding badly. I went to report at Greytown police station, who told me to go to Rietvlei. At Rietvlei I asked them to open a case, but the officer there, who is now station commissioner, said it was not worth it because I would just be running up and down and nothing would happen, so it was not worth bothering."[184]

The research carried out by Human Rights Watch was not statistically based, and cannot indicate how widespread the problem of assaults on farmworkers or residents by farm owners or others really is. The accounts below aim rather to give an indication of the sort of abuse that occurs on South African farms, and the lack of accountability through the criminal justice system where that abuse takes place.

---

[182] Human Rights Watch interview, Greytown, April 3, 2000. Following their eviction, these former farm residents were assisted to bring a civil claim by the Association for Rural Advancement, Pietermaritzburg.

[183] Human Rights Watch interview with station commissioner, Northern Province, March 31, 2000.

[184] Human Rights Watch interview with farm resident, April 4, 2000.

Abuse by Farm Owners

        At intervals, a particularly shocking case in which a farm owner has abused a farm resident or worker will reach the South African media, such as the April 1998 incident in which a smallholder near Johannesburg shot and accidentally killed a small baby being carried in her sister's arms across his land[185]; or the Mpumalanga farmworker painted in silver from top to toe for allegedly trespassing on a farm in July 1999[186]; or the January 2000 beating of a farmworker so severely that he died several days later[187]; or the September 2000 case in which a farmer appeared in court accused of murdering his employee by tying him to the back of his pick-up truck with wire and dragging him along the ground for almost six kilometers[188]; or the March 2001 beating to death of a black trespasser, allegedly by members of the Pieterburg rugby team.[189] Alternatively, a story will attract attention when it concerns a well-known figure.[190] However, advocates for farmworkers' rights state that it is not so much the headline cases of extreme

---

[185] The case was extensively reported. See, for example, Anso Thom, "Farmer who shot baby charged with murder," *Star* (Johannesburg) April 16, 1998; Mike Masipa, "Bigwigs descend on grieving family's shack," *Star*, April 17, 1998; "The day an innocent baby died," *Saturday Argus*, May 8, 1998; "Political slogans and threats greet baby Zwane's killer," SAPA, March 23, 1999; Chris McGreal, "The hate that won't go away," *Guardian* (London), July 26, 1999.

[186] "Two appear in court after painting of farmworker," SAPA, July 14, 1999; Justin Arenstein, "Silver paint farmer in court," *ZA Now*, July 14, 1999; Selby Bokaba, "Outrage over sentence for painting worker silver," *Star* (Johannesburg), February 23, 2000.

[187] It was reported that Adolf Moore, an Mpumalanga farm owner, had beaten Themba Mkhaliphi, one of his workers, so severely that he died several days later. The assault was reportedly for using a tractor, to collect firewood for his own use, without permission. Moore was arrested. Dumisani Lubisi, "Mpumalanga farmer beat worker to death," African Eye News Service, posted on *ZA Now*, January 31, 2000.

[188] Pieter Odendaal was charged with murdering his employee, Masolo Rampuru. Odendaal's lawyer requested that he be sent for psychiatric evaluation. "Racial tension bursts in Sasolburg," SAPA, September 4, 2000; "Sasolburg community demands town's transformation," SAPA, September 9, 2000.

[189] Chris McGreal, "Teamwork session that ended in murder charge," *Guardian* (London), April 7, 2001. Nine white members of the rugby team were charged with murder.

[190] For example, Tommie Laubscher, a former player for Western Province rugby team, was reported to have assaulted workers on his farms on numerous occasions, including a case in which he broke the jaw of a worker. Judy Damon, "Farm workers fear rugby star: regular beatings alleged," *Cape Times*, August 18, 1998.

violence as a constant lower level of abuse, often for "disciplinary" reasons, that forms the daily reality of the lives of many farmworkers.

A smallholding near Tarlton on the West Rand, Gauteng, growing vegetables for the Johannesburg market, provides an example. Among the testimonies received by Human Rights Watch were the following comments from women working on the farm, and one man (names have been changed):[191]

> Elizabeth: I have lived on this farm since 1986. Sometimes the farmer hits us. We work morning to dark for R110 (U.S.$14.50) a week. He beat me once when I spilt some flour.
> Meisie: We are working long hours. I have seen people being beaten by that guy; sometimes he hits me because I don't know Afrikaans.
> Lettie: We were in the field cutting broccoli, and he came and saw one was not cut and so he hit me on my side with his fist.
> Julia: We work hard and we are beaten. We work six days a week, 6 am to 6 pm. Once when I was working I fell from the tractor and injured my foot. I was in hospital several months and I was not paid during that time. I used to see other people being beaten by him.
> Palesa: One time I was asking the owner how to cut properly and he hit me on the head with the blunt side of the knife. Another time he hit me with a carrot when some vegetables fell from the belt in the storeroom.
> Baleka: I was arguing with the foreman, and then he told Joubert who came here and hit me with flat side of a knife on the back and head. Then he came to the house and took my possessions and took them to the tar road and left them there until I came back and begged for my job again. He calls the workers kaffirs. Another time he hit me with fists because I was absent the day before.
> Jacobus (a tractor driver): He hit me once last month because we had a problem with the wheel we were trying to fix, and after we came back from lunch break the owner kicked me, saying I was destroying his trucks. He hurt my hand when I tried to stop him.

---

[191] Human Rights Watch interviews, April 20, 2000. Translated from Tswana and Sotho.

When asked whether they had ever complained to anyone about this constant low-level violence the workers commented: "We have never reported these incidents to the police because there is no use in doing so. We have no place to run. There is no other place to work."[192]

A similar pattern was reported to Human Rights Watch by a former farmworker from a farm near Levubu, Northern Province: "The farmer was never treating us well, he would assault us while we were working. If he saw you could fight back then he would be hiding and kicking you when you don't see him. If you were weak he would assault you anyhow, with anything near to hand, even a spade. He was always blaming us if the crop was not of good quality, especially the avocadoes, if they were falling and getting bruised. There were cases of serious injuries, a lot of them. There was one old man who was beaten every day; he was even walking like a cripple, one side of his body was not right. Another one was injured with a splinter in his eye. The farm owner used to tell his workers that around here in Louis Trichardt or Levubu there was no policeman who could arrest him, and so we were thinking there was nothing we could do."[193] Another worker from Northern Province told of the same sort of low-level aggression: "When we were working they would come and say we were not working the right way. When you were packing oranges they would take an orange and throw it at you, or hit you with their hands if they were closer."[194]

Hendrik Regis (not his real name), a farmworker in the Western Cape, is fifty years old and has been working as a tractor driver for eleven years on a farm earning R250 (U.S.$33) per week. In 1999 Regis went to visit his brother who works at a neighboring farm. When he got there, the farm owner started beating Regis, accusing him of being drunk. Regis told Human Rights Watch:

> The owner of the farm, known as Cassie, beat me for no reason.
> He kicked me hard on the chest several times, rolling my body
> on the ground. I spent some days being very sick and could not
> report to work. I went to see a doctor at Piketberg. The doctor
> who treated me also took some X-rays of my chest and told me
> that I had a fractured rib. I was hospitalized for one week. After
> discharge from hospital, I reported the case to the police. The

---

[192] Human Rights Watch interview, April 20, 2000.

[193] Human Rights Watch interview with former farmworker, Louis Trichardt, March 29, 2000. Translated from Shangaan.

[194] Human Rights Watch interview Maswiri Boerdery employee, March 28, 2000. Translated from Venda.

> investigating officer gave Cassie a warning against beating me
> and asked him to pay a fine. I do not know how much he was
> asked to pay. I wanted Cassie to be sent to prison for beating me.
> To date, I still suffer from chest pains.[195]

Human Rights Watch interviewed another farmworker who was assaulted by his employer in May 1998 and dismissed from his employment on the same day. Paul Muzambi (not his real name) was born on a farm in the KwaZulu-Natal midlands in 1936, and lived on the same farm since his birth. He worked as a headman and earned R160 (U.S.$21) per month.

> In May 1998, I was taking the cattle to the grazing yard. The
> farmer asked me why I was taking the cattle to the grazing
> yard—but I did not understand why he was asking me that,
> because I have always been taking the cattle there. He picked up
> a thick stick and hit me on my left leg. He told me that I was
> dismissed from employment and I should leave the farm. I went
> to the police station and reported the case. My leg was seriously
> swollen. The police recorded my statement and referred me to
> the doctor. The doctor treated me and completed a form that I
> took back to the police. After a couple of weeks, I went to the
> police station to inquire about the status of the case and the
> investigating officer told me that the case had been forwarded to
> the prosecutor, who declined to prosecute it.[196]

When Human Rights Watch interviewed Muzambi, he was still staying on the farm, but no longer working. He complained to Human Rights Watch about the constant threats of eviction and harassment by the farm owner. Muzambi still limps when walking.

There are frequent allegations of theft and other property crime against those who live or work on farms. Many of these allegations are well-founded: both petty theft and stock theft by well-organized gangs is common. Altercations over allegations of theft or other crimes or misdemeanors by farmworkers can often precipitate violence.

---

[195] Human Rights Watch interview with farmworker, Western Cape, April 11, 2000.
[196] Human Rights Watch interview, New Hanover district court, KwaZulu-Natal, April 6, 2000.

The wife of a farmworker from the Northern Province, who herself worked as a domestic servant, reported how the farm owner assaulted her husband in December 1999, when he tried to deny that he had stolen R100 (U.S.$13) worth of paraffin (kerosene): "I was watching with my two children as the farmer beat him with his fists. Then the farmer said to me 'take your dog home.' The farmer said he doesn't want to see him on the farm any more; he was dismissed and they told us we must leave the farm."[197] The woman also lost her job. In another case, farmworkers told Human Rights Watch of abuse which resulted from an allegation that they had been poaching animals from a game farm:

> On June 30, 1999, the farmer who is the owner of the neighboring farm, came to our residence and told me and George to get into his car. He made us get into his car, with another white person. He was carrying a rifle. We went with him to his farm, and we met two other black security guards there from Messina, and one white security guard. The security guards did not have firearms. The security guards used our own t-shirts to blindfold us so we would not see where we were going. They took us to a dam. When we got there they took off the t-shirts and told us to get in the dam. When we refused they were assaulting us with fists, and they tied our hand behind our backs with rope. They drove us into the water and kept us there for two hours, from about 5 pm to 7 pm. Every time we tried to get out they were assaulting us again, and the security guards even got in the water and held our heads under water so we could not breathe. At 7 pm they took us out and left us there. When we asked them why they were doing this they said they had information that we were poaching animals from the game farm. We were asking them 'Where is your evidence?' but they couldn't show anything. They have not opened any case against us for poaching. We did open a case of assault, but up to today

---

[197] Human Rights Watch interview with farm resident, near Naboomspruit, Northern Province, March 30, 2000. Translated from Pedi. In this case the Nkuzi Development Association negotiated for the family to stay on the farm, but the husband has not been reinstated to work.

we have not been for trial. The police in Messina say that when the papers come from Pietersburg they will let us know.[198]

In some cases, the police are alleged to be willing participants in such assaults. Human Rights Watch interviewed a farm resident tried and sentenced to thirty months in prison for stock theft in March 2000:

On 24 December 1999 eleven people came to my house, including the farm owner, his son and grandson, farmworkers from the farm and a police detective from the stock theft unit. They dragged me outside and beat me, accusing me of stealing a sheep, and also beat my mother (aged about sixty) and my two children (nine and ten). They were beating me with fists, kicking me, and hitting me with gun barrels. They were using electric cattle prods on my body and on my genitals. They put a plastic fertilizer bag over my head and then covered it with another cloth bag, so I couldn't breath, and laughed at me when I started vomiting. They threw me in the dam and kept putting my head under water. They were doing all this for a long time, more than an hour, even though I admitted that I had stolen the sheep. Then they put me in the back of a bakkie [pick up truck] and left me near my bus stop and said I must not do it again.

Some days after Christmas, when I could walk again, I went to Louwsberg police station and opened a case of assault. A policeman took a statement and the police took me to a doctor in Ngotshe who filled in a form saying that he found injuries on my body but he didn't give me any help. I still have scars on my abdomen, and I am still sore on one rib today. I think it may have been broken. I have heard nothing about the case I opened since then. I don't have a case number.[199]

The man believes he was victimized for reporting the assault:

---

[198] Human Rights Watch interview with farmworker, Northern Province, March 28, 2000. Translated from Venda.
[199] Human Rights Watch interview, Vryheid Prison, September 15, 2000.

On 24 February 2000 seven detectives, three white and four black, came in two police vehicles to my house at night, and arrested me. I heard a knock and saw the searchlight. I opened the door and asked what was going on. They told me to dress and said I was going with them and I must show them my friend who was involved with me in stealing the sheep. When we reached my friend's house they said I must show them his bedroom, and they beat me again. The owner of the house came out and said my friend was not there. The policemen were drunk, and they beat me again in the car when they took me to the police station at Driefontein where they kept me in the cells for two days.

They took me to the magistrate in Ngotshe on the third day, and then I was transferred to Vryheid prison awaiting trial section. When I was tried in March, I asked the magistrate how I could be tried without a lawyer and why I had to be beaten, when I had admitted that I stole a sheep—why couldn't they just take me to the police station. The magistrate, who was white, said that I had been arrested for theft and I shouldn't complain.[200]

Nowhere are the huge economic inequalities in South Africa so marked as on the "front line" between commercial farmland and former homeland areas, where there is great poverty and land hunger. Farms that border the former homelands are often the site of confrontations between farm owners and their neighbors, especially over stock theft, collection of firewood, and other property crimes; in some cases over land invasions. Rather than go through the criminal justice system, which is slow and often ineffective, the temptation for farm owners is to take the law into their own hands. These confrontations can be abusive. For example, Josephine Thenga, who lives in a village in the former Venda near Louis Trichardt, was found with others collecting firewood from a neighboring farm in April 1997. The farm owner, Roelf Schutte, fired in the air at first:

I was so afraid I couldn't run away. Then he started assaulting me, with his fists and boots. There was a black man with him, but only the farmer was assaulting me. I couldn't even ask for forgiveness or anything because he was just assaulting me.... He

---

[200] Ibid.

took me to his house inside the farm and put me in his bakkie [pick up truck] and drove me to his workshop at the garage he owns in Levubu. He put me on a chair, and I started asking forgiveness, begging with my hands. There was a young boy there and I asked him to interpret from Venda for me. The farmer gave me a choice between being killed and being arrested. He untied the dog that was outside the workshop and came in holding it on a leash, threatening that he would let it loose. [The farmer went away in the bakkie and came back.] He asked the black man who was with him on the farm to carry a coffin he had brought back with him to the workshop, and he told me to undress to my underwear and get inside the coffin and lie down. I said, 'No, I will lie down only when I am dead,' and he ordered me to go and sit in the chair again. After a long time he told me to help the other man to carry the coffin back to the bakkie [pick up truck]; we then drove to the mortuary and we were ordered to take the coffin back into the mortuary.... He then took me to the police station and he got a policeman to come back to the farm with us. We went back to the police station and they opened a docket. I spent the night in the police cells and was released on R100 (U.S.$13) bail. I then went to court at Louis Trichardt and I pleaded guilty and was fined R800 ($105) for trespass and theft of the wood. I didn't lay any charge of assault against the farmer; I took it that since I was on his farm without permission I had no right to lay a charge. While I was there at Levubu police station I was complaining that I was feeling pain, but a black policeman said not to talk about that because of the firewood I had stolen. Now we get firewood on the other side, within the tribal area. But he does nothing on the farm, there are no crops, no cattle, no game, he uses it just to live; and we have no electricity here.[201]

The South African Human Rights Commission heard evidence from Ms. Thenga in the course of an inquiry into farmworkers' rights in the Northern Province, and concluded that "while the initial arrest of Ms. Denga was lawful in all the circumstances, her subsequent treatment at the hands of Mr. Schutte amounted to a violation of her right to dignity and her right to the freedom and

[201] Human Rights Watch interview, March 27, 2000, translated from Venda.

security of her person."[202] The commission recommended that "the Prosecuting Authority should consider the findings, the reasons for them, and the full record relevant to the allegations against Mr Schutte."[203] Thenga commented to Human Rights Watch on the SAHRC investigation: "The inquiry was helpful. It can change his behavior. He came and testified, which is useful. The hearing was indicating that things have changed; you can't just be beaten any more and say nothing."[204] Whatever the failures of the criminal justice system, direct action of the kind taken in this case is not permissible, and should result in prosecution.

A district surgeon (government-employed doctor, responsible for medico-legal services in addition to other duties) in KwaZulu-Natal told Human Rights Watch that he had received many cases involving dog bites from the farming community in that area—cases in which the dogs had been deliberately set on the person injured.

> Farm owners have a tendency to set their dogs on farm workers, often causing them serious injuries. In one critical case involving a dog bite, the farm worker had an argument with the farmer after he was evicted from the farm. The farmer then set his dogs on him and the dogs bit him severely. When the farm worker was brought to me for treatment, he had serious cuts all over the body and was bleeding seriously. I referred him for hospitalization. The case was reported to Waterburg police. In another case in January 2000, a farm owner let his dogs on the farm worker who had trespassed on his farm. The dogs bit the farm worker severely causing him serious injuries all over his body. I referred him to Matebelo Hospital where he was hospitalized.[205]

Again, attempts to get farm residents, especially labor tenants, to reduce the number of their own livestock or vacate the land, can lead to violence; tension over grazing rights is a significant cause of tension between farm owners and labor

---

[202] *Investigation of Alleged Violations of Farmworkers' Rights in the Messina/Tshipise District*, Report of the South African Human Rights Commission, (Johannesburg: February 1999). Although Thenga is the spelling preferred by the witness, Denga is what appears on her identity book.

[203] Ibid.

[204] Human Rights Watch interview, March 27, 2000. Translated from Venda.

[205] Human Rights Watch interview, KwaZulu Natal, April 4, 2000.

tenants.[206] An elderly woman from a farm in the KwaZulu-Natal Midlands told Human Rights Watch about a saga of confrontation that began in 1998:

> The induna [headman] came to my house and started counting my goats one evening. I asked him why he was counting my goats and he said I should ask my husband since he was the one who was working. He came back the next day with the farm owner who questioned us about the goats and why I wouldn't let the induna count them. Then [the farm owner] went straight past me and started beating up my sons, who are working on the farm, with a stick. When I tried to stop him he threatened to beat me as well, but then he left and said he would come back to kill us. A few days later around sunset the farm owner came and parked here [on the public road close to the farmworkers' houses] and dropped off the induna and three security guards that he has. We heard them talking and after a few moments the dogs barked, and then they lit up the thatch on the roof of my house, and then the house where my daughter-in-law and her children were sleeping. I heard them screaming, 'We are burning.' I came out of my house and saw the two houses burning. The farmer was still on the road and we heard him laughing loudly. Then they left. The next morning the farmer came and said that he had heard that we were suspecting that he had burnt down the houses, but that the burning down was just a small thing, the serious things were coming later. The same day after sunset we heard the dogs barking and footsteps. Apparently someone put down poisoned pieces of meat, because one of the dogs became sick and then vomited, and then we saw other pieces of meat around. The dog died anyway.
>
> The next day the farmer came and he was boasting that no matter where I went for help I wouldn't succeed because he works with everyone from the police station at Rietvlei to Zibambeleni [a community development association] in Muden. I said of course

---

[206] One survey of farmers in KwaZulu-Natal found that in 81 percent of farms where employees owned cattle, the farm owners said that they had to keep talking to their employees about their numbers of cattle, with overgrazing always a danger. Johnson and Schlemmer, *Farmers and Farmworkers in KwaZulu-Natal*, p.29.

> I can't do anything because I don't have land. You've got the
> land and the world belongs to you.[207]

Nevertheless, the woman who talked to Human Rights Watch did report the case at Rietvlei police station, where a police officer made an appointment to meet her in nearby Greytown. On three consecutive days he failed to turn up, until she went to the magistrate's court and was advised by a magistrate to phone the station commissioner and given the number. The station commissioner confirmed that the police officer was coming, but said that the farmer had also reported that some fence was missing. The investigating officer did eventually come to the farm several times and take a statement from two members of the family, but only after a fieldworker from the Pietermaritzburg-based Association for Rural Advancement (AFRA) had inquired about the case.

> About a month after the houses were burnt down, security
> people came to the farm early in the morning. There were ten of
> them in six vans, Coloreds, Indians, and Africans, wearing green
> and white camouflage uniform. Three of the vans were of the
> kind the police normally use. They had dogs as well. They
> parked on the road and came to our houses and started looking
> in boxes and searching. One of the Indians, who seemed to be
> in charge, said 'stop looking, we were not asked to search, only
> to beat up the old woman and the son.' They ordered me and
> my son to stay separately. I thought they would shoot at any
> minute, they were armed with rifles and revolvers. But the
> Indian guy told his people to leave. I think he was touched,
> because he was asking where is my son's gun, and I said that
> there was no gun, if there had been a gun my other son wouldn't
> have died. [He had been shot by cattle thieves earlier.] More
> than one of them was wearing police uniform, navy with tabs on
> the shoulders. The Indian officer did not want to beat about the
> bush, he just said that they had been told by the farm owner to
> chase us away from the farm because we didn't want to leave
> voluntarily. I heard from someone who works on the farm that
> now he is threatening to send people to shoot me because I have
> reported the case to AFRA.[208]

---

[207] Human Rights Watch interview with farm resident, April 4, 2000. Translated from Zulu.
[208] Human Rights Watch interview with farm resident, April 4, 2000. Translated from Zulu.

Often, violence or the threat of violence is used by farm owners in an attempt to induce farm residents who are not currently employed on the farm to leave the property. Some of the more serious cases of violence are reported below, in the section on evictions, but many lower level incidents take place short of actually forcing a family to leave the property: "Earlier this year the farmer came to my house and destroyed my garden. There were banana trees, sweet potatoes, strawberries. I was not there, but he told my children that he was cleaning his farm. I don't know what he meant by that; perhaps it was dirty! When the farmer was destroying the place the [private security company employees] were there, looking high and low; they didn't say what for. They locked one young man up with handcuffs for a short while, saying that he looked like a criminal, and they took away my brother's tool box that he uses as a builder and never brought it back. The farmer said he was not allowed to build any more because he was no longer working on the farm."[209]

In some cases, an individual farmer engages in a range of abuse of those who live on his farm, the lesser incidents leading up to more serious assaults. For example, a number of witnesses described to Human Rights Watch the behavior of a farmer who owns several farms and a poultry business near Estcourt, KwaZulu-Natal. From their accounts, there appears to be a war of attrition between the farm owner and the long term residents who no longer work on the farms but want to continue living there. The previous owner of the farm, with whom the residents had a good relationship, sold up and went overseas. As he was leaving he said to the residents, according to one who was there, "I'm not sure if the new owner will be good to you; he has said he will burn all of you."[210] The new owner has allegedly engaged in a range of abusive behavior. One elderly man recounted a relatively minor assault: "I have been living on this farm for many years. I was working there but I am not any more. I had built a large rondavel [hut] but it was not yet thatched. In March 1999, the farmer came with guns and security people and gave me a saw to cut down the hut, which I did because the barrel of the gun was pointing at me. The farmer said 'I have been trying to evict you all this time and you must go; why are you still building?' About two weeks later I was coming back from town on a cold day and the farmer saw me at the bus stop and he looked around to see if there were any other people around; then he jumped out of the car and started kicking me and hitting me. He kicked me twice and then he jumped into

[209] Human Rights Watch interview with farm resident, Eston, KwaZulu-Natal, April 4, 2000. Translated from Zulu.

[210] Human Rights Watch interview with farm resident, near Estcourt, KwaZulu-Natal, April 5, 2000. Translated from Zulu.

his car again and drove away. I was confused, I didn't report the case."[211] Other serious incidents were described by a middle-aged woman living on the farm:

> On May 13, 1999, I was going to a neighbor's place, on a path that is not much used. After I had crossed the river, I heard the farmer calling me. I thought of running away, but I thought, 'no, let me go to him' and so I went. The farmer was on the river bank. When I got to him I crossed the river to the fence separating us. The farmer was standing on the steeper side. He had a big stone in his hand, and he put it on top of a big pole and asked me to cross to his side of the fence and asked me where I was going. I said I was going to my neighbor and he then said 'when are you going to leave the farm.' And I said I would not leave because the previous farm owner said we should stay on the farm. He then crossed the fence to my side and grabbed me and started assaulting me. He was hitting me until I fell to the ground and then he pressed me to the ground and started banging my head against the ground and strangling me. Then he tried to pull me to the river down the steep bank, saying 'today I am going to kill you.' I was sure I was going to die anyway so I pulled at his balls and started screaming; he let go and I could run away.... I ran to my neighbors bleeding and told them he had assaulted me. The following day I went to the police station and reported the case. They took a statement and came back with police officers to the farm. When we got there the farmer said he had never seen me. The police wanted him to come to the police station, and he said 'no, I am busy with my accounts.' Some of the other workers had heard me screaming, but when I later went to the police station to see what had happened with the case, the investigating officer said the farmer had come to cancel the case with several workers from the farm who were witnesses for him saying they had heard nothing.
>
> After they canceled the case, one day in August in the late afternoon I was with my daughter and we saw a car passing by. The car stopped and the farmer asked me who was collecting

---

[211] Human Rights Watch interview with farm resident, near Estcourt, KwaZulu-Natal, April 5, 2000. Translated from Zulu.

firewood on the farm. I said no one is carrying firewood here. Then the farmer took my child, she is thirteen, and left with her and took her to the house. At 8 pm he came back with her and with the police. The police came to arrest me at the place I stay with my sister. They stopped at the door and called us out. When we went out the farmer said 'our people said you were collecting firewood.' I said I never went there. He said 'this child—indicating my daughter—was collecting wood.' My daughter later told me he was asking her about trespasses, people hunting, people collecting firewood. She said he had a big gun with him while he was talking to her. My daughter went into the police van, and I went with my sister in the farmer's car and we went to the police station where I was held overnight in the cells, though the farmer took my daughter and my sister back to the farm. The police came to write a statement that evening. They said that the farmer had come to the police station and told them that my daughter had told him that I had opened the dam and all the water had drained out and he had lost livestock as a result, which is not true. I can't read but I fingerprinted the statement. They took me to Estcourt prison and I spent one night in prison. On Monday I went to court and I was released on free bail. The prosecutor canceled the case because there was no evidence.[212]

In other cases, farm owners' own fear of violent crime leads to violence against people who seem to them to be suspicious, even those on public property. One paralegal working with farm residents in northern KwaZulu-Natal reported an occasion in 1995 when he had been assaulted: "I was coming back from Durban, when I was stopped at about 11 pm, just outside Vryheid after I had fetched my wife from the farm where she works. A farmer stopped me on the public road, he was standing in the road with his vehicle, and asked me where I am coming from. I explained I was fetching my wife. He said that all the farmers had gathered together the previous Saturday and decided that no one is allowed to travel at night because they are scared. He grabbed me by the shirt through the window, pulled me out of my car and started to hit me with his gun, with stones, and threatening to kill me. We were fighting until the police came by on a stock theft patrol. They also said I was not allowed to travel at night. I said 'he assaulted me, what are you

---

[212] Human Rights Watch interview with farm resident, near Estcourt, KwaZulu-Natal, April 5, 2000. Translated from Zulu.

going to do?' and they said they couldn't help me and I must go home. I went to the police station the next day to report the case, but the prosecutor eventually declined to prosecute."[213]

Many farmers reported to Human Rights Watch that fear of violent crime had led them to be more suspicious of black people generally, and in some cases assaults of farm residents can be directly linked to farm owners' fear and desire for revenge. At its most extreme, this reaction has led to killings. In September 2000, farmer Albertus George van Aswegen, from the Paulpietersburg area of northern Natal, was found guilty and sentenced to twelve years in prison on charges of murder and attempted murder. He had shot dead Bheki Bulunga and wounded Teys Simelane in October 1997, suspects apprehended in connection with a farm robbery. Aswegen had been returning from a funeral of a farmer who had been killed, when he found other farmers with Bulunga and Simelane lying on the road. He got out of his vehicle and shot the suspects, execution-style. At the trial he testified emotionally how robbery and murders had affected the white farming community, and claimed not to remember actually firing the shots.[214]

Abuse by the Commandos

> *The main problem in the farming areas is the police that are working on the farms, the private security and the commandos. Any time there is a dispute, the farmers say they will call the soldiers.*[215]

Some of the most serious abuse of farmworkers is carried out by members of the commandos, a system of reserve soldiers operating under the control of the South African National Defence Force (SANDF). Human Rights Watch heard credible reports of abuse—ranging from the staging of illegal roadblocks to murder—by commando units in many areas, including several in KwaZulu-Natal as well as the Wakkerstroom commando in Mpumalanga.

---

[213] Human Rights Watch interview with Philip Shabalala, paralegal, Christo Loots Attorneys, Vryheid, April 6, 2000.

[214] Christi Coetzee, "Accused farmer weeps in court," *Natal Witness*, September 13, 2000; "Farmer gets 12 years for 'execution,'" SAPA, September 19, 2000. Aswegen was sentenced to twelve years for murder and five for attempted murder, to run concurrently.

[215] Human Rights Watch interview with farm resident, Vryheid, KwaZulu-Natal, April 6, 2000. Translated from Zulu.

According to information received from attorneys acting for the victims, for example, members of the Umvoti commando in KwaZulu-Natal severely assaulted Stofu Dladla, a community leader of local standing, in the presence of the station commissioner of the Muden police station, on October 14, 2000. Dladla was allegedly handcuffed, assaulted, and "tubed" with a rubber bag over his head, after his house was searched for firearms, without a warrant. He had produced three firearms and their respective licenses. The station commissioner denied that he was present during the raid, though he agreed that three other police had been, and stated that one unlicenced pistol had been found.[216] In August 1999, four white men appeared in court in Vryheid, KwaZulu-Natal, facing various charges including attempted murder, assault with intent to do grievous bodily harm, and malicious damage to property, in connection with a severe assault on four black men in September 1998. S'busiso Hadebe, Thokozane Mdunge, another Thokozane Mdunge, and Mbongi Mdunge had a puncture on the road between Vryheid and Paulpietersburg. While they were stopped, they were approached by a group of men who forced them to lie on the ground while they searched the car, and then beat them with rifle butts. An army-type vehicle with six men dressed in military clothing, presumably commandos, then arrived and joined in the beating. The victims told the police they were taken to a farm dam, made to strip and jump into the water, and subjected to further assaults. When they were finally able to return to their car, they found it burnt out.[217] Three of the accused were acquitted; the fourth, Daniel Van Rooyen was convicted on four counts of assault with intent to do grievous bodily harm. He was sentenced to a fine of R2,000 (U.S.$264) or one year of imprisonment, and a further two years of imprisonment suspended for five years.[218]

When abuses by the commandos are raised, the response from the police, army, and agricultural unions can be to dismiss such allegations as attempts by criminals to discredit an effective system, while emphasizing the fear of violent crime faced by all farmers and recognizing that there may be individual cases of

---

[216] Letters dated October 18, 2000, from Jordaan Geldenhuys, attorneys, to the Independent Complaints Directorate, Durban; October 24, from Mary de Haas, violence monitor, to the station commissioner, Muden; and October 26, from Capt. C. Steyn, station commissioner, Muden, to Mary de Haas.

[217] Letter dated September 14, 1998 from Mary de Haas to the station commissioner, Vryheid; Ingrid Oellerman, "Four in court over attack on motorists," *Mercury* (Durban), August 3, 1999.

[218] Letter from Director of Public Prosecutions, KwaZulu-Natal, to Human Rights Watch, December 18, 2000.

excessive force. Others point to resentment if members of the commandos are arrested on assault charges when they have been carrying out anti-crime duties—given the perception and reality that many crimes in South Africa go unpunished, and that a high proportion of cases opened with the police are dropped before they reach court. But the perspective from those working with farmworkers is different. As one trade union organizer commented: "The commandos are a law in those areas: you can feel the chill in a remote rural area, you feel threatened there and then as a stranger if you see a bakkie [pick up truck] and the way they look at you."[219]

The most serious reports of abuse concerning commandos, both in number and type, came from southern Mpumalanga and northern KwaZulu-Natal, in the triangle formed by Piet Retief, Vryheid, Volksrust, and their surrounding districts. This is an area where the majority of farm residents have historically been labor tenants and where reports of serious abuse by white farmers and police date back many years.[220] It is also an area where white farm owners historically have been highly mobilized for self-defense.

The Wakkerstroom Commando

In recent years, there have been ongoing reports of abuse by the Wakkerstroom commando, one of several commando units controlled by local farmers operating in this border region. These abuses have led to successive attempts since 1994 to engage government action. In early 1995, for example, thousands of labor tenants and farmworkers marched to the Piet Retief magistrates' court to protest evictions, harassment, the impounding of livestock, and alleged assaults by the commando. Among them was elderly labor tenant Joseph Mabulwa Mavimbela, who claimed that members of the commando had evicted him, using electric cattle prods to drive him and his family off the land, then burning their houses.[221] Community representatives attempting to organize against forced

---

[219] Human Rights Watch interview with Howard Mbana, SAAPAWU, March 24, 2000.

[220] See *A Toehold on the Land* (Johannesburg: Transvaal Rural Action Committee, May 1988), a report which describes the eviction of labor tenants from the Wakkerstroom area, the violence visited on them, and the failure of the police to act—as well as torture and killings by the police themselves; also Davies, *We Cry for Our Land*, which describes several assaults in the Piet Retief area, including a case where a farmer was fined R100 (£25/U.S.$39, at that time), for assaulting a farmworker who later died.

[221] Mono Dabela, "Labourer (72) run off farm," *City Press* (Johannesburg), February 26, 1995; "Farm evictions that abide by the law, but are they moral," *City Press*, March 12, 1995.

evictions, such as the farm residents participating in a short-lived Mpumalanga Land and Labor Rights Committee that brought together farm owners and labor tenants in discussion, have themselves been subject to assault, harassment, and eviction.[222]

During the second half of 1996, the situation was especially bad. In October 1996, members of the commando rounded up more than thirty people and seriously assaulted them. Human Rights Watch spoke to several of the victims. Fana Mthethwa, a twenty-nine year old man now living in Johannesburg, who lived from 1987 to 1996 on a farm owned by Cornelius L. Greyling, working as a "garden boy," was one of those arrested. He told Human Rights Watch how on October 9, 1996, the farm manager collected him, his older brother and his uncle from the farm and took them to another farm owned by C.L. Greyling's son, Barend P. Greyling. When they arrived there they found a group of men from the commando, both white and black, wearing brown army camouflage uniform. Mthethwa knew many of those present by name. The three of them were separated and taken into different buildings. Mthethwa was handcuffed by one of the black commandos and put into a small room, where he was assaulted from early afternoon until late in the evening. "They all had electric cattle prods and were carrying pistols. There were five black guys, first assaulting and then electrocuting, beating me while I was still handcuffed. Towards the end they closed the windows and sprayed us with a canister and left us for thirty minutes. It was difficult to breathe, we were crying, our lungs were burning. I still have a problem with my eyes today.... They were asking me who steals things on the farm, and I gave names of people even though they had never stolen anything. I still feel bad about this today."[223] After the black members of the commando tired, Mthethwa told Human Rights Watch, the white members took over. "At the end of the assault, I was given a document to sign. I didn't want to sign it but had no choice. When I signed it they told me that now I would be on the commando and we would work together." He and others were taken to another room where they slept the night, still in their handcuffs. In the morning, the police from Dirkiesdorp, a nearby town, came to take them away. Mthethwa was kept for three days in the lock-up cells at the police station, and was then released without charge; after reporting the case in Piet Retief, he left for Johannesburg for safety.

Alfred Hlatshwayo was born in 1965 on a farm owned by C.L. Greyling. He was evicted from the farm in 1999, and Human Rights Watch met him in

---

[222] Human Rights Watch interview with Signet Mashego, Rural Development Support Network, Johannesburg, September 4, 2000.

[223] Human Rights Watch interview, Johannesburg, March 26, 2000.

Johannesburg where he was living with his brother and working repairing shoes. He was one of those arrested in the October 1996 incident.

> I was accused of stealing mealie-meal [cornmeal] from the farm. The farm security came to search my house and arrested me. I was locked in a small house at the farm and sprayed with tear gas. The security commander choked me with an iron bar and beat me. I was bruised all over my body and bleeding form the nose and mouth. When the farm owner, C.L. Greyling, saw me, he said, 'this man is going to die,' because I was seriously injured. I was released in the afternoon and taken to my house. I reported the assault at police station, but they never investigated the case. When I asked why this case was not being taken to court, the police told me that the case had been closed. I was seriously injured and received hospital treatment.[224]

Moses Mayisela, rounded up during the same incident, suffered more serious consequences. He lives today and used to work on the Rooikop farm near Driefontein owned by the Greyling family, where he was born thirty-six years ago.

> I was looking after cattle with another worker, Mnisi, when C.L. Greyling's two sons came with four black members of the commando, saying they were looking for illegal firearms and stolen goods. They were all in soldiers' clothes. The black ones are also from around here, on the farms. They said I should bring our hands forward, put us in handcuffs, and took us to a different farm in their bakkie [pick up truck]. At the other farm we were taken into a small building, and they assaulted us until late at night, always asking for firearms. They were choking us with electricity wire, hitting us everywhere, using electric cattle prods to shock us, and spraying something into our faces. My eyes were full of blood. Then they took us to their father's place and we slept there, with our hands still tied. The next morning the father saw that we were hurt and tried to put ointment in my eyes. When they saw it was not working, after some days, they took me to see a doctor in Piet Retief. The doctor gave me some painkillers. I asked for a doctor's letter, but he refused and said

---

[224] Human Rights watch interview, Alfred T. Hlatshwayo, Johannesburg, March 26, 2000.

he would give it to Greyling. Then they took us back to his home and I spent three days taking the medication before the induna [headman] was told to bring me home.[225]

Mayisela is now completely blind. "I went to Greyling for help because I can't work any more, and all they said was they wished the doctors could help me. Then they came here looking for money saying that because I am no longer working I must pay for grazing for my cows, so we have paid for three years now."[226]

Fourteen members of the commando were eventually charged in the Wakkerstroom magistrates court in connection with this mass round-up by the commando. The cases were, however, withdrawn by the state in May 1999, due to "insufficient evidence."[227] Mayisela has filed a R1,467 million (U.S.$193,000) suit in the Pretoria High Court against Cornelius Greyling and his sons Barend and Willem Greyling, claiming for medical expenses, lost wages, and his pain and suffering.[228] Another farmworker, Richard Hlatshwayo, has laid a claim for R300,000 ($40,000) in connection with the same incident.[229] The state is paying for the legal costs of defending these cases, on the basis that they related to actions

---

[225] Human Rights Watch interview, Driefontein, Mpumalanga, April 12, 2000, translated from Zulu. See also Aaron Nicodemus, "Farm worker sues boss for R1.4 m," *Mail and Guardian* October 15, 1999.

[226] Human Rights Watch interview, Driefontein, Mpumalanga, April 12, 2000. Translated from Zulu.

[227] "Task team probes alleged farmer racism in Piet Retief," SAPA, February 28, 2000; information supplied by South African Human Rights Commission. These cases represented only a sample of a substantial number (in double figures) of charges laid against members of the Wakkerstroom commando for assault or worse, many of them dating from the same period in late 1996. In all cases, the charges had been withdrawn, the prosecutor declined to prosecute, or the accused found not guilty. Correspondence between the South African Human Rights Commission and the Volksrust police station.

[228] Particulars of Claim in the matter of Mvimbi Moses Mayisela and Barend Petrus Greyling, Cornelius Lourens Greyling, and Willem Hendrik Greyling (Case No. 28249/99 Transvaal Provincial Division, High Court), September 28, 1999. Aaron Nicodemus, "Farmworker sues boss for R1.4 m," *Mail and Guardian*, October 15, 1999; Sizwe SamaYende, "Tales of terror," *Rural Digest* (Johannesburg) May/June 2000.

[229] Aaron Nicodemus, "Farmworker sues boss for R1.4 m," *Mail and Guardian*, October 15, 1999. Particulars of Claim in the matter of Mgezeni Richard Hlatshwayo and Barend Petrus Greyling, Cornelius Lourens Greyling, and Willem Hendrik Greyling (Case No. 28250/99 Transvaal Provincial Division, High Court), September 28, 1999. The exact amount claimed is R291,300.

taken "within the course and scope of their duties" as members of the Wakkerstroom commando.[230] Members of the Mpumalanga Department of Land Affairs are distressed by what they see as their lack of capacity to act in such cases; all they can do is refer complainants to the police. "They do these things in commando uniform, and then the government pays for their defense."[231]

Two of those rounded up in the October 1996 incident were again assaulted in 1998. Hlatshwayo described what happened:

> In 1998, [one of the commando leaders] accused me of owning a gun. The farm security and [the commando leader] came to my house and started beating me. They ordered me to get into their helicopter, and there was a dog inside the helicopter. The dog was biting me all the way. When we got to the police station, [the commando leader] and his farm security brought two boxes of dagga [marijuana] which they gave to the police, accusing me of being the owner of the dagga. I did not possess any dagga and I do not know where they had found these boxes of dagga. The police arrested and detained me. The following day I was taken to court and when the magistrate asked me about the dagga, I decided to admit that it was mine because I was tired of being beaten by the police and [the commando]. The magistrate asked me to pay a fine of R120 rand [U.S.$16]. I paid the fine and was released from court. I went back to my home at the farm only to find my house had been burnt and all the property destroyed. I ran away from the farm because I was afraid of being killed by [the commando leader] and his farm security.[232]

Fana Mthethwa also told Human Rights Watch about the use of a helicopter, repeating allegations he had made in a statement to the South African Human Rights Commission on February 12, 1999:

---

[230] Aaron Nicodemus, Marianne Merten and Mungo Soggot, "SANDF foots farmers' defence bill," *Mail and Guardian*, October 22, 1999. The minister of defense has been joined as a defendant to these cases, and has filed a defense denying all charges and pleading proscription (that it the cases happened too long ago). The state attorney is acting for both the individuals defendants and the minister.

[231] Human Rights Watch interview with Mpumalanga Department of Land Affairs officials, April 12, 2000.

[232] Human Rights Watch interview, Alfred T. Hlatshwayo, Johannesburg, March 26, 2000.

On July 26, 1998, at approximately 11:30 a.m., a helicopter landed near my house on a farm at Wakkerstroom, Mpumalanga. A group of men got out of the helicopter armed with guns. My house was surrounded and the men entered my house. I hid in the wardrobe with the assistance of my sister who pulled clothes on top of me. I recognized people who were working for B.P. Greyling against whom I laid a charge of assault. Amongst those I recognized were [several commando members, black and white], and a known policeman from Wakkerstroom.... The policeman took out a piece of paper indicating that they were allowed to search for me. They policeman said if they found me they were allowed to shoot me. A police dog was also used in the search. I was afraid for my life because I believed that they were only searching for me because I had laid a charge of assault with approximately 30 others against [several of the same people].... Most of these defendants had come to my house to search for me. I am very afraid to return to my home and feel intimidated because of the fact that I laid an assault charge against these people. Two of the other complainants who laid the charges with me have already been shot in suspicious circumstances.[233]

Human Rights Watch interviewed the widow of Jabulani Simelane, one of those other complainants who was shot. In February 1997, Simelane, who lived in Driefontein, visited the graves of his family on the farm owned by B.P. Greyling on which he used to live. During the visit he encountered members of the Wakkerstroom Commando, and was shot and seriously wounded. He was taken to hospital, where he spent several weeks before he died. "A policeman came to tell us that he had been shot at Rooikop farm and taken to hospital in Piet Retief. We went to visit him, and he told us that the soldiers had asked him where he was going, because there was a fence around the farm. He had told them that he was visiting the graves, and then they shot him. He said ... who shot him. A case was opened but we were never called to court. No one ever came here to take a statement from me or anyone else from his family. They didn't even tell us when he had passed away, and they wouldn't let us bury him with his grandparents on

---

[233] Copy of statement taken by the South African Human Rights Commission, February 12, 1999.

the farm."[234] As far as his widow knew, her husband was not interviewed by the police before he died. The case never came to court, despite protests made by the Farmworkers Research and Resource Project (FRRP) at the time.

Some of the targets of assaults by the commando appear to be at random: Human Rights Watch interviewed Sipho Dlamini (not his real name), a kombi taxi driver, who one evening in 1997 was sheltering from the rain in his taxi in Driefontein (tribal land, Piet Retief magisterial district) on the public road. A group of white men wearing military uniform surrounded the vehicle with several bakkies (pick up trucks). The other people in the taxi (six or seven of them) ran away, but the men dragged Dlamini out of the vehicle and assaulted him severely, with sjamboks and fists, for no reason that they explained. They were carrying firearms and shot at those who ran away, though no one was injured. Eventually the police arrived and rescued Dlamini, who assumes they were attracted by the shots fired. Dlamini went to the police station, was referred to the district surgeon for a medical report, and laid a charge. The case was called to court, but as he told Human Rights Watch "when I arrived a policeman called me outside and said, 'since you didn't see who attacked you, who are you going to contest the case with?' And so the case was dropped."[235]

There are also more recent cases implicating the commando. David Nxumalo (not his real name) spoke to Human Rights Watch in Driefontein, near the farm where he has lived for many years. One day in July 1999, "two white people and one black, whom I didn't know, just came and loaded me into their bakkie (pick up truck), accusing me of stock theft. They took all my eight cattle away. They took me into the veld and started assaulting me with sticks. Then they took me to a different place where they put me alone into a railway container, and they kept me for two and a half days, without any food or water. My whole back was raw, and I still can't see properly with one eye because of the beating."[236] Nxumalo, a man of over sixty, was found in the container by members of his community who obtained the help of the Driefontein police, after someone had seen him in the back of the bakkie (pick up truck) with his face badly swollen. According to a community leader, "We laid two charges with the police here at Driefontein, for kidnapping and assault and for the theft of the cattle, and Nxumalo

---

[234] Human Rights Watch interview, Driefontein, Mpumalanga, April 12, 2000. Translated from Zulu.

[235] Human Rights Watch interview, Driefontein, Mpumalanga, April 12, 2000. Translated from Zulu.

[236] Human Rights Watch interview, Driefontein, Mpumalanga, April 12, 2000. Translated from Zulu.

stayed here by the police station for two weeks and didn't go back to the farm, but they didn't take a statement from him. On the sixteenth or seventeenth day, two bakkie-loads of police came from Piet Retief and Wakkerstroom and said that charges of stock theft had been laid against Nxumalo that morning in relation to cattle that had gone missing eight months ago by the farmer who had assaulted him—and yet they hadn't been able to take a statement about the assault for two weeks."[237] The case is still going on, but when Nxumalo has appeared in court in Volksrust, there have been farmers from around the area at the court house intimidating him.

In January 2000, *City Press*, a Sunday newspaper published in Johannesburg, reported further allegations of brutality over the previous Christmas period by the commando, including the serious assault of a labor tenant, Simon Vilakazi, from a farm outside Piet Retief.[238]

Despite such incidents, a representative of the Mpumalanga Agricultural Union told Human Rights Watch that the commandos were doing a good job. "In Piet Retief and Wakkerstroom the role the commandos play is very good, a positive proactive role. They are visible in the area and it helps a lot in curbing violence. But now it seems to be targeted that those are the areas from which people are reporting human rights abuses. I can't believe that people from outside are saying human rights violations are occurring when the only action being taken is prevention of crime. The national government puts systems in place, but then the provincial and local people are not satisfied and they say there is intimidation: what do they want? Do they want crime to get out of hand so anyone can do what they want, or do they want crime to be prevented? And where they are operating there were attacks a number of years ago, but now the figures show that crime has dropped in those areas."[239]

In July 2000, in response to these allegations of abuse, Defense Minister Mosiuoa "Terror" Lekota visited SANDF Group 12 headquarters near Ermelo, to which the Wakkerstroom commando reports, together with Correctional Services Minister Ben Skosana and Intelligence Minister Joe Nhlanhla. The delegation spoke to SANDF Colonel Anton Kritzinger, and also to representatives of farm

---

[237] Human Rights Watch interview with Yunus Cajee, ANC Councillor, Driefontein, April 12, 2000.

[238] Phalane Motale, "Terror of nightly 'kaffir bashing,'" *City Press*, January 9, 2000.

[239] Human Rights Watch interview with Lourie Bosman, Mpumalanga Agricultural Union, Ermelo, April 12, 2000.

residents who came to Ermelo to meet the minister.[240]   The Mpumalanga Department of Safety and Security, under the direction of MEC (provincial minister) Steve Mabona, has also conducted an investigation into violence on farms, including crimes allegedly committed by the Wakkerstroom commando.[241] A team of policemen based in Middelburg has been appointed to reinvestigate outstanding cases and follow up on any new cases involving farm violence. Since the visit of Lekota and other government ministers to Ermelo, there are no further reports of serious assaults committed by members of the Wakkerstroom commando.[242]

Abuse by Private Security

Many farmers, especially in the wealthier farming areas, are turning to private security companies to protect their assets from theft and their families from violence. Security companies vary considerably, but there are many reports of assaults by private security operatives, and in some areas the same company is repeatedly named. In Greytown, in the KwaZulu-Natal midlands, the police have charged a few private security guards for assault, including one case of attempted murder after a guard had brutally beaten up a teenager. The guard was released on bail following the charge, on condition he remained office-bound.[243]   In another case, a man reported that he had been badly assaulted, but he did not lay a charge, because he said he feared reprisals.[244]   A district surgeon in a village nearby commented that he saw about thirty patients a year who had been victims of assault committed by private security companies.[245]   An inspector at Mid-Illovo police station, also in the KwaZulu-Natal midlands, commented, "We've had allegations of assault, but nothing seriously overstepping the lines, no case for which we would consider charging them so far.   If there were a serious allegation we would

---

[240] "Lekota satisfied by explanation of Mpuma commandos," SAPA, July 27, 2000; Justin Arenstein, "Farm labourers speak out about abuse," African Eye New Service, July 27 2000.
[241] Human Rights Watch telephone interview with officials of the Mpumalanga Department of Safety and Security, April 18, 2001.
[242] Human Rights Watch telephone interview with community leader, Driefontein, April 18, 2001.
[243] Human Rights Watch interview with Capt. Moodley, acting station commissioner, Greytown police station, April 3, 2000.
[244] Human Rights Watch interview with Dave Carol, Greytown 911 Center, September 13, 2000.
[245] Human Rights Watch interview with district surgeon, KwaZulu-Natal, September 13, 2000.

investigate and leave to the court prosecutors to decide whether to prosecute. But there is a case against [a private security company] that is going through court from this area, when they used tear gas to disperse people at a compound and someone also alleged an assault."[246] In May 1998, a security guard on a farm near Kroonstad in the Free State reportedly shot dead a teenaged boy, Lethusang Mohloane, who was shooting birds on a farm belonging to Theo Delport, after beating him and three other younger boys he accused of stealing sheep. The security guard, James Morungo, was arrested and released on R5,000 bail (U.S.$660), paid by his employer.[247]

The use of military-type uniform by private security operatives (many of whom are ex-soldiers) causes particular problems, even though camouflage is supposed to be worn only by the army.[248] As one police officer from the detective branch noted, "it can be hard for victims to tell if they people who attacked them are private security or the commandos, since everyone wears camouflage uniform."[249] Some of those running commando units acknowledge that the unauthorized use of military uniform is a problem, noting that abuses committed by criminals who have stolen uniform can be attributed to the commandos.[250] A paralegal working with farm residents was more forceful: "The situation with assaults is terrible, in most cases during the night. You can't even say who the person is. The assaults have got worse since private security have become involved. You can't even walk at night.... It's got worse especially since 1998. These people are wearing old SADF [the pre-1994 army] uniforms; if they come to your place you can think they are soldiers. They are mostly black people; but some of them can't speak Zulu" (meaning they are not local people).[251]

---

[246] Human Rights Watch interview, Insp. Stuart Brodie, Mid-Illovo police station, April 4, 2000.

[247] Bongani Siqoko, "Killed for shooting birds," *Mail and Guardian* June 12 to 18, 1998. Human Rights Watch was not able to find the result of this case.

[248] Section 115 of the Defence Act (No. 44 of 1957, as amended, currently under review) provides that anyone who wears an army uniform or any dress or decoration "having the appearance or bearing the marks of any such uniform" commits an offence, unless he is a member of the army or is properly authorized to wear such a uniform. There have, however, been few if any prosecutions under this law in recent years.

[249] Human Rights Watch interview with detective inspector, SAPS, southern Mpumalanga, April 13, 2000.

[250] Human Rights Watch interview with Dave Carol, Greytown 911 Center, September 13, 2000.

[251] Human Rights Watch interview with Philip Shabalala, paralegal, Christo Loots Attorneys, Vryheid, April 6, 2000.

Some private security companies appear to be particularly abusive, and to be able to function despite repeated accounts of assaults and worse. Human Rights Watch interviewed a range of witnesses, from police to court officials to victims of assault, who complained of the behavior of employees of a private security company based in Levubu, near Louis Trichardt, Northern Province. The company employs seventy people, and offers a variety of security services to commercial farmers, including comprehensive armed security, patrolling fences, or simple installing of alarms. Most of the crimes the company responds to are burglaries and theft, with the majority of suspects in theft cases being people resident on the farm itself. According to the co-proprietor, the security company works closely in coordination with the police and (in accordance with the law) does not carry out any arrests on its own account, rather waiting for police to arrive to arrest suspects, after conducting a preliminary investigation. She noted that the farmers the company deals with have complaints about the slowness of police response.[252] Local police also note that some farmers tend not to rely on the police for security since the white station commissioner was replaced with a black officer, preferring to rely on the private security company, who would begin the investigation and then hand over any suspect to the police. However, the security company would continue to monitor the case closely and would attend court with the farmers when their cases were heard.[253]

The control prosecutor at the magistrates court in Louis Trichardt noted that the court was seeing an increasing number of cases of assault involving private security companies, protecting both businesses and farms. The same Levubu company, in particular, had figured in many complaints relating to intimidation, and techniques such as keeping suspects in a dark room for a long time until they confessed. There had been more than one prosecution in relation to those cases, and one admission of guilt and R1,000 (U.S.$132) fine for pointing a firearm.[254] A murder case against the proprietor of the company had also been opened in Messina, in connection with the death in early 1998 of one of the guards employed by the company.[255] In another case, a police officer told how a white employee of

---

[252] Human Rights Watch interview, March 28, 2000.

[253] Human Rights Watch interview with Inspector Risimati Robert Maluleke, Levubu Police Station, March 28, 2000.

[254] Human Rights Watch interview with control prosecutor, Louis Trichardt district magistrates court, March 29, 2000.

[255] Human Rights Watch interview with Inspector Risimati Robert Maluleke, Levubu Police Station, March 28, 2000; Human Rights Watch interview with control prosecutor, Louis Trichardt district magistrates court, March 29, 2000.

the company had kicked a pregnant woman outside the Levubu police station and seriously injured her; a case of attempted murder had been opened and was still pending in April 2000.[256] Again, a former farmworker reported to Human Rights Watch that he had seen a co-worker accused of stealing bananas after he had been badly assaulted by members of the same security company. He was able to walk following the assault, but was badly swollen around the face. "I don't believe he reported the assault; many farmworkers don't know there is a right to report a case."[257]

In KwaZulu-Natal, several different sources mentioned problems concerning one large private security company. One farmer based outside Howick, in the KwaZulu-Natal midlands, described to Human Rights Watch how he was approached by the company to join a scheme that was presented to him as a conservation effort, to stop poaching. He refused to sign up, because of fears that his staff would be harassed. "My fears came true. About a year or eighteen months ago one of my workers was beaten up just outside my farm. He was accused of stealing compact discs, and this was a guy who probably doesn't even know what a CD is. They came and hauled him out of his house at night time, took him to another place, beat him up and left him there. He couldn't work for six weeks. We went to the police, who just laughed [when we named the company].... They knew all about them."[258] The farmer and his worker laid a charge against the company, and the police came to the farm and asked the worker if he could identify the people who assaulted him. "He said he couldn't identify all eleven, but they were all wearing [the company's] uniform. The police took down the details, but we've heard no more."[259]

Serious reports of abuse were also made against a private security agency operating in the Commondale area in Mpumalanga, on the border with KwaZulu-Natal. Commondale borders the Piet Retief and Wakkerstroom districts, where commandos are also accused of serious abuses, and appears to benefit from the same impunity from the criminal justice system. "Since 1995 when [the security company] came to our area they have been assaulting people. Three have been killed. But nothing has happened. Some people say to me that they won't report an assault to the police because there is no use. They say they are looking for

[256] Human Rights Watch interview with Inspector Risimati Robert Maluleke, Levubu Police Station, March 28, 2000.
[257] Human Rights Watch interview with former farmworker, Louis Trichardt, March 29, 2000. Translated from Shangaan.
[258] Human Rights Watch interview with farmer, KwaZulu-Natal, September 12, 2000.
[259] Ibid.

firearms or for stolen cattle, or if the farmer doesn't want someone on his farm he just sends them to chase the people away."[260]

Human Rights Watch spoke to relatives of one man who died following an assault by employees of this company. Moses Hlatshwayo (not his real name) was assaulted in February 1997, and later died of his injuries. His son told Human Rights Watch: "They came to the house during the night, at about 9 pm. There were four of them, two whites and two blacks. They kicked the door down, and asked for my father. We said he wasn't there, but they went to the other rondavel [traditional dwelling] and the dog found him at the back of the door, and they took him away, naked.... He came back about 8 pm the next day. He had been badly beaten. His whole body was swollen, as though he had been beaten with an iron. He said that the security people had said he had stolen cattle. We gave him *muthi* [traditional medicine] and took him to hospital in Piet Retief and then to Johannesburg, but he died two months later."[261] The family laid a charge at Piet Retief police station, but no police ever came to take statements from family members and other witnesses, and the case has not gone forward.

Human Rights Watch interviewed a schoolboy, Sipho Khumalo (not his real name), who was assaulted in June 1999 by members of the same company. "Five of them, one white and four blacks, came to our house at night, 2 or 3 am, and kicked the door down. My mother asked them what they were looking for, and I tried to run away, but they caught me, shone a torch in my eyes and beat me, asking me if he had a firearm. I asked to put on my clothes but they refused, and they took me outside into the forest naked and they beat me, using a gun butt and a stick from the forest. They took a twenty liter container of water and poured it into my nose. Then they left me in the forest after it was light. They were wearing camouflage uniform and driving a 4x4."[262] The boy's father complained to the owner of the farm where the family was living, who employed the company to provide security. The farmer said he would report the case to the police, but the police had not been to take a statement, and no case had been opened so far as the boy knew. Following further intimidation of the family by the farm owner, who threatened to send the same security company to evict them, they left the farm where the boy had been born, and moved to live in a forest site owned by the large wood and paper company, Mondi.

Daniel Dlamini (not his real name), a young man living in a forest area near Commondale, said he had been picked up on the road in 1998 by employees

---

[260] Human Rights Watch interview with Chief D.T. Hlatshwayo, April 13, 2000.

[261] Human Rights Watch interview, Commondale, April 13, 2000. Translated from Zulu.

[262] Human Rights Watch interview, Commondale, April 13, 2000. Translated from Zulu.

of the same company, who questioned him about where he lived and asked him about illegal firearms. He was taken to the farm owner, who did not know him, and then severely assaulted. "They kicked me and beat me with gun butts and left me for dead. There were five of them, four black and one white, all wearing camouflage uniform. I came back here, though it was difficult to walk. I went with my father to see a doctor in Piet Retief, and we reported the incident to the police, but we've heard nothing since, although they said they would contact us."[263] Human Rights Watch also spoke to family members of Kumisani Hlatshwayo, a middle-aged man who was killed in 1998, apparently by members of the same company. He was seen being taken from his place of work (a security guard at the CTC timber company) by employees of the company, and his body was later found in their vehicle, although they claimed that they had only found the corpse. CTC stated that they had reported the case to the police, but family members are not aware of any progress on the case since then.[264]

Abuse by Vigilante Groups: Mapogo a Mathamaga

Mapogo a Mathamaga, "colors of the leopard" in Northern Sotho (SiPedi), is a vigilante group formed in 1996 in Sekhukhuneland, Northern Province, in the former homeland of Lebowa. The group was formed by John Monhle Magolego, a local businessman, in protest at attacks on local businesses to which he felt the police response had been inadequate. Immediately successful in attracting business people to its ranks, across Northern Province and beyond, the association also accomplished the rare achievement in South Africa of uniting whites and blacks in a common approach. By the end of 1999, Magolego claimed a membership of 35,000, including about 10,000 white members, in ninety branches in Northern Province, Mpumalanga, North West Province, and Gauteng. Fees are levied on a sliding scale from R50 (U.S.$6.50) up to R10,000 (U.S.$1,320) for large businesses with fleets of trucks. Members, or black members at least (most whites are passive members), are expected to take part personally in exacting punishment on alleged criminals.[265]

The police do not like Mapogo or other similar vigilante groups, though they recognize at senior level that these vigilante structures are a response to the

---

[263] Human Rights Watch interview, Commondale, April 13, 2000. Translated from Zulu.
[264] Human Rights Watch interviews, April 13, 2000.
[265] Constanza Montana "Day of the leopard," *Focus* no. 15 (Johannesburg: Helen Suzman Foundation, December 1999); "Using Crime to Fight Crime: Tracking Vigilante Activity," *Nedbank-ISS Crime Index*, vol. 4, no. 4, July-August 2000, available at <www.iss.co.za> accessed February 28, 2001.

inadequacies of the state law enforcement agencies on the ground. Commenting on Mapogo's methods, a spokesman for the Northern Province Department of Safety and Security (responsible for the police) noted that, "if I assault you badly enough, you will be anything I want you to be, even if you're not guilty."[266] As a result of their methods, Mapogo members have faced more than 300 criminal charges, including thirteen of murder and nineteen of attempted murder; more than twenty people have reportedly died at the hands of Mapogo since 1996.[267] A large number of assault charges have been filed by people who claim mistaken identity and other errors in Mapogo's choice of victim. Among these are several cases involving farmworkers.[268] In June 1999, three Mapogo members were convicted of assault and illegal possession of firearms at the Groblersdal magistrates court, and sentenced to a R10,000 (U.S.$1,320) fine and three months imprisonment.[269] In August 2000, twelve members of Mapogo, including Magolego, were acquitted on charges of murder and assault; the police claimed the acquittal was due to Mapogo's intimidation of witnesses.[270] In 2000, stories of a split in Mapogo, over its brutal methods, involvement in protection rackets, and the dictatorial style of Magolego, surfaced in the press.[271]

Among the issues reportedly dividing the group were Magolego's decision to sign up large numbers of right-wing farmers, symbolized by the decision to launch a branch in Ventersdorp, North West Province, stronghold of the Afrikaner Weerstandsbeweging (AWB, Afrikaner Resistance Movement). Many farmers in Northern and North West Provinces display the distinctive Mapogo symbol of two leopard heads on their gates, and some are enthusiastic personal participants in the organization: one farmer went to Mapogo's inaugural meeting in his area, ordered all of his sixty workers to pay the fee and join the group or leave the farm, and now supervises the beating of alleged thieves and other criminals all round the neighborhood. "The thing that shocks me, is that I'm degraded to the level where

---

[266] Human Rights Watch interview with Dion Pelser, Director of Support Services, Northern Province Department of Safety and Security, Pietersburg, March 29, 2000.

[267] "Using Crime to Fight Crime."

[268] Human Rights Watch interviews with control prosecutor, Louis Trichardt district magistrates court, and with Dion Pelser, Director of Support Services, Northern Province Department of Safety and Security, Pietersburg, March 29, 2000.

[269] Constanza Montana "Day of the leopard," *Focus* no. 15 (Johannesburg: Helen Suzman Foundation, December 1999).

[270] SABC News Agency, August 15, 2000; Evidence wa ka Ngobeni, "What's cooking... with Mapogo," *Mail and Guardian*, December 12, 2000.

[271] Evidence wa ka Ngobeni, "Vigilante group faces split," *Mail and Guardian* May 9, 2000.

I actually have to go out and lynch these people. I don't want to have to degrade myself like that. It's the government's job."[272]

In March 2000, the Congress of South African Trades Unions accused Mapogo of targeting its members, following the death of a Mozambican farmworker and severe beating of another near Brits, North West Province. The two Mozambicans were reportedly assaulted and kept in closed sacks overnight, and one of them was found dead the next day. They had been accused of stealing tomatoes, but COSATU spokesman Solly Phetoe alleged that the vigilante group had ignored previous allegations of theft made against others who were not members of a union. The farmer on whose farm the incident took place was arrested by the police, and released on R30,000 (U.S.$3,950) bail the next day; four members of Mapogo were also arrested.[273] The case had not been brought to court by March 2001. Lawyers acting for farm residents and others reported several cases to Human Rights Watch in which Mapogo had been involved in carrying out illegal evictions of farm residents.[274]

---

[272] Peter Drake, commercial farmer and Mapogo member, quoted in Decca Aitkenhead, "Rough justice," *Observer Magazine* (London), May 28, 2000.

[273] Cathy Thompson, "Farmer arrested for death of farmworker," *Citizen* (Johannesburg), March 3, 2000; Mahap Msiza, "Murder of farm labourer: COSATU accuses Mapogo a Mathamaga of targeting its members," WOZA, March 14, 2000; Human Rights Watch telephone interview with Solly Phetoe, June 22, 2000. Undocumented migrant farmworkers, often Zimbabwean or Mozambican, are particularly vulnerable to abuse because their lack of legal status makes complaint to the police or other authorities extremely difficult. See Human Rights Watch, *"Prohibited Persons": Abuse of Undocumented Migrants, Asylum Seekers, and Refugees* (New York: Human Rights Watch, 1998).

[274] Human Rights Watch interview with Oupa Maake and Charles Pillai, Legal Resources Centre, Pretoria, April 10, 2000.

VIOLENCE ACCOMPANYING EVICTIONS

I cannot remember my exact age, but my son said I am seventy-two years old. What I know is that my grandfather was also born here. This umlungu [white man] started evicting me seven years ago when he bought the farm from the one who stayed here only five years. He wanted me to stop plowing my field and ordered me to sell my cattle and work for him for R30-00 a month. I told him that I cannot survive on this money. He then got angry and ordered me to leave 'his farm.' Since then he has evicted me six times and I kept on coming back. I was taken to umaje [the magistrate] several times and I told him I was born here and know no other place. I was born here and so were my parents. There is no reason why I should leave. I will die here. This is my father's place, and as an elder son I have inherited it.[275]

Historically, evictions of black workers and tenants from South Africa's farms have been carried out with the explicit and active use of force, whether by individual farmers or by the state security forces. The transition period from 1990 to 1994 and the early years of the new government saw a fresh wave of farm evictions, as farmers acted pre-emptively to remove workers and tenants from their land, for fear that they would acquire permanent rights. There were further surges during the periods leading up to the passing of the Labour Tenants Act and the Extension of Security of Tenure Act (ESTA) in 1996 and 1997.[276] Although these peaks in the rate of evictions have flattened off, anecdotal evidence from those working with farm residents indicates that evictions of farm residents are still carried out in violation of the law. Moreover, although the law reform measures introduced by the government since 1994 have provided greater protections for

---

[275] Witbooi Khubeka, a labor tenant from Dirkiesdorp, Mpumalanga, interviewed July 1994, as quoted in Abie Ditlhake, "Labor Tenancy and the Politics of Land Reform in South Africa," in Richard Levin and Daniel Weiner (eds.), *No More Tears: Struggles for Land in Mpumalanga, South Africa* (Trenton, NJ/Asmara, Eritrea: Africa World Press, 1997).

[276] See, for example, Thabo Thulo, "Flotsam from the farms," *Sunday Independent*, October 8, 1995; Ann Eveleth, "Farmworkers evicted before a new law," *Mail and Guardian*, August 29 to September 4, 1997.

farm residents, they do not provide a right to secure tenure, but only a regulated procedure for allowing tenure to be terminated, and evictions also continue in accordance with the legal procedures. Though there are still difficulties with getting farmers to follow the letter of the law, even when attempting to obtain a legal eviction, the financial costs incurred by some farmers who have been taken to court for failing to follow the rules have served as a warning to others. Several lawyers representing farm residents reported to Human Rights Watch that they now find it easier to deal with farmers than in the past. Most of the cases in which the legality of an eviction has been challenged before the Land Claims Court appear to be the Western Cape, and the areas of northern KwaZulu-Natal and southern Mpumalanga where there are still many labor tenants.[277]

In November 2000, the National Assembly adopted a report on farm evictions in four provinces prepared by the parliamentary portfolio committee on land affairs.[278] The report concluded that "It is nearly impossible to attach a figure to the total number of evictions taking place throughout these provinces." While the report noted that many problems with the existing laws on security of tenure related to implementation rather than loopholes in the acts, it concluded that "the biggest flaw in ESTA is that the Act merely regulates tenure rights without actually providing security of tenure," and recommended a review of the legislation. The report also urged an investigation into the role of the commandos, police and sheriffs in evictions.

In May 2000, following reports of several especially brutal evictions, and against the context of contemporaneous violence on farms in Zimbabwe, President Mbeki expressed his concern, stating that he was "deeply disturbed by these practices."[279]

The Department of Land Affairs has sought to monitor evictions in contravention of the Labour Tenants Act and Extension of Security of Tenure Act. DLA officials are required to collect information relating to all evictions reported to the department or to other bodies, such as NGOs. In KwaZulu-Natal, KWANALU, the agricultural union, has also participated in the information

---

[277] Human Rights Watch interview with Judge Justice Moloto, Land Claims Court, Randburg, September 18, 2000.

[278] *The Extent and Nature of Unfair Farm Evictions in KwaZulu-Natal, Freestate, Mpumalanga and the North West Province*, available on the Parliamentary Monitoring Group website, <www.pmg.org.za> as at November 21, 2000; "Assembly adopts farm evictions report," SAPA, November 2, 2000.

[279] "Mbeki disturbed at SA farm evictions," SAPA, May 10, 2000.

collection process. The statistics remain sketchy and incomplete: many evictions, especially those carried out family by family rather than of a group of households at once, still go unreported. However, they indicate that there were hundreds of threatened evictions countrywide during the period from November 1999 to August 2000, and at least 125 illegal evictions in the same period. Thousands of people were affected by these threats or evictions.[280] Those who are evicted face further impoverishment, loss of their housing, and disruption to the education of their children.

In many cases, evictions are carried out not by the direct use of the law or the application of force, but through the creation of conditions that cause farm residents to leave their homes "voluntarily." The methods used include the cutting off of water or other services, the closure of schools or clinics, or the denial of grazing or cultivation rights. "When the current owner bought the farm in 1995 he tried to evict us all because we were not working. Before he came we had enough grazing and land for cropping but now he has taken it away."[281] At Mooiplaas farm near Piketberg in the Western Cape, the farmer cut the water supply to the farm residents in 1999: as a result, residents had to walk long distances in search of water, and basic hygiene and sanitation suffered, with adverse health consequences.[282]

A woman resident on a farm near Estcourt, KwaZulu-Natal described some of the farm owner's efforts to make life difficult for those he wanted to leave:

> In January 2000, the farmer took down all the fences from the fields round our houses and let all his livestock graze on our fields, and his cattle destroyed what we had planted. I told the induna [headman] that he must tell the farmer that his cows are destroying our property, and he came back and said that the farmer had said that we must put a fence around our fields—but he was the one who had taken down the fences which were put there by the previous owner. I was born there and the fence has been there ever since I was born. Since then the cows are grazing on our fields and roaming around our homesteads and we can't collect firewood any more. There is a neighboring

---

[280] Tables supplied to Human Rights Watch by the Department of Land Affairs.

[281] Human Rights Watch interview, farm resident, near Estcourt, KwaZulu-Natal, April 5, 2000.

[282] "Labor Rights are Human Rights," *HRC Quarterly Review* (Johannesburg: Human Rights Committee, June 2000), p.42.

farm where we are allowed to collect firewood, but the farmer
has telephoned the farmer to say he should not allow us because
we are breaking the fence, and he now says if he sees us going
to the neighboring farm he will shoot us and take us to the police
station. Before, he allowed us to collect firewood on his farm,
but not now; he has burnt all that forest so we can't collect
there.[283]

Today as in the past, many evictions are accompanied with violence or the
threat of violence, violence that seldom enters the official record. As one
Pietermaritzburg lawyer handling eviction cases commented: "The great majority
of evictions are under threat of violence, obviously. We have become so used to it
that we don't even record it any more, since there's not much we can do."[284]

Farmworkers remain vulnerable to forcible eviction, including some
forced evictions carried out in accordance with the terms of the law. In particular,
farmers are anxious to remove from the farm all those who do not have a family
member actively working on the farm; in some cases, only the working member is
allowed to be resident, even in areas of labor tenancy where work on a farm
traditionally brought rights of residency and cultivation for the whole family.
"What is my main worry now is that he does not want my children on the farm....
He says that he does not want them because they are not working on the farm."[285]
From one day to the next an apparently secure position with a good relationship
with the farmer, including land to cultivate, can be destroyed, because the farm is
sold to a new owner, or the person who had been working on the farm is no longer
available. "I was evicted in 1996. My son was working as a tractor driver but he
asked the farmer for a raise, and when he refused he went to work for a
construction company instead and left the farm. The farmer said I must then go as
well because my son was not working. I went to look for a place but when I was
still looking my children came to me and said the farmer was at my house with the
security people chasing us away. So I had to take all my possessions and move out
of the farm. I did not report this to anyone because there was no time, I was taken
by surprise. This was his land and he can do as he likes. He started by moving us

---

[283] Human Rights Watch interview with farm resident, near Estcourt, KwaZulu-Natal, April
5, 2000. Translated from Zulu.
[284] Human Rights Watch telephone interview with Christo Loots, Attorney,
Pietermaritzburg, May 10, 2000.
[285] Human Rights Watch interview, farm resident, Eston, KwaZulu-Natal, April 4, 2000.
Translated from Zulu.

from our own houses to a compound, but then he bulldozed the compound too. There were about three families chased away at the same time. There was no notice, they just came. We couldn't even get all our possessions."[286]

In some cases, evictions from farms appear to be driven by security concerns. As one survey of farm owners noted: "those who had recently cut back the number of workers on their farm were somewhat less worried [about crime] than those who had done the opposite. That is to say, those who dispensed with farmworkers or evicted them did not seem to worry about revenge.... On the other hand, those farmers who had taken on more labor were more anxious than others—suggesting, all too nakedly, that the reverse did not apply and that for some white farmers, at least, having more black people living nearby simply increased one's sense of insecurity."[287] Such concerns have also contributed to the increasingly close controls some farmers have introduced over those who live on the farm and their would-be visitors. "Since 1996 the farmer has taken photographs of all the people working on the farm. They want to stop people living on the farm who have no permit. If there is a visitor from outside the farm they must get a permit letter, say how much time they will spend there, etc. You are allowed to visit your family but you are not allowed to stay without a permit; and the security come and check during the night. We used to live in our own houses, but now we are all moved into a compound which used to be a butchery."[288]

Sibongile Ndlela (not her real name) is twenty-nine years old with one child. She stayed with her four brothers and a sister, on a farm in KwaZulu-Natal where both her parents had died and were buried. Problems with the farm owner started when Sibongile's eldest brother, who was then the sole worker in the family, died in January 2000. The farm owner demanded that Sibongile hand over all her deceased brother's property to him. When Sibongile refused to do so, the farm owner told her that she and her other siblings were evicted from the farm. Sibongile told Human Rights Watch:

> The owner of the farm bought my brother a wheelchair in March
> 1998 after my brother got injured while he was working on the
> farm. A straw bale fell on my brother breaking his spinal cord
> and he became paralyzed. When my brother died in January this
> year, [the owner] demanded the wheel chair as well as my

---

[286] Human Rights Watch interview with farm resident, Eston, KwaZulu-Natal, April 4, 2000. Translated from Zulu.

[287] Johnson and Schlemmer, *Farmers and Farmworkers in KwaZulu-Natal*, p.54.

[288] Human Rights Watch interview, farm resident, Eston, April 4, 2000.

brother's clothes claiming that all this property belonged to him. When I refused to give him the property, he took the wheel chair only and told me that he did not want to see me on the farm anymore, as well as my remaining siblings. I reported the case to the local council who advised me to go and report the case to the Department of Land Affairs in Pietermaritzburg. When I reported the case to the Department of Land Affairs, they called [the owner] and told him not to evict us from the farm. We are still staying on the farm, but receive threats, occasionally, from the farm owner that he will send the farm security to evict us.[289]

Another resident of the same farm told Human Rights Watch how he was evicted in 1997:

I was born on the farm and lived there all my life. We were living in houses that we built by ourselves on the farm. The farm owner did not provide us with housing, until in 1997 when he built some nice houses for farm workers. However, only people who were working on the farm were allowed in the new farm compound, though my mother and brother who still worked on that farm were allowed to stay with the rest of us. Myself, my father and my sister were denied accommodation in the new compound. One morning during October 1997, the farm owner sent the farm security to destroy the old houses where we stayed, leaving us with no accommodation. The security were instructed to evict us from the farm on the same day. They killed all our livestock, about five goats and several chickens and doves. They even threatened to shoot us. We fled to my sister's house in Hammersdale. Many families were evicted as well, and their livestock was shot. Approximately sixty people were evicted from the farm. We reported the case to Mid-Illovo police but they did not help us. We also asked the Department of Land Affairs to help by reinstating us onto the farm, but they kept promising to look into our case since 1997.[290]

---

[289] Human Rights Watch interview, KwaZulu-Natal Province, April 3, 2000. Translated from Zulu.

[290] Human Rights Watch interview with farm resident, Eston, KwaZulu-Natal, April 3, 2000. Translated from Zulu.

Even when an evicted family has considerable assistance, it can be difficult to get action from the courts. One couple interviewed by Human Rights Watch had lived on a farm for twenty-six years, and had therefore acquired rights under ESTA. They had an excellent relationship with the farm owner, were paid well, and had land of their own to cultivate. The farm owner went bankrupt and the farm was sold; the new owner said that he wanted them to leave: "He chased us away saying that he didn't want to see a kaffir on this farm; he had bought the farm not us, and that if we stayed he would fight."[291] Even though the previous owner took his former employees to the magistrates' court for assistance the day they were evicted, and a magistrate advised that they were allowed to stay there, they were forced to leave, their belongings thrown out on the road. The magistrate took no action himself, nor did he send them to report the matter to the police, even though the farmer's action was apparently in violation in the law. Rather, he directed them to seek assistance from the land rights organization Nkuzi, based in Pietersburg.

Evictions of this type are often accompanied by assaults or other explicit violence. A former farm resident from Ingogo, KwaZulu-Natal, told Human Rights Watch "I was on the farm for many years, then the sheriff of the court came with a letter and said I must leave. A long time after the letter, in about November or December 1997, the farmer came with some other farmers and about five policemen and they demolished some of my buildings and took my belongings and took me away. Then the crisis committee [formed in response to illegal evictions] intervened and took me back to the farm. About three weeks later soldiers and police came, together with the farm manager. They came with a bulldozer and about six people. There were many, more than twenty, in three vehicles for the soldiers and two vans and a car for the police. They ordered us to go outside and then they demolished the houses and collected some of our belongings and put them on a truck and took us to the road; there were twenty-nine people. My daughter was beaten up badly. She went to get my money from my house, and they were threatening to shoot her, and they beat her. They were heavily armed. We walked to find our things which they had dumped at different places."[292]

Another former farm resident from the same area reported a similar case: "I was living on the farm for some years, since 1982. I had twenty cattle, forty goats, three pigs and two horses. Then in August 1999, the farm was sold. The previous owner said we would work for the new owners too, but they said no and

---

[291] Human Rights Watch interview with farm residents, Northern Province, March 30, 2000.
[292] Human Rights Watch interview with former farm residents, Ingogo, April 7, 2000. Translated from Zulu.

asked us to leave. Many of us left, but I did not leave, I stayed on by myself with my family. Then one day the [owners] came in the afternoon and demolished my houses with a bulldozer. The crisis committee people then came, but they were chased away by the [owners]. They fired some shots, though nobody was hurt. After that they called the police and soldiers. They came at about 7 pm with some other farmers I did not know, and took me to the old railway station [state land now occupied by a number of mostly evicted families]. There were many, I don't know how many because it was night, but there were two vehicles, one for soldiers and one for police. They were armed. I had received no letters and was not called to court. I am living by the railway station now. I have had to sell some livestock; I am renting grazing land for my cattle."[293] A member from the Ingogo Crisis Committee confirmed the story, and told how she was also assaulted: "Around 10 pm, I was called by the wife of [the previous witness] who came to say that they were being harassed. We went to help, and we found soldiers there and the station commissioner from the Ingogo police station, and the [owners]. I asked what they were doing, since it didn't look like they had a court order, but then they chased me away. When I was at the gate one of the two brothers [who owned the farm] came rushing and held me by my neck and I fell, and he beat me with a gun, hitting me on my forehead. My sister came to ask what was happening and they beat her too with a gun, around her middle. I went to report the case to the police, but the station commissioner, the one before this one, said no, because the police had been there and they knew I was lying that I had been assaulted. Eventually they did refer me to a doctor in Newcastle and the case was opened, but it did not go anywhere."[294]

A former farm resident from near Commondale told of a case in which a private security company [the same one involved in the cases described above] had assisted in an eviction. "Our home was burnt down by the farmer in 1997. We reported to the Department of Land Affairs but they did not help. The farmer was using the [private security company] to help him. They were beating us during the night, and we had to sleep on the mountain. There were five or six people from [the private security company], one white and the others black, all wearing uniform, and the farm owner. They were all carrying big guns. The whole family was beaten. We were evicted because my husband died. They burnt all our

---

[293] Human Rights Watch interview with former farm residents, Ingogo, April 7, 2000. Translated from Zulu.
[294] Human Rights Watch interview with member of the Ingogo Crisis Committee, Ingogo, April 7, 2000. Translated from Zulu.

property and burnt the house; everything is gone. They gave us two days notice, but there was nothing like a court hearing."[295]

The large paper and timber company Mondi Ltd, a member of the Anglo-American group of companies, generally has a good reputation when it comes to the thousands of people living on its forest land, many of whom are not its employees. The company has provided school buildings in many cases, and there are few allegations that it has illegally evicted or otherwise mistreated people; unions are permitted to operate freely among those who work for the company. Yet workers living on one of the plantations owned by Mondi near Tzaneen, Northern Province, which it is in the process of selling, found themselves evicted and their accommodation bulldozed without a court order. Although there was no physical violence involved, the difficulty in obtaining police assistance is illustrative of the problems faced even by a well-organized resident population faced with arbitrary action by the land owner. In December 1998, workers at the timber factory on the plantation were called to a meeting and told that the factory would be closed temporarily and that the management did not know the new terms on which it would reopen. The workers carried on living in the accommodation provided by the company. Several months later they started receiving letters saying that on September 16, 1999, the water and electricity would be cut and that the buildings would then be destroyed. At a meeting between shop stewards representing the workers and the Mondi area manager, this was repeated, and they were told they should seek accommodation in the villages of the surrounding former homeland areas. None of the people living on the plantation agreed to go. About a month later, a bulldozer simply came to the settlement and started knocking down the buildings, under the direction of a Mondi manager. The people sought help from the Pietersburg-based Nkuzi Development Association, who came the next day and went to the Tzaneen police station to open a case under ESTA.

> At Tzaneen police station it seemed to be the first case they had
> dealt with like this, so they didn't know how to approach it.
> They fetched the station commissioner, and he also didn't know.
> The Nkuzi fieldworker had to give them a copy of the law, then
> he began to understand. They opened a case, and said they

---

[295] Human Rights Watch interview, near Commondale, April 13, 2000. Translated from Zulu.

would come the next day, but took no statements. They have never come to talk to us.[296]

When the people working for Mondi returned the next day and were shown Nkuzi business cards, they agreed to stop the destruction. About half of the 600 people who used to live on the estate have left; thirty-one dwellings are left standing. Mondi's senior management has stated that the demolition of the houses was not in accordance with company policy, though no compensation was paid to those whose homes were destroyed. Nkuzi entered into negotiations with Mondi with a view to obtaining the transfer of the land to the occupiers; during the process, the land was sold to a new proprietor, with whom they are now also in negotiation.[297]

For more vulnerable groups, the consequences can be even more severe, and the violence much more explicit, even where a court order has been obtained. Members of a large group of former residents of a farm near Greytown, totaling about twenty-six families, told how they were evicted in November 1997:

> He gave us papers and ordered us to go home and not come back to work, but we were not sure what was written on the papers. On November 10, he started burning houses, if they were thatched, or knocking them down with a bulldozer if they had zinc roofs. We had no warning. Prior to that, a few weeks earlier, the police came and raided the place in about seven vans. There were about twenty policemen, and dogs. The police were searching all over for guns but they found nothing. They asked us, 'where are your guns,' and we said we had none. They said they would come back with dogs, but they still found nothing. Then they just left. We don't know who sent them. The day they came to destroy the houses there were more than ten people with different roles. Some would surround the houses with guns while others destroyed them. They were all armed. We were not even given time to take our property out of the houses. Most of us just left everything. They just arrived one morning and then stayed about a week. It was raining. There were police present when the bulldozers were there, one van with two officers. They were quite sympathetic; in fact they advised us to

[296] Human Rights Watch interview with residents of the Mondi plantation, March 31, 2000. Translated from Pedi.

[297] Email from Nkuzi Development Association to Human Rights Watch, April 10, 2001.

come to Greytown police station and ask the station commissioner to stop these guys bulldozing our houses. So a committee went there, but the station commissioner said that he couldn't do anything because we were being evicted with a court order (but we hadn't heard anything about a court order), and in any event it was not his jurisdiction and we should go to Muden. So we went to Muden but the station commissioner there said that it was not his jurisdiction either. After that we gave up. We were all scattered, we only had somewhere to sleep because a fieldworker from AFRA found us on the side of the road and organized a hall for us out of the rain.[298]

Residents of the "Joe Slovo" squatter camp, a group of no more than ten houses on land owned by an absentee farmer near Lanseria airport, northwest of Johannesburg, told Human Rights Watch of harassment by a neighboring farm owner. During 1998, the farm owner told the residents of the settlement that they should leave, and one morning he came right into the camp, demanding that they go. "One of us, Obed, approached him and said that he could not tell us to go, and he fired three shots, to either side of him; they hit the wall behind. Then he beat him [Obed] with the butt of the gun. We picked up the cartridges and took them to the police station in Randburg with a delegation from the camp. They just said we were on the land illegally, and we should move off the property. Then we went to the ANC office, and they asked for details of the farmer, and I think someone from the ANC phoned him, and since then he has not come here again."[299]

In 1999, the Pietersen family was evicted from a state-owned farm in the Western Cape by the premier of the Western Cape, who had failed to follow the provisions of ESTA. When representatives of Lawyers for Human Rights, an NGO, arrived at the farm at the request of the Department of Land Affairs, they found about thirty policemen firing tear gas and rubber bullets into the air, amidst an angry crowd of community members, including school children, who had tried to prevent the police and court sheriff from removing the Pietersens' belongings by placing burning tires at the entrance to the residential area. One woman was injured and taken to hospital.[300]

In another case, Lawyers for Human Rights approached the Land Claims Court on an urgent basis in August 2000, on behalf of sixteen people who had been

---

[298] Human Rights Watch interview, Greytown, April 3, 2000. Translated from Zulu.
[299] Human Rights Watch interview, September 5, 2000.
[300] "Labor Rights are Human Rights," *HRC Quarterly Review*, p.43.

living on Weskus Farm in Brackenfell, Western Cape for various periods of time, some as long as seven or eight years. On the morning of Saturday, July 29, 2000, the soon-to-be-new owner of the farm arrived with two bulldozers and workers to level the land where Lawyers for Human Rights' clients were living in informal structures of wood, plastic and other materials. During the ensuing destruction of their homes, some of those living there tried to grab a few of their personal belongings; others were away at the time, and most were left with only the clothes that they were wearing. Among the things destroyed or lost were identity documents, clothing, cooking utensils, bedding and other possessions. Other occupiers living on the farm were served with a letter stating that they must leave the farm, and then alerted Lawyers for Human Rights, who intervened with the landowner. The reaction from the landowner was that the people were not living in houses but in the bushes and that he was not prepared to replant the bushes.[301]

As Lawyers for Human Rights pointed out:

> A case of this nature is extremely time consuming. The two attorneys worked many after hours, weekends and public holidays. The case took eight days to get to court. Some of the challenges of this type of litigation included: Clients did not know the address of the current owner. We therefore had to get special instructions from court to serve the papers. The attorney had to collect the client who had been to the owners house previously and drive 1.5 hours. They then had to drive around this place until the client recognized the house. The police were willing to accompany the lawyers to the house to serve the papers, but would not serve the papers as the court had instructed. Clients were so poor and did not have money for transport. Therefore, when urgent replying papers had to be drafted, other members of staff had to fetch and carry clients. This occurred on the day of court as well. At certain stages, we could not get hold of our clients as they had managed to find work for the day. Most clients did not have permanent employment. They had lost everything and therefore had to work in order to get money for food.[302]

---

[301] Email from Judith Robb, Lawyers for Human Rights, Stellenbosch, to Human Rights Watch, September 19, 2000.
[302] Ibid.

A settlement was eventually reached and made an order of court. In terms of the settlement agreement, clients received blankets, mattresses, pots, buckets, three rooms, and two container structures to live in. It was recognised that clients were occupiers in terms of South African law and protected by the Extension of Security of Tenure Act.

The Maswiri Boerdery

The complex interlinking of a range of different types of abuse is epitomized by the case of the Maswiri Boerdery, an orange farm in the Messina area, close to the Zimbabwe border, owned by Andries Fourie. Conditions on the farm were poor, and wages low. In early 1998, several hundred workers from the farm were dismissed when they joined a union. They were replaced with Zimbabwean migrant workers. After the employees were dismissed, which the employer stated was on account of an illegal strike, they were given notices to leave the farm. A court interdict was granted in favor of Maswiri Boerdery restricting the movement of the dismissed workers to certain defined areas of the farm; according to the former workers, this interdict was never properly served and they were not made aware of its terms.[303] The eviction case is still going through the courts.

According to workers at the farm who spoke to Human Rights Watch, at around the same time as they were dismissed they heard that workers on another farm owned by Fourie had also been fired, and the farmer had called the police to collect them and take them away; they were believed to be Zimbabwean migrant workers. A delegation of union shop stewards then went to Fourie to ask why the others had been fired, but were not satisfied with his response. The delegation came back and agreed with their colleagues that they would demand an explanation on why the others had been arrested. When they staged a sit-down near the school, Fourie called the police. The subsequent events formed the subject of a South African Human Rights Commission (SAHRC) inquiry.

On March 3, 1998, about thirty policemen came to the farm, in response, as they later stated to the SAHRC, to a complaint from Fourie that his former employees were contravening the court order. According to some of those present, the police were mostly white with some black police handling dogs.

---

[303] Sizwe SamaYende, "Outrage over conditions on farms in Northern Province," *Star* (Johannesburg), September 3, 1998; Mukoni T. Ratshitanga, "Farm workers jailed, beaten during strike," *Mail and Guardian*, March 6 to 12, 1998; Ann Eveleth, "Farmers sow the seeds of xenophobia," *Mail and Guardian*, February 12, 1999.

We sat for a long time waiting.... The police captain then gave an order that he wanted all of us inside the van in fifteen minutes. But we didn't want to get into the van because we didn't know any crime we had committed. After fifteen minutes, he gave the order 'one minute,' and after that minute 'on your marks, get ready, go'; and then they started grabbing people, assaulting them, kicking them, trampling on people. When I got up I was trying to run because I didn't want to get in the van, but the captain started assaulting me and telling me to get in the van. I asked what crime did I commit that I should get in the van, but he just said, 'get in the van, or we can make it difficult for you,' and carried on hitting me. Everyone else got in when they saw me being beaten up. About 150 people were arrested that time, and eighty-five later. More women were arrested than men, and there were also school children and infants. One was bitten by dogs.[304]

According to the police version of this incident, the police were met on arrival at the farm by a crowd, including some who were armed with sticks, stones, and metal pipes, and adopted a "threatening, violent, and provocative attitude." The South African Human Rights Commission found that this version of events was "highly improbable."[305]

The workers were taken to Messina police station, where they were locked in the cells overnight and taken to court the next day. After much legal argument, they were released on free bail. Those arrested were initially charged with contravening the court interdict, later with trespass, and in some cases with resisting arrest; according to the Nkuzi Development Association, those arrested included people who were in no way connected with the farm or the interdict.[306] All charges against the farmworkers were, after numerous court appearances, subsequently dismissed by the Messina magistrates court.[307]

---

[304] Human Rights Watch interview, Tshipise, Northern Province, March 28, 2000.

[305] *Investigation of Alleged Violations of Farmworkers' Rights in the Messina/Tshipise District*, Report of the South African Human Rights Commission, (Johannesburg: February 1999).

[306] *Response to the Human Rights Commission Report on Farmworkers' Rights in Messina/Tshipise*, Nkuzi Development Association, (Pietersburg: April 1999).

[307] "Farm workers fight for rights and win," SAPA, November 12, 1998.

Three of those assaulted laid charges against the police, but these have not led to prosecutions. Shirhami Shirinda of the Nkuzi Development Association reported to Human Rights Watch that the police were reluctant to follow the case up, saying that they could not find witnesses. Only when Shirinda took the witnesses to the police station did the police take statements from them.[308] Nkuzi also complained to the Independent Complaints Directorate, responsible for investigating complaints against the police, but received a response indicating that the investigation was proper, an assessment Nkuzi challenges.

Azwindini Maggie Randima, a middle aged woman with three children, was born on the farm and had been working there all her life since she became a teenager:

> After we were dismissed we were given notices to leave the farm. They threatened to call soldiers, but only lots of white people came from the neighboring farms. They were using horses and coming in the night into the village and threatening us. One day, May 29, 1998, I woke up in the morning and I was just in my underwear going to the toilet in the bush. Before I even got there I was arrested by the farm security. They took me to Mr. Fourie and he said he was calling the police to arrest me because I had entered an area that was restricted by a court interdict that ruled that we were only allowed to stay in our houses.... I had to stay there under the jacaranda tree the whole day until 6 pm still in my underwear with the security guarding me. When the guards went away they locked me in the store room, then took me to another farm and I was kept in the back of the car until 11 pm. They then took me to Messina police station. The police inquired what offence I was charged with and the security guard said I was found in a restricted area. I tried to explain I was in an area where I was allowed, but they insisted on arresting me. At around 1 am they said I should sleep and I was locked in the cells with two other women. In the morning they took my fingerprints but they said that since it was Saturday I would have to wait till Monday to go to court and so I stayed

---

[308] Human Rights Watch interview March 28, 2000; letter from Nkuzi Development Association to the Pietersburg office of the Independent Complaints Directorate, March 1, 2000.

there all weekend. A Zimbabwean gave me a t-shirt and a towel to wear as a skirt over my underwear.[309]

According to Nkuzi, the police refused to intervene on behalf of Randima, even after they were informed that she was being held on the farm.[310] The South African Human Rights Commission, considering this case, found that, on the basis of Mr. Fourie's own evidence, he was "aware of the inhumane manner in which Ms. Randima was detained" by the farm security, a company known as Pro-Tek. While, "on the evidence before us," the commission found that the arrest was lawful, it also ruled that "Holding people for long periods in private detention is simply unacceptable.... [T]he conditions under which Ms. Randima was detained amounted to cruel, inhuman and degrading treatment."[311] On the grounds that Mr. Fourie had undertaken that no such incident would happen again, the commission made no specific recommendation regarding redress, though "it is open for Ms Randima to pursue whatever action she may think is appropriate."[312]

---

[309] Human Rights Watch interview, Tshipise, Northern Province, March 28, 2000.

[310] Email from Nkuzi Development Association to Human Rights Watch, April 10, 2001.

[311] *Investigation of Alleged Violations of Farmworkers' Rights in the Messina/Tshipise District*, Report of the South African Human Rights Commission, (Johannesburg: February 1999). The Human Rights Commission's investigation and report were heavily criticized by the Nkuzi Development Association, which had been key in arranging for the hearings to be held, as overly legalistic and failing to take the "opportunity to speak out forcefully on the institutional racism and violence that permeates the agricultural districts of the Northern Province." *Response to the Human Rights Commission Report on Farmworkers' Rights in Messina/Tshipise*, Nkuzi Development Association, (Pietersburg: April 1999). See also the chapter on South Africa in Human Rights Watch *African Human Rights Institutions* (New York: Human Rights Watch, 2000).

[312] South African Human Rights Commission, *Investigation of Alleged Violations of Farmworkers' Rights.*

GENDER ASPECTS OF VIOLENCE

The practice is to keep women hostages in fear: Fear of more
violence at the work place, in the home, and in the community.
The male farm worker becomes yet another level of
management and social control. If a woman complains of
violence, whether perpetrated by the farm owner or foreman,
or by a male farm worker, the idea is to keep her silent about
the violence.[313]

Scope of the Problem

Placed low in the farming community hierarchy, black women living on farms are subjected to sexual and physical violence by farm owners, managers, other farmworkers, and from within their own families, from husbands and intimate partners.[314] As with assaults on farm residents generally, it is difficult to establish the extent of sexual violence, given that many cases of rape and other physical violence go unreported.[315]

Women farmworkers or residents who are raped by other farmworkers face a different situation from those who are raped by their supervisors or farm owners. In both situations, however, to speak about the rape would be to risk serious retaliation, and many women will not speak about the rapes while they are still working on farms. Women are prevented from reporting rape or sexual violence against them by dependency on the perpetrator or fear of being evicted from the farm, fear of rejection and ostracization by their families and society, by the belief that the police may not be receptive to their complaints, and other

---

[313] Human Rights Watch interview, Rita Edwards, director, Women on Farms Project, Stellenbosch, April 13, 2000.

[314] Human Rights Watch did not document any cases of rape against wives or female relatives of farm owners, although we received allegations that such women are often targets of rape on farms in the context of violent crime against farm owners. The absence of accounts of such rapes in the section that follows is due only to the difficulty of arranging to speak to such victims, and does not in any way imply that we regard the trauma of white women in such circumstances as in some way less than that of black women. A separate research project focusing on this issue would certainly be valuable.

[315] One study of women migrant farmworkers in the Free State found that 15 percent of the women interviewed reported having experienced or knowing of women who were raped or subjected to sexual harassment while working on farms. Ulicki and Crush, "Poverty and Women's Migrancy," pp.79-80.

reasons. On one hand, women who report rape perpetrated by other farmworkers may be assaulted again by their assailants or be blamed for the rape by their families, community, and even law enforcement officers. On the other hand, those who report cases of rape by their employers or supervisors face possible violent retaliation, dismissal from employment, or eviction from the farm.[316]

Levels of domestic violence are also reported to be high on many farms, though again the extent of the problem cannot be accurately gauged because many cases are unreported.[317] According to researchers in the Western Cape, women are most often targets of domestic violence because of their unequal status to men within the farming community. The stereotypical attitudes held by some farm owners as well as male farm workers, that farm labor is predominantly a masculine domain, often results in the legitimization of women's economic dependence on men. The fact that a woman who is employed on a temporary basis only has access to continuous income through a male relative's or a husband's wages, further entrenches male dominance over women and leaves women vulnerable to violence.[318] Although this was not the focus of our research, Human Rights Watch documented a few cases of domestic violence on farms, including one fatal case.[319]

---

[316] Human Rights Watch interview, social worker, Victim Support Centre, Estcourt, KwaZulu-Natal, April 4, 2000.

[317] In 1998, the South African legislature adopted the Domestic Violence Act, which came into force on December 15, 1999. This law replaced and significantly improved on the 1993 Prevention of Family Violence Act, in particular by adopting a broader definition of domestic violence. Under the Domestic Violence Act (1998), domestic violence includes, "physical abuse, sexual abuse, emotional, verbal and psychological abuse, economic abuse, intimidation, harassment, stalking, damage to property, entry into the complainant's residence without consent where the parties do not share the same residence, any other controlling or abusive behavior towards a complainant, where such conduct harms, or may cause imminent harm to, the safety, health or wellbeing of the complainant." For more information on domestic violence in South Africa, see Yoon Jung Park, Joanne Fedler, and Zubeda Dangor (eds.), *Reclaiming Women's Spaces: New Perspectives on Violence Against Women and Sheltering in South Africa* (Johannesburg: Nisaa Institute for Women's Development, 2000).

[318] Waldman, "'This house is a dark room': Domestic violence on farms in the Western Cape," in Glanz and Spiegel (eds.), *Violence and Family Life in a Contemporary South Africa*; Human Rights Watch interview with Rita Jones, Women on Farms Project, Stellenbosch, April 13, 2000.

[319] The absence of detailed accounts of cases of domestic violence against women farm workers in this report is due to a realization of the need to conduct a more in-depth research and review of the impact of the 1998 Domestic Violence Act on women farm workers. For

We also interviewed officers of the Women on Farms Project, a South Africa-based nongovernmental organization conducting a project to address domestic violence on farms in the Western Cape, and received reports that perpetrators of domestic violence on farms are seldom made accountable.[320] A fieldworker coordinator with the Women on Farms Project told Human Rights Watch, "A lot needs to be done to pierce through the fence of the farms and empower women to use the law. Despite the existence of a law punishing domestic violence, women are not familiar with it and are too intimidated by their husbands and farm owners to report cases."[321]

Rape and Assault by Farm Owners and Supervisors

Human Rights Watch documented cases of rape of women farmworkers or residents by farm owners or supervisors. Our research cannot indicate the true scale of the problem, but does indicate the need for more in-depth investigation of this issue. While farm residents will, if they believe the information to be given in confidence, talk readily about general physical assaults, it is much more difficult for women to speak out about sexual abuse. The following cases are illustrative.

In April 2000, Human Rights Watch visited the housing compound for workers on a vegetable farm near Tarlton on the West Rand. This farm grows produce for the Johannesburg market. Most of the workers on the farm were women, and virtually all had tales of abuse by the farm owner. In some cases, this abuse was more serious, involving sexual harassment and in at least one case, rape. Dipo Masotsha,[322] a sixteen-year-old girl living on the same farm since she was ten years old, described to Human Rights Watch how the farm owner repeatedly attempted to rape her:

> [The farm owner] sends his foreman to tell me to come and work, but when I get there he says he doesn't want to work with

---

that reason, we narrowed the focus of our current research to documenting rape and sexual harassment on farms. A separate research project focusing on domestic violence on farms would certainly be valuable.

[320] Human Rights Watch interviews, Rita Edwards, director, Dinna Bosch, Field Workers Coordinator, and a group of field workers working with Women on Farms Project, Stellenbosch, April 13, 2000.

[321] Human Rights Watch interview, Dinna Bosch, Field Workers Coordinator, Women on Farms Project, Stellenbosch, April 13, 2000.

[322] Unless otherwise noted, all names in this section have been changed, and the ages given reflect the age of the person at the time of the interview.

a prostitute. He is hitting everybody. He is sleeping with people
here. Once when I was working here he took me from this side
of the farm to the other side and tried to have sex with me, but
then other people came and so he couldn't. He used to try often
to have sex with me. Even when he pays us sometimes he gives
a lot of money to one woman and when people want to know
why he says she is good. He tries to have sex with anybody,
even with my [younger] sister. If somebody comes to ask a
question he hits them. There is a rumor that people have become
pregnant. He kicked one who was pregnant and the rumor was
that it was his baby. She went home to Pietersburg to have the
baby.[323]

Dipo told Human Rights Watch that on at least one occasion the farm
owner had succeeded in raping her. Human Rights Watch also visited several
farms in Northern Province and spoke to dozens of male and female farmworkers
there. At one farm near the town of Messina, Human Rights Watch spoke to Hilda
Rutenga, a farmworker, who told us that Mr. Wilbert, the owner of the farm, raped
his domestic worker and impregnated her. "When his wife left for work, Mr.
Wilbert remained, raping Elizabeth Mate, his domestic worker. After his wife
found about the rape and pregnancy, she fired Mate from her job," said Hilda
Rutenga.[324] Mate gave birth to a baby girl. In April 2000, she was still living at the
farm with the child, now aged between four to six years old. She did not report the
case to police.
      In September 2000, Human Rights Watch visited farms in the Piketberg
area of the Western Cape. Human Rights Watch learned about the case of Lucy
Fernson, a woman farmworker who alleged that she was raped by the owner of the
farm on which she lived. She visited the Piketberg advice office to seek help:

Lucy came to our office in March 1999 to report a case of rape.
She was thirty-one years old when I interviewed her.
Unfortunately, she refused to disclose the name of the farm
owner who had raped her because she was afraid of possible
retaliation. Lucy told me that on several occasions the farm
owner raped her in his house. Sometimes the farm owner raped
Lucy in the field when his wife was present in the house. Lucy

---

[323] Human Rights Watch interview, Tarlton area, Gauteng, April 20, 2000.
[324] Human Rights Watch, interview, Northern Province, March 28, 2000.

did not want to work on the farm anymore. She used to work in the kitchen as a domestic worker. She was four months pregnant as a result of the rape when I interviewed her. She wanted assistance with how to obtain social welfare funds once she delivered her baby. She refused to report the case to police because she was afraid of the farm owner. She did not revisit our office [the advice office] since I spoke to her in March 1999. I do not know what finally happened to her and I still do not know who raped her. She refused to disclose the name of the farm owner. She was in a very terrible state when I spoke to her.[325]

In the Free State, young woman of eighteen reported to researchers how a supervisor had sexually assaulted her, but that she was fearful of reporting it:

I went out and never went to his office again. I did not tell anybody except one of my friends at home. I felt like telling the farmer, but I was afraid that the same thing would happen or I would get fired. Since it happened to me secretly, I think it happens to others, but they are afraid to say anything.[326]

In another case, a young woman about twenty years old who lived and worked at a vegetable farm near Tarlton, on the West Rand in Gauteng, told Human Rights Watch how she was threatened and physically assaulted by the farm owner:

One day last August at 6:30 in the evening I came home and that man [the farm owner] came here. He doesn't knock, he just kicks the door down, and found me undressing. He took me out of the bedroom to the kitchen and laid me down on the floor and stood over me and hit me with his fist on my chest and threatened to have sex with me. I went to the Tarlton police station the next day and reported a case of assault.[327] I went to

---

[325] Human Rights Watch interview, advise office coordinator, Piketberg, Western Cape, September 12, 2000.

[326] Ulicki and Crush, "Poverty and Women's Migrancy," pp.79-80.

[327] Case no. 71-08-99, assault and grievous bodily harm, Tarlton police station, Gauteng. As of October 2000, the case was still being investigated. Human Rights Watch telephone interview with Sgt Motlabane, Tarlton police station, October 13, 2000.

see the doctor after the police gave me a form to take to the doctor. The police recorded a statement from me and said they would come and see the farm owner. They have not come here to talk to other people who witnessed the incident. The case occurred at night and I was alone but there were others when I was running away after he hit me, so there were witnesses. I don't live here any more, I came only to see my mother.[328]

Rape by Other Farm Residents

Women farm residents are also raped and sexually assaulted by other farmworkers. Women farmworkers may be more likely to speak about the rapes perpetrated by other farmworkers (except marital rape),[329] than rapes perpetrated by farm owners and managers. Nonetheless, there are no statistics of rape of women farm residents in either circumstance, since police do not break down reported rapes by place of residence. Women and girls are raped by men well known to them, such as neighbors, husbands, or work mates. The poor housing conditions prevalent on farms, including hostels or compounds in which single migrant workers, men and women, are housed in close proximity, and where there is poor security, increase the likelihood of such violent interactions.[330]

In many cases, known perpetrators are left unpunished for their actions. Farm owners often distance themselves from violence involving farmworkers against each other. In the context of the quite closed community of the farm, where farm residents are unlikely to have their own transport or phone connections, this may mean that no outside assistance is available to farmworkers. In many cases, farm owners consider violence among those working or resident on their farms as "none of their business," and may trivialize its consequences on women.[331] For example, the Centre for Rural Legal Studies, a research and advocacy group working on labor rights for farmworkers, encountered a farm owner and his wife who made a joke out of a case of rape of a woman farmworker that occurred at their farm in the Karoo region of the Western Cape in 1999. In this case, the victim

---

[328] Human Rights Watch interview with farm resident, near Tarlton, Gauteng, April 20, 2000.

[329] Like incest, reporting of marital rape is less likely to happen, among farm workers as in other communities, because of the intimate connection between the perpetrator and victim and because the concept of marital rape may not be understood.

[330] Ulicki and Crush, "Poverty and Women's Migrancy," pp.75-78.

[331] Human Rights Watch interview, Jackie Sunde, Department of Sociology, University of Cape Town, April 14, 2000.

allegedly owed rent to her assailant and she had failed to make payment of the rent on the due date. The assailant then went to her house and raped her. After raping her, the assailant told the farm owner that he "just collected the 'rent' she owed him," meaning that raping the woman was equivalent to obtaining the rent she owed.[332] The farm owner had made no effort to tell the woman of her rights to report the matter to the police, or encouraged her to seek other assistance. In another case, a group of women reported to researchers that men had been threatening them with sexual assault for several nights at their hostel, and had broken windows. Although they had complained to the farm owner, no action had been taken.[333] The same researchers found that cases of rape and sexual harassment among migrant farmworkers were left for supervisors to handle, often permanent male employees.[334]

Thirteen-year-old Kasy Mwale was raped by a man she identified as an employee of Thomson farm near New Hanover, KwaZulu-Natal. When Human Rights Watch interviewed her, Mwale stayed with her mother on a farm where her mother worked as a domestic worker. Mwale was a student at New Hanover Primary School. She encountered the rapist while on her way to the farm store:

> I knew the man who raped me before the rape occurred. He works at Thomson farm. He is married and has four children. Two of his children go to the same school with me. On March 29, this man followed me while I was on my way to the store. He dragged me into a bush and raped me. He beat me on the face and head while he was raping me. He threatened to kill me if I told anyone about the incident. When he left me, I went back home and told my mother about the rape. My mother reported to the police. The rapist was arrested on the same day. Police also took me to the doctor on the same day. I was examined by the doctor who wrote the results and gave them to the police. The doctor also gave me an injection. The police, however, released the rapist after he denied having raped me.[335]

---

[332] Human Rights Watch interview, Jackie Sunde, Department of Sociology, University of Cape Town, April 14, 2000.

[333] Ulicki and Crush, "Poverty and Women's Migrancy," p. 80.

[334] Ibid., p.80

[335] Human Rights Watch interview, Kasy Mwale, New Hanover, KwaZulu-Natal, April 5, 2000.

When interviewed by Human Rights Watch, Mwale complained that she still suffered from vaginal pain and had difficulty walking because of it.

Human Rights Watch met with a group of children who are now housed at the Sithabile Child and Youth Care Centre, a shelter project for child survivors of abuse from the farms in the East Rand in Gauteng.[336] Many of these children came from the East Rand farms where they experienced abuse, including sexual violence by farmworkers. Most of the children complained to Human Rights Watch about their parents' neglect of them. Many of them had been used as child labor on the farms, daily loading vegetables and other produce on tractors and trucks.

Ten-year-old Moretse Mhlothi was one of the children who had been sexually assaulted by more than one male farmworker at a farm where her parents worked. Mhlothi told Human Rights Watch that "rape and sexual abuse had become a way of living for many girls on the farms."[337] She came to the Sithabile Centre in 1996, aged six, after having lived all her life on a farm in the East Rand area:

> It was painful staying on the farm. On many occasions when my mother sent me to the shops, I encountered a male farmworker who took me to his house and raped me. Another man, a tractor driver, also used to do the same to me. They were both elderly men. I did not report the case to anybody, because I was afraid of the assailants.[338]

Mhlothi came to the Sithabile Centre on her own after she heard about the center from other children on the farms. She did not want to go back and live on the farm with her parents.[339]

A fourteen-year-old girl, who lived with her aunt on a farm in the East Rand told Human Rights Watch about the rape that she suffered:

---

[336] Human Rights Watch interview, Thabisile Msezani, director, Sithabile Child and Youth Care Centre, Boksburg, Gauteng, April 15, 2000.

[337] Human Rights Watch interview, Moretse Mhlothi, Sithabile Child and Youth Care Centre, Gauteng, April 15, 2000. Translated from Sotho.

[338] Human Rights Watch interview, Sithabile Child and Youth Care Centre, Gauteng, April 15, 2000. Translated from Sotho.

[339] Human Rights Watch interview, Sithabile Child and Youth Care Centre, Gauteng, April 15, 2000. Translated from Sotho.

> My aunt used to make me do a lot of work in the house, including going out to fetch firewood in the forest. One day while I was in the forest collecting firewood, I encountered a man who worked on the same farm where we lived. The man beat me and raped me. When I told my aunt's friend about the rape, she in turn went and told the assailant's wife who beat me so badly. I left the farm after my friend told me about Sithabile Centre in 1998. I did not report the case to anybody else except my aunt's friend.[340]

Sexual Harassment

Women farmworkers experience sexual harassment from their employers and managers, and from other farmworkers. Sexual harassment happens in the packing rooms, in kitchens, and in the field. Sexual harassment commonly takes the form of persistent requests for sexual favors in exchange for better working conditions, unwanted flirting, sexualized language, and other degrading treatment.[341] Victims of sexual harassment in general suffer a number of negative consequences, including poor job performance, persistent absenteeism, victimization by other workers, victimization by employer, guilt, loss of promotion or salary, and resignation or dismissal.

Human Rights Watch interviewed many women farmworkers who had been victims of sexual harassment from KwaZulu-Natal, Western Cape, and Gauteng. Some of the victims told Human Rights Watch about the negative side effects they suffered as a result of the harassment. Some had been assaulted by their employers or managers as punishment for resisting advances. Twenty-year-old Deliwe Hlabathi was sexually harassed by the foreman on several occasions. When interviewed by Human Rights Watch, Hlabathi was a single mother with one child.

---

[340] Human Rights Watch interview, Sithabile Child and Youth Care Centre, Gauteng, April 15, 2000.

[341] Sexual harassment is defined in South African civil law as "unwanted conduct which is persistent or serious and demeans, humiliates or creates a hostile or intimidating environment or is calculated to induce submission … and which is related to sex, gender or sexual orientation." Promotion of Equality and Prevention of Unfair Discrimination Act, No. 4 of 2000, section 1(xiii). Article 3 (1) and Article 4(1) of the National Economic and Development Labor Council (NEDLAC)'s *Code of Good Practice on the Handling of Sexual Harassment Cases* of 1998, refer to "criminal conduct of a sexual nature," which may include "unwelcome physical, verbal, or non-verbal conduct."

She was dismissed from her job on a farm in KwaZulu-Natal after she complained about the sexual harassment:

> I worked at the farm for ten months, from August 1999 until June 2000. I was employed as a domestic worker, cooking for all the farmworkers. I earned R150 [approximately U.S.$20]. I was not getting any additional benefits. Since my first day of work, the foreman started to propose love to me. He is married with three children, who all live on the farm with him and his wife. I refused his requests, and he started treating me badly. He spoke to me with a harsh voice each time he saw me. In August 1999, the foreman came into the kitchen and hit me hard on the back with a cooking stick while I was working. He accused me for delaying to prepare food for the farmworkers, but I had spent all morning helping others extinguish the fire that broke out on the farm. I went to report him to the farm owner. Surprisingly, the farm owner rebuked me for disrespecting the foreman. The farm owner dismissed me from work on the same day. I reported the case of assault to the police at Redfree. A case of assault was opened and we went to court. The foreman denied that he had beaten me. [The case was dismissed.] The foreman was left unpunished for beating me and for causing me to be dismissed from employment for no reason. Instead, I was punished on top of having gone through all this.[342]

Women also complained to Human Rights Watch that they were often subjected to other degrading treatment by farm owners. In some cases farm owners used highly sexualized language when speaking to women. In other cases, farm owners subjected women to humiliating treatment either in the context of pursuing an eviction or in situations where they found the woman trespassing on the farm. For example, thirty-nine-year old Josephine Thenga (her real name), whose case is reported above, was beaten seriously by the farm owner, Roelf Schutte, after he found her fetching firewood on his farm. The farm owner forced Thenga to undress in the presence of men unknown to her, violating her rights to dignity and privacy,

---

[342] Human Rights Watch interview, KwaZulu-Natal, April 4, 2000.

Moses Mayisela, blinded following an assault by the Wakkerstroom Commando.
Bronwen Manby/(c) Human Rights Watch, 2000

Farm workers cottage, Northern Province.
Bronwen Manby/(c) Human Rights Watch, 2000

Farm workers houses, KwaZulu-Natal.
Bronwen Manby/(c) Human Rights Watch, 2000

Sign on farm gate, Northern Province, advertising that the farmer employs the services of the vigilante group Mapogo a Mathamaga.
Bronwen Manby/(c) Human Rights Watch, 2000

Living conditions for evicted farm workers from Weskus Farm in the Western Cape Province.
(c) Lawyers for Human Rights, 2000

Demolition of the homes of residents of Weskus Farm, Western Cape Province.
(c) Lawyers for Human Rights, 2000

Demolished house of farm worker, Northern Province.
Bronwen Manby/(c) Human Rights Watch, 2000

before forcing her to lie in a coffin and threatening her with further violence.[343] Similarly, Azwindini Maggie Randima (her real name), a middle aged woman with three children, whose case was reported above, was arrested by farm security on May 29, 1998, when she awoke one night to go to the toilet in the bush, and kept all day in the open wearing only her underwear.[344]

---

[343] Human Rights Watch interview, March 27, 2000; see also *Investigation of Alleged Violations of Farm workers' Rights in the Messina/Tshipise District*, Report of the South African Human Rights Commission.

[344] Human Rights Watch interview, Tshipise, Northern Province, March 28, 2000.

ASSAULTS AGAINST FARMWORKERS' ADVOCATES

It is very difficult to get access to farms in South Africa. Farms are private property and unauthorized visitors are potentially subject to charges of criminal trespass. Section 6 of the Extension of Security of Tenure Act, however, provides that farm residents have the right "to receive *bona fide* visitors at reasonable times and for reasonable periods," subject to "reasonable conditions" imposed by the owner. ESTA explicitly attempts to strike a balance between the rights of farm owners (who often assert that a commercial farm should be no different from any other private workplace, where the proprietor has a right to decide who may enter the premises); and the rights of farm residents (for whom the farm is also a home), to dignity, privacy, freedom of movement, family life, and other rights.[345]

Farm owners have legitimate concerns about the presence of strangers, especially in the current climate of insecurity on commercial farms. Agri-SA is developing a "protocol" to be followed in order to obtain access to farms or farmworkers, including requirements that all visitors make a prior appointment to obtain access, with "more flexible" arrangements for members of the security forces.[346] In some cases, however, these concerns lead to a violent response: persons on a farm without permission can risk assault or worse from the farm owner. Those working with farm residents, from NGOs or unions, face particular difficulties, and the consequence can be to deprive farm residents of assistance in asserting their rights under the law. In 1997, the Free State Agricultural Union warned that it took exception to the "unauthorized and unreasonable" access to farms by trade union officials and others who entered property without permission.[347] In isolated farming areas even people meeting on public land can

---

[345] Section 5 of ESTA provides that "Subject to limitations which are reasonable and justifiable in an open and democratic society based on human dignity, equality and freedom, an occupier, an owner and a person in charge shall have the right to—(a) human dignity; (b) freedom and security of the person; (c) privacy; (d) freedom of religion, belief and opinion and of expression; (e) freedom of association; and (f) freedom of movement, with due regard to the objects of the Constitution and this Act." Section 6(2) provides that the right to receive *bona fide* visitors is "without prejudice to the generality of the provisions of section 5 ... and balanced with the rights of the owner." Section 6(2)(d) adds to the right to receive visitors, the right "to family life in accordance with the culture of that family."

[346] "Farmers must now lock their farm gates," statement on Agri-SA website <www.agri24.com>, as at November 21, 2000, no date.

[347] "FSAU warns against trespassers on farms," SAPA, June 23, 1997, quoting Pieter Moller, FSAU's manager of human resources.

129

face suspicion, and a close watch is kept on those who may be deemed "troublesome." At Ingogo police station, in northern KwaZulu-Natal, the station commissioner requested that the local crisis committee, offering support in cases of illegal evictions, report the presence of all outsiders visiting even public property, including Human Rights Watch.[348]

The situation may have improved in some areas: another community leader working with labor tenants commented to Human Rights Watch that, though threats from farmers were still frequent, farmers were not able to use the police to harass activists as in the past.[349] Other fieldworkers have built up relationships with the police and are able to obtain police escorts to farms.

In some cases, advocates for farm residents face serious harassment. For example, Shirhami Shirinda, fieldworker with the Nkuzi Development Association, has faced threats and harassment on several occasions from farmers and police, as a result of his work. On October 20, 1999, he was traveling to attend a meeting in the Messina area, at a holiday resort near the Maswiri Boerdery, where he had been involved in the case of the dismissed workers, described above. He was stopped outside the meeting hall by two police vans with five policemen, who stated that they came from the Masisi police station and that they had come to arrest him in connection with a case from Gumbu village. When Shirinda demanded a warrant of arrest or statement showing his name as a suspect, it became apparent that the police did not know his name. As Shirinda attempted to enter the meeting hall, since there was no warrant of arrest, he was seized by the policemen.

> I was grabbed from behind by the five policemen who were talking to me about the arrest. I started to struggle to get loose but they were holding me with both legs and hands. I didn't walk with them voluntarily, but they dragged me on a tarred surface up until where the police van was parked. At the police van I grabbed the door and then the struggle to put me in and for me getting loose started again. The ones who were holding me by my hands twisted my wrists and I felt pain and they managed to get my upper body into the van. There was another struggle to get my lower body into the van and one policeman hit me on my left foot with the door of the van, I felt pain again and they

---

[348] Human Rights Watch interview with Insp. De Klerk, station commissioner, Ingogo police station, April 7, 2000.

[349] Human Rights Watch interview with Jotham Myaka, Zibambeleni, New Hanover, September 13, 2000.

succeeded in getting my whole body into the van. During the struggle, I sustained several injuries and my jersey was torn apart as a result of the police conduct. Then they drove with me to Masisi police station where I was detained. I was detained as an unknown person as the police who arrested me failed to give the police in the charge office my name. At the police station I insisted to see a docket or a warrant of arrest but they told me that they were not in possession of any.

Shirinda was taken to court the next day and the court ordered that he should be released on bail of R1,000 (U.S.$132). He was not freed, but instead was immediately redetained by another policeman who said he was arresting him in connection with a case in Messina and held for another night. The next day he was taken to Messina, charged with resisting arrest and assaulting a police office, brought before court, and released on free bail.[350] This case was still outstanding as of April 2001, when it was postponed because the police failed to come to court.[351]

Philip Shabalala, a paralegal based in Vryheid, northern KwaZulu-Natal, told Human Rights Watch of a raid on his house, after he had been making inquiries in relation to assaults on farm residents:

Around Christmas 1998, or early 1999, some security came to my house; I'm not sure if it was private security or the commandos. There were two whites and about ten blacks, all wearing army-style camouflage uniform. I asked them why they had come, and they said they were looking for cellphones, because one of the farmers had phoned them to say that I had phoned him and threatened to kill him and so they have come to check if I have a cell phone. I denied this, and asked if they had a search warrant. They said they did not, but they came in anyway and checked all over inside and outside the house. They had big guns, radios, and they were driving four vehicles of the type used by the SANDF. But they couldn't find anything. Then they left. Next day I went to Vryheid police station and spoke to the station commissioner and asked if he had sent those

---

[350] Statement of Shirhami Shirinda, March 24, 2000; "Land activist appears on assault charges," SAPA, October 22, 1999.
[351] Email from Nkuzi Development Association to Human Rights Watch, April 10, 2001.

people. He said he knew nothing about it. I told him I was visited by these people who said they were the police, and I reminded him of a case at around that time of a certain Mr. Masondo from Vaalkop who was taken in a white police van to Paulpietersburg and assaulted very badly and left for dead, and asked him how we could trust the police. The station commissioner promised he would bring the person from the roadblock and find out if he was the one who instructed these people to come to my place. He phoned me afterward to say that the person at the roadblock knows about the raid, and I said he must bring him to me so that we can talk to find out why they came. We are just scared now that if white people visit us at home at night they can just assault us or even kill us. But up to now he has not brought this man to me. I tried to open a case: I went to the charge office here in Vryheid, and they said 'how can you open a case when you don't know who you are talking about.' I said they must talk to the station commissioner who knew about it, and they said he was on leave. So I just gave up.[352]

The attorney for whom Shabalala works, Christo Loots, has his main office in Pietermaritzburg. He told Human Rights Watch that, when he was opening the office in Vryheid, no white property owner would rent premises to him when it became known the type of work that would be handled. He therefore had to purchase the building where the office is located. He himself had received anonymous phone calls threatening him for his work on land rights, while he has completely ceased to receive instructions from the agricultural cooperatives, for whom he was previously also acting.[353]

In 1997, local farmers told members of the Ingogo Crisis Committee, formed in 1994 in response to a spate of local evictions, that they would be held responsible for any future attacks on farms in the Ingogo area. They accused Shadrack Kubheka, a member of the committee, of threatening that farmers would be slaughtered, following the eviction of several families from a farm, a charge he

---

[352] Human Rights Watch interview with Philip Shabalala, paralegal, Christo Loots Attorneys, Vryheid, April 6, 2000.
[353] Human Rights Watch interview with Christo Loots, Pietermaritzburg, September 11, 2000.

denies.[354] "When there is a murder of a white farmer they blame us. When [a farming couple] were killed, we didn't know who did it, but because it happened when we had been telling people their rights, they assumed it was us. The farmers came here and wanted to know why they were killed. But then a person was arrested [for the murders] who had been working for them and we didn't know. They had hired him from outside, and then those people cause problems, not us. We live nearby, but we don't know what is happening on the farm, that is the employees."[355]

Solly Phetoe, working for the union federation COSATU in North West Province, was threatened and nearly killed by members of Mapogo a Mathamaga when he became involved in a case in which one Mozambican worker was killed and another seriously injured by the vigilante group. Following verbal threats when they met at the police station or court, there was an attempt to kill him. On April 7, 2000, he was driving alone in his vehicle on a deserted stretch of road near Hartebeestpoort dam. A bakkie [pick-up truck] behind flashed at him to stop, which he did not do until he was obliged to do so at a four-way stop. The bakkie [pick up truck] then drew up alongside, Phetoe saw the double leopard head Mapogo symbol, and drew away as quickly as he could. The bakkie [pick up truck], which had three white people and one black in it, attempted to force him off the road, and then shots were fired that broke the back window of Phetoe's car. Fortunately, he was not injured and managed to escape. He reported the case to the

---

[354] "Tension mounts over death threats," *Newcastle Advertiser*, December 19, 1997. Kubheka was convicted in 2000 on a charge of incitement which he believes is an attempt to silence him. "They said I told someone to kill an Indian who rents a farm, when all I was doing was telling the residents their rights under the new laws, that he couldn't close a road. The incident happened in January 1999, but it was only after I argued with the station commissioner later that it was really pushed forward. They removed him [the commissioner] at the end of 1999, but the last thing he said was that he was going to get me. There is a statement on the docket saying that I agreed that I incited the person, but I didn't. And the affidavit was not sworn before a magistrate. They have made up the confession and put it on my docket." In August 2000, Khubeka was convicted of incitement and sentenced five years in prison, suspended for five years, and to one year six months or a R5,000 fine. According to Kubheka, the prosecution witness in fact denied that he had incited anyone, but the magistrate had chosen to believe the account of the police. Human Rights Watch interview, Shadrack Kubheka, Ingogo, April 7, 2000, and Utrecht, KwaZulu-Natal, September 15, 2000. Human Rights Watch has not itself investigated the circumstances surrounding the charge, and cannot comment on whether Khubeka was wrongly convicted or not.
[355] Human Rights Watch interview, Ingogo, KwaZulu-Natal, April 7, 2000.

Hartebeestpoort police, but they said since he could not identify his attackers—the bakkie [pick up truck] had no registration plates—there was nothing they could do.[356]

In December 1997, Sam Moyo, a campaigner for the rights of farmworkers in the Lanseria area near Johannesburg, Gauteng, was arrested by police at his home on a farm in the district. He was kept in prison until May 1998, when the family finally obtained funds to take the bail application to the Johannesburg High Court, which released him on R3,000 (U.S.$395) bail. Moyo was reportedly arrested on charges of intimidation based on information from a security guard employed by a local businessman and farmer. "When Sam was arrested," according to his brother Farayi Moyo, quoted in the *Mail and Guardian*, "he had laid another charge against one farmer who had beaten a farmworker and then threw him on the fire. But due to his arrest that case vanished into thin air. More surprisingly, three months prior to his arrest, he had laid a similar charge of intimidation against [the farmer who employed the security guard whom Sam Moyo was alleged to have intimidated], but no arrest was made. The investigating officer said there was no valid evidence."[357]

In September 1999, Rural Action Committee fieldworker Alfred Ngomane attempted to intervene in a case in Arnot, near Middelburg, where a farm owner was not complying with a court order that his labor tenant be given grazing land. According to Ngomane, "I went with a member of the Transitional Local Council to the farm, and talked to the tenant, and then went to the farmhouse to talk to the farmer. He said he didn't like the guy I was with, and said that if we didn't leave he would drive over our car with a tractor. We had no option but to leave. We immediately went to Middelburg police station and reported the case, but I've heard nothing until now."[358] It is an offence to "wilfully obstruct or interfere with an official in the employ of the State or a mediator in the performance of his or her duties under ESTA,"[359] yet even officials with the Department of Land Affairs can face harassment. According to one DLA employee, "There was one case where the farmer locked us inside the farm, when we had been there to negotiate a burial. The landowner had been informed through an attorney that we were coming, but he

---

[356] Human Rights Watch telephone interview with Solly Phetoe, June 22, 2000.

[357] Thokozani Mtshali, "Mysterious death in farm 'paradise,'" *Mail and Guardian* December 18-23, 1998; Human Rights Watch interview with Farayi Moyo, September 5, 2000. Sam Moyo died four months after being released from detention.

[358] Human Rights Watch interview with Alfred Ngomane, The Rural Action Committee (TRAC), April 12, 2000.

[359] Section 23, Extension of Security of Tenure Act, 1997.

deliberately locked us in. We subsequently laid a charge with the police, but at no stage did any police official come back to us, and then two or three months later we were told that the prosecutor had declined to prosecute."[360]

A private landowner who allowed twenty-three families to stay on her land near Lanseria, Gauteng, after they were evicted from a nearby farm told newspaper reporters that she had been threatened as a result: "I don't know who they are, they disguise their voices and say ugly things to me. They even threatened my children and said they would mutilate them and me." The families had also been threatened by neighboring landowners.[361]

Harassment of Individuals Involved in Union or Political Activities

Farmworkers or farm residents who attempt to join a union, a political party, or speak to the press may also face harassment or eviction. Farmworkers only obtained the right to organize in 1993, and union organizers still report problems in obtaining access to farmworkers, and harassment of workers who attempt to join unions. Though legalized, farmworkers' unions remain weak.

The workers for the Maswiri Boerdery whose case is highlighted above were dismissed after they joined a union. The farm owner allegedly then began various forms of harassment which culminated in their dismissal. Similarly, in October 1998, eight workers from the Sandfontein Boerdery near Louis Trichardt were dismissed after union officials came to the farm and workers indicated their interest in joining. The farmer himself was present at the meeting, which went ahead without incident, but when individuals put down their names indicating they were interested in joining the union, eight of thirty-three workers, regarded as the ringleaders, were dismissed. The case was taken to the Commission on Conciliation, Mediation and Arbitration, and those dismissed still live on the farm. One of these told Human Rights Watch: "The owner sent someone working with him to call me. He said 'are you the one causing the trouble?' and he took out a gun and said, 'this is an automatic gun, with twenty-one bullets; I could shoot you.' Then he turned and went back to his room."[362] The former worker attempted to open a case with the police about this threat, but they refused to do so until he returned to the police station with a fieldworker from the Nkuzi Development Association. The same informant told Human Rights Watch that "the farmer used

---

[360] Human Rights Watch interview with Mpumalanga Department of Land Affairs officials, April 12, 2000.

[361] Melanie-Ann Feris, "Squatters must move away, say neighbours," *Star*, September 15, 1997.

[362] Human Rights Watch interview with farm resident, Northern Province, March 28, 2000.

to beat people so much. Hitting them with his fists, kicking them. He would follow us with his motorbike, chasing us and saying that he was doing it because we had joined COSATU [the Congress of South African Trades Unions; in fact an umbrella body, rather than an individual union]. But COSATU wouldn't help us because when I phoned they said they didn't know us because we had not actually paid up our membership dues. Since this business the clinic has not come, and the farmer says that he won't buy medicine because COSATU will buy us everything."[363]

A woman working on the same farm, who had lived there all her life, told Human Rights Watch:

> We wanted to know our rights as workers. The salary was very little. At the end of the year we were not getting bonuses. One time when we asked [the farmer] for bonuses, he said 'I cannot squeeze my penis to produce money.' We worked overtime and were not paid for that. He only gave us tea when we worked overtime. The current problem started in April 1998 when our trade union representative came to meet with [the farmer], to talk about the conditions on the farm in general. After the trade union representative left, [the farmer] called us individually to his office. He did not want us to become members of a trade union, hence he was angry with us. He told each one of us that she would be dismissed from their job if she kept demanding to be paid more money, because he did not have that money. From that day, [the farmer] made the working conditions on the farm even more difficult. He started to ask us to pick forty, rather than the twenty crates we used to pick per day. When we asked why he had doubled the number of crates per day, he responded sarcastically, by saying, 'SAAPAWU trade union asked me to do so.' He followed behind us riding on his motor-cycle while we were carrying heavy crates of avocados commanding us to 'hurry up.' He even followed us to the toilet and waited by the entrance shouting, 'do it quickly or else get an axe to cut that shit if it's not coming out.' When we asked why he was behaving that way, he always said, 'SAAPAWU trade union asked me to do so.' In March 2000, he evicted us from the farm.[364]

---

[363] Ibid.

[364] Human Rights Watch interview, Northern Province, March 28, 2000.

Farm owners can be hostile towards workers who are actively involved in politics. Human Rights Watch interviewed a young man who is an ANC councillor and former resident on a farm near Eston, in the KwaZulu-Natal Midlands, and his sister, who was still resident on the farm. "I was born on the farm twenty-seven years ago, and started becoming active in the ANC in the late 80s. I started having problems with the farmer in 1996 when he was evicting some people and I was objecting.... He pointed to me as the one who was encouraging them to go to the Department of Land Affairs and told my parents that he didn't want to see me around here any more. He sent the private security people to tell me to leave.... Early this year we were launching ANC branches in Eston. On February 19, all the farmers gathered at Eston primary school and instructed the [private security company] and the police and told them to come and remind me that I am not allowed here. The station commissioner from Mid-Illovo came to my home where I was staying on the farm with my parents and told me he had been instructed by the farmers to tell me to go. I said that I know my rights and am not going anywhere without a court order for eviction."[365] His sister corroborated this to Human Rights Watch, stating, "In February this year the station commissioner from Mid-Illovo police station came with two other people and said that he had received an instruction from the farm owner that he did not want Sipho here; in fact they don't want anyone who is ANC on the farm. The same day at about 2 pm the [private security company] members also came to our house, four people, and also said we don't need Sipho here and will come again later to check whether he is in or not."[366] Sipho has in fact left the farm.

Even talking to journalists about farm conditions can cause serious problems: In 1997, farmworker Samuel Moabi was evicted from the farm where he lived and worked after he talked to reporters from the *Mail and Guardian* about his brutal assault and eviction from his previous place of employment.[367]

---

[365] Human Rights Watch interview with ANC councillor, Eston, KwaZulu-Natal, April 4, 2000.

[366] Human Rights Watch interview with farm resident, Eston, KwaZulu-Natal, April 4, 2000. Name of activist changed.

[367] Ann Eveleth, "'Sadist' grins at light fine," *Mail and Guardian*, November 7 to 13, 1997.

"FARM ATTACKS":
VIOLENT CRIME AGAINST FARM OWNERS

The first time I was attacked was in August 1998. I came back home and parked my van. My boy said there were three people looking for work. I said I only want one, and I went out to meet them in the garage. They said they wanted work, but then one with a revolver signed to the other one, who grabbed my boy; the first one pulled out his gun, but it jammed. I grabbed a broom and hit him, and then the other one, and then I ran inside to get my gun. But they knocked me down and fractured my skull, so I was unconscious. They chased my boy, but the dogs went after them, and they ran out. The fellows from the farmwatch picked them up on the road. They shot one, arrested another, and the third one later gave himself up. But all three later escaped from the police cells.

One of my neighbor's boys must have seen what was going on and ran to my neighbor who pushed the panic button and alerted the farmwatch cell. It was the commandos who dished out the treatment, not the police. I came to, and identified the guys who were caught before they took me to hospital.

The farmwatch were here twenty minutes after the incident, the police in forty-five minutes. They left a policeman here overnight, and they did the usual jobs that they do, taking statements, but to this day we have no information from our local police station about what happened—I only got any follow up by calling Pretoria. They never interviewed my laborers to find out if they had seen anything, there was no follow up.

Six months later they broke into the house again... I phoned a neighbor and pushed the panic button in our bedroom, and then the phone started ringing and the boys got a fright and ran off.... They had the room stripped and everything out of it ready to go.... Lying in the dark waiting is an awful feeling, if

the commandos hadn't come I don't know what would have happened.[368]

---

[368] Human Rights Watch interview, Bapsfontein, September 19, 2000.

Over the last decade, there has been an increasing incidence of violent crime against the owners and managers of commercial farms or smallholdings and their families: according to statistics collected by police, between January 1997 and December 1999, 356 people on farms or smallholdings were killed by intruders.[369] Farm owners' organizations claim that more than 1000 people have died in such circumstances since 1991.[370] The escalation in violent crime against white farm owners and managers, disproportionate in relation to general crime trends in South Africa (though high, the overall murder rate has declined somewhat in recent years), has drawn significant media and political attention. Crimes committed against commercial farmers have come to be given the description of "farm attacks," although the description is often used to refer to any burglary of a farmstead and not only those where violence is used. Human Rights Watch prefers to describe such incidents as "violent crime."

In the past, commercial farmers, isolated from the urban environment and relatively wealthy, largely escaped the violence plaguing many areas of South Africa—though farmers living along the border areas with Zimbabwe and Mozambique were mobilized for the defense of the state against incursion by the liberation movements and in turn were the victims of landmines planted by Umkhonto we Sizwe (Spear of the Nation, known as MK, the armed wing of the ANC) or the Azanian Peoples Liberation Army (APLA, the armed wing of the Pan Africanist Congress, PAC). APLA explicitly stated that it regarded white farmers in general as legitimate targets in the liberation war (in violation of international humanitarian law), though few were actually killed. With the political transition of the last decade and the repeal of the pass laws, violent crime has spread from the black townships and former homelands, at the receiving end of the social dislocation and economic hardship caused by apartheid, to touch all South Africans, including those in formerly privileged white enclaves. Nevertheless, as in other countries, most perpetrators of violent crime are known to their victims, according to police: one of the reasons that violent crime against farm owners has received such prominence is that, after police officers, farm owners and their

---

[369] *Attacks on Farms and Smallholdings: Report by the Crime Information Analysis Centre, No.1 of 1999*; email dated August 15, 2000, from SAPS to Human Rights Watch. The totals for murders committed in each year under these statistics are: 84 in 1997, 142 in 1998, and 144 in 1999.

[370] "Farm killers trained and paid: Agri bodies," SAPA, March 29, 2001; "Agri Securitas Trust Fund contributes to obelisk for murdered farmers," Agri-SA press release, March 8, 2001.

families are probably the group of people most likely to fall victim to violent crime committed by people they do not know. Among white people—who, due to their relative affluence, are mostly protected from stranger violence by ownership of private vehicles, expensive private security guards, and other means, to a degree not possible for most black South Africans—their vulnerability is even more striking. Crime committed by strangers arouses particular fears; in part, because it is unpredictable. It remains the case, however, that the vast majority of victims of violent crime in South Africa are black and poor.

Statistics: What is a "Farm Attack"?

From October 1997, the SAPS Crime Information Analysis Centre (CIAC) based in Pretoria has collected statistics on "attacks on farms and smallholdings." There is no "crime code" providing for a category of crime with this definition in the general collection of police statistics, so the statistics are based on questionnaires distributed from Pretoria and completed by individual police stations.

> To ensure consistency, a definition was formulated to describe attacks on farms and smallholdings. The definition refers to acts aimed against the person of residents, of workers at and/or visitors to farms or smallholdings, whether with the intent to murder, rape, rob or inflict bodily harm (cases related to domestic violence, drunkenness or resulting from commonplace social interaction between people—where victims and offenders are often known to one another—were excluded from the analysis). In addition to the above, all actions aimed at disrupting farming activities as a commercial concern, whether for motives related to ideology, labor disputes, land issues, revenge, grievances or racist concerns, like eg intimidation, were also considered.[371]

Using this definition, the SAPS has charted a consistent rise in the number of "attacks on farms and smallholdings" since 1997, with a sharp rise in early 1998. This increase exceeds general increases in the recorded incidents of aggravated robbery (within which category the majority of these crimes would be recorded). The murder rate within these statistics has increased less quickly, running at about

---

[371] *Attacks on Farms and Smallholdings: Report by the Crime Information Analysis Centre, No.2 of 1998*, available, with other crime statistics, at <www.saps.org.za>.

twelve a month during 1999, up from around seven a month during 1997. The CIAC itself admits that part of the increase may be due to better collection of information from police stations as the process of collection has become routinized.[372] Figures for 2000 are not available, due to a moratorium on publishing police statistics (due to be lifted in July 2001). However, during an April 2001 briefing to the parliamentary portfolio committee on safety and security, the police reported that the incidence of "attacks on farms and smallholdings" stabilized during 2000, and that the number of people killed during such attacks decreased compared to 1999.[373] Given definitional issues (what is a farm?) and problems in collecting accurate information, it is not possible to establish any reliable comparison between the murder rate and other crime for farm owners and the general population, though some have tried to do so.[374]

The statistics for "attacks on farms and smallholdings" are problematic for a number of reasons. In the first place, the bundling together of farms and smallholdings has skewed the figures. There is no definition of either "farm" or "smallholding," which in itself creates difficulties, though the categories are understood to refer in the first case to large commercial farms which provide the sole or main form of income to those who own them; and, in the second, to the small plots of land mostly surrounding the big cities, where people live and may grow some crops, but which do not form the principal source of livelihood for their owners, who usually work in other employment or are retired. People living on this type of smallholding are particularly vulnerable: effectively part of the city crime environment, where strangers do not attract attention, they are also quite isolated from their neighbors and distant from police assistance. According to the police statistics relating to "attacks on farms and smallholdings," attacks on smallholdings have increased much more quickly than attacks on the more distant commercial farms; this is reflected in the fact that attacks have increased especially rapidly in Gauteng, the province housing the Pretoria-Witwatersrand-Vereeniging urban conglomeration, where a majority of the incidents would relate to smallholdings.[375]

---

[372] Human Rights Watch interview with J.C. Strauss, SAPS Crime Information Analysis Centre, Pretoria, April 10, 2000.

[373] "Farm and Police Murders: SAPS Briefing," *Minutes of the Parliamentary Safety and Security Portfolio Committee*, April 4, 2001.

[374] Human Rights Watch interview with J.C. Strauss, SAPS Crime Information Analysis Centre, Pretoria, April 10, 2000.

[375] Gauteng accounted for 54.1 percent of all reported "attacks" reported countrywide between January and June 1998. *Attacks on Farms and Smallholdings, No.2 of 1998.* The eleven areas that are mainly metropolitan in character accounted for 36 percent of all

Bundling the figures together generates a picture of remote commercial farms based on information that is in fact derived partly from the very different environment of the semi-rural areas surrounding the big cities.

Secondly, while the definition does not refer to race, in practice racial issues dominate the way the statistics are collected—just as they dominated the decision to start collecting the statistics in the first place. According to the CIAC, police stations are asked to note "attacks" on a non-racial basis: so a crime by a stranger against anybody living or working on a farm would be reported. One study found that of murdered victims, 74 percent were white, 17 percent black, 3 percent Asian, and 6 percent colored.[376] In practice, however, based on Human Rights Watch's interviews with station commissioners in different parts of the country, in many cases the statistics collected relate to violence or property crimes against white farm owners or managers, and to violence against their black farmworkers only if it is carried out in the course of a crime against the (white) farm owners. Station commissioners usually had detailed knowledge about violent crime or burglaries against white farmsteads, but when questioned about violent crime against farm residents committed by unknown outsiders in their district that had come to the notice of Human Rights Watch, they tended not to be aware.

Furthermore, the exclusion from the definition of crime resulting from "commonplace social interaction" means that many crimes affecting farm residents are not included in the statistics for "farm attacks," whether carried by outsiders against black farmworkers or residents or by black farmworkers or residents against each other—what in the 1980s would have been referred to by the South African Police as "black-on-black violence." Equally, violence within the family of the white farm owner, for example, would not be recorded. Most assaults reported to the police by farm residents are in fact by other farm residents or visitors with permission. At least part of the reason for this exclusion in the collection of police statistics is an attempt to analyze a category of premeditated violent crime, which may be more susceptible to a law enforcement approach, rather than violent crime deriving from, for example, the use of alcohol.[377] The particular fear created by crime committed by strangers, which drives forceful lobbying from organized agriculture for a response to the issue, is undoubtedly also a key factor. But the

---

"attacks" in 1998, and 25.4 percent of murders. *Attacks on Farms and Smallholdings: Report by the Crime Information Analysis Centre, No.1 of 1999.*
[376] *Attacks on Farms and Smallholdings No.2 of 1998.*
[377] Human Rights Watch interview with J.C. Strauss, SAPS Crime Information Analysis Centre, Pretoria, April 10, 2000. This report has made a similar distinction by excluding, in the main, information related to assaults among farmworkers.

low priority given to "social crime" also excludes the violence that most affects most farm residents, and gives them—according to interviews carried out by Human Rights Watch—the impression that only violent crimes affecting property owners are of importance to the state. At many police stations in farming areas, serious assaults among farmworkers are the most common violent crime reported to the police, yet farm residents noted that in such cases there was little or no police response. The statistics also do not include assaults committed by farm owners against farm workers, which go largely unreported; to a large extent this type of crime appears to be invisible to the criminal justice system, except in the most extreme cases.

Whatever the faults of the statistics, it is clear that many white farm owners are living in fear. "People are living with guns all the time, they are being terrorized. There was one murder when the victim was chopped with a cane knife, and when the farmwatch arrived the perpetrators were sitting there having breakfast. These guys feel nothing."[378] In several areas, farmers reported to Human Rights Watch that local commando units conducted patrols not only at nights, but also every Sunday when the white farming community is at church, since farmsteads have become a target from crime during that period, and it is usually the old or sick who may be left at home alone. In some cases, the same farm owner has been the victim of repeated crimes, or of ongoing low-level harassment punctuated by more serious incidents. One woman in her seventies living alone on a smallholding just east of Johannesburg, told Human Rights Watch of a series of security incidents escalating since 1994:

> I was attacked in 1994 in winter. I woke up suddenly, heard nothing, but just as I was turning over to go back to sleep, I heard a window being smashed. I sat up in bed. At that time I had no burglar bars or anything. I came into this room [the living room] and found the whole place smashed up and everything stolen. They'd come with a truck.
> In June 1997 it happened a second time. By then I had burglar bars on all the windows, and security doors, and lights put up, and I felt safe. But one night I suddenly woke up and heard a smash. I jumped out of bed and got on the radio alarm and called Pieter [a neighbor]. I got dressed in no time and took my Beretta that I had next to my bed—before, I used to keep it in a

---

[378] Human Rights Watch interview with Mike de Lange, formerly KWANALU security desk, Eshowe, September 14, 2000.

safe—and stood next to the wall. They must have had a crow bar because they had lifted up the steel door, and then must have woken me smashing the wooden door, then they'd climbed on the deep freeze to break the window and get in. They were in the kitchen, and I heard one say 'baas, mos ek nou skiet?' [master, must I shoot now?].... Then I fired a shot. Then there was no sound, they were bundled together in the kitchen. I thought to myself, I have three more cartridges, but then I heard Pieter's gun firing outside... he shot their sentry. Pieter called me and I came outside. They had run away....

The police only came the next day.... they took fingerprints, but I found the cartridges they had used. I don't know if anyone was arrested, the police tell you nothing anyway, but I've never been called to court.

About eighteen months later my black was also attacked... they tied him up hands and feet and asked him for his gun. They wanted him to come and ask me to open the door. But then the cell group started and things have been fairly quiet since then—though I still get stones thrown at my roof at night, and I had visitors trying to break into my garage, they came back again and again...[379]

The Motives for "Attacks on Farms and Smallholdings"

Many farm owners and some of the representatives of the agricultural unions believe that the motive behind the violent crime committed against farm owners is explicitly racial or political, a conspiracy aimed at driving white people off commercial farmland. As noted by one senior police officer with responsibilities for rural safety and security, "It is a complicated issue, an emotional issue, and political because of some of the things that have been said about the land belonging to all. Every attack is perceived by the farmers as having a political motive, based on an organized political attempt to dispossess them, though we can't find a shred of proof that that is the case."[380]

To a great extent, the debate over "farm attacks" has been driven by some especially brutal killings, rather than by the overall numbers of murders—though these are certainly high. According to Jack Loggenberg of the Transvaal

---

[379] Human Rights Watch interview, Bapsfontein, September 19, 2000.
[380] Human Rights Watch interview with Commissioner Johann Burger, SAPS, Pretoria, April 10, 2000.

Agricultural Union, "We say it is not only crime but something else; they way the people are handled, not only killed, but also tortured brutally, and sometimes nothing is stolen. And not doing anything about it gives the impression that this is acceptable. It could be organized, but we don't have the facts. We find that in farm murders a lot of research is done, in 100 percent of cases there is prior reconnaissance and then there is extreme violence used. This is planned, very organized, a sweeper involved in removing evidence. It is usually outsiders; often the farmworkers try to stop them and they are also killed. If it is to do with bad relations with farmworkers we can do something about it, but this is more worrying, there is nothing leading up to the attacks."[381] (Others who have investigated farm killings, however, note rather that in many cases "their hallmark is extreme amateurishness," with evidence frequently left at the scene.[382]) In May 2000, Agri-SA, the Agricultural Employers Association, and the Transvaal Agricultural Union launched a countrywide signature campaign called "Action: Stop Farm Attacks," noting "the attackers do not merely kill the victims, but inflict pain, humiliation and suffering, especially on elderly people. Women and children are not spared."[383] The campaign was endorsed by the Freedom Front and Afrikaner Eenheidsbeweging, two conservative political parties.[384] By November, the petition had gained 372,000 signatures.[385]

Farm owners' organizations have pointed to the campaign against white farmers carried out by APLA during the 1980s and early 1990s, as evidence for the existence of a political movement to drive them off the land.[386] At one point, slogans often heard at PAC and some ANC rallies included "one settler, one bullet," or "kill the boer, kill the farmer." In September 1999, the Truth and Reconciliation Commission (TRC) granted amnesty to three APLA cadres convicted for the murder of Sandra Swanepoel and attempted murder of her

---

[381] Human Rights Watch interview with Jack Loggenberg, Transvaal Agricultural Union, April 17, 2000.

[382] E-mail from Jonny Steinberg, a researcher based at the Centre for the Study of Violence and Reconciliation who has carried out extensive research into the phenomenon of "farm attacks," November 16, 2000.

[383] "Aksie: Stop Plaasaanvalle / Action: Stop Farm Attacks," media briefing by the Agricultural Employers Association, Agri-SA, and Transvaal Agricultural Union, May 31, 2000. Available at <www.agriinfo.co.za/>, accessed October 6, 2000.

[384] Freedom Front press release, June 1, 2000; SAPA, May 31, 2000.

[385] "Farmers plead for international help against killings," SAPA, November 7, 2000.

[386] Justine Nofal, "Apla blamed for farm murders," Mail and Guardian, October 24-30, 1997.

husband Johannes Swanepoel, farmers near Tzaneen, Northern Province, in 1993.[387] To some, this decision, which under the terms of the Promotion of National Unity and Reconciliation Act included a finding that the crime had a political motive, is proof that similar killings today are also part of an organized terror campaign.[388] Alternatively, a correlation is drawn between the TRC hearings themselves and a rise in violent crime against farm owners.[389] Again, the Freedom Front, a right wing political party, picked up on the statement by a soldier from the Lesotho Defense Force, on trial for treason in connection with an alleged attempted coup in 1998, that he had been trained to regard South African "boers" as the enemy, linking it with news of land confiscation in Zimbabwe and the ANC's proposal to reform the law on gun control, as well as "farm attacks" in South Africa. The Freedom Front called for an independent investigation by the African Commission on Human and Peoples' Rights, set up under the African Charter on Human and Peoples' Rights, into "the ANC government's racist approach."[390]

At their most extreme, these views lead to a belief that the government is training former members of MK or APLA to assassinate white farm owners, possibly even under the direction of some shadowy international force. "There's someone very clever behind these blacks telling them what to do. Someone is orchestrating the farm attacks; there's a central place where they are being planned. The government wants land prices to go down, and one way is to make the people on the land want to leave. And the farm attacks are professional, carried out with military planning."[391] The Transvaal Agricultural Union sees "farm attacks" as "ideologically driven; we are rushing into a situation similar to that in Zimbabwe with the pressure on agriculture in general and the transformation regarding land. The intent is to make land reform affordable, and the farm attacks are part of the

---

[387] "Amnesty granted to APLA members," press release from the Truth and Reconciliation Commission, September 23, 1999.

[388] Human Rights Watch interview with Jack Loggenberg and Boela Niemann, Transvaal Agricultural Union, April 17, 2000; Justine Nofal, "Apla blamed for farm murders," *Mail and Guardian*, October 24-30, 1997.

[389] Prof. C.J. (Neels) Moolman, "An investigation into farm attacks in South Africa," *Landbouweekblad*, November 1998, section 5.3.2, available at <www.landbou.com>, accessed October 6, 2000.

[390] SAPA, March 3, 2000; "Racism in Africa," press release from the Freedom Front, March 3, 2000.

[391] Human Rights Watch interview with members of the Northern Natal commando, Vryheid, September 14, 2000. The same speaker commented that "There's people behind this thing, not the blacks—and your organization [Human Rights Watch] is part of it." The others present at the meeting, however, did seem to believe that this was going a little far.

pressure applied to speed up the process. You must see the total picture. We can't come to another conclusion."[392] TAU admits that it has no evidence for an orchestrated campaign of violence: "At this stage we haven't got it, but there is circumstantial evidence that suggests we must put these attacks in perspective," noting that the 1955 Freedom Charter promises that "the land shall be divided among those who work it."[393] Even those with more moderate views wonder aloud if the unnecessary brutality involved in some killings of farm owners is aimed at driving farmers off the land, in the context where the Department of Land Affairs is not delivering on its promises for redistribution through the use of the law. Similarly, there are numerous rumors of "hit squads" made up of criminal elements in the big cities that can be hired if someone has a problem with a farmer, such as a threatened eviction; while links are seen between violent crime against farm owners and land invasions, drawing parallels with the government-backed take over of white farms in Zimbabwe. In March 2001, the chair of "Action: Stop Farm Attacks" told reporters that six suspects in a "farm attack" case had been found in possession of a video including instruction material on how to carry out a farm attack. It later appeared that there was no substance to these claims.[394]

Some academic writing supports the view that violent crime against farm owners is driven by a desire to intimidate farmers to leave their land, though it relies on media reports, police statistics, and theorization about the impact of apartheid on black South Africans and their world view, rather than on studies of particular cases, interviews with perpetrators, or other empirical evidence.[395]

---

[392] Human Rights Watch interview with Jack Loggenberg and Boela Niemann, TAU, Pretoria, September 19, 2000.

[393] Ibid.

[394] "Farm killers trained and paid: Agri bodies," SAPA, March 29, 2001; Carolyn Dempster, "SA farmers 'prove' killing campaign," BBC website <www.bbc.co.uk>, March 30, 2001; "Farm attack training video a myth: prof," SAPA, April 5, 2001.

[395] See, for example, C.J. (Neels) Moolman, "A Criminological Perspective on Property Rights and Violence Against Farmers: Summary of a research report on farm attacks," in Henk van de Graaf and Chris L. Jordaan, *Property Rights in South Africa* (Pretoria: Transvaal Agricultural Union, 1999); C.J. Moolman, *Farm Attacks and the African Renaissance: Opposite Reactions to a Devastating European Culture* (Pietersburg, 2000); C.J. Moolman, *Bloodstains on Your Food: An investigation into farm attacks in South Africa* (Pietersburg, 1998), a version of which is available at <www.landbou.com>, accessed October 6, 2000; B. Haefele, "Violent Attacks on Farmers in South Africa: Is there a hidden agenda?" *Acta Criminologica* (Johannesburg), vol. 11, no. 2, 1998. The studies do not, for example, consider the reasons behind the sometimes apparently gratuitous violence used in burglaries in urban areas, in order to compare motivations with "farm attacks"— burglaries

Several farmers interviewed by Human Rights Watch reported that they had received threats of various types, ranging from anonymous telephone calls to letters warning them to leave their farm or face the consequences. For some, these are an indication of an organized campaign, others see them as isolated threats from the land-hungry. Extracts from one such letter were published in the Helen Suzman Foundation's *Briefing* magazine:

> Dear Mr L,
> We write this letter to warn you concerning hiring a part of Mr B's farm. The time now is ripe for the Amachanu tribe to act vigorously to show all the conservative Boers our concern about our ancestors' land which was taken from them forcefully by your nation. We know that you are dealing with livestock to make profit out of them and be able to support your family. Think about the people of B's farm and their livestock. They are still oppressed. We feel that you are part of oppression, but don't be fooled by Mr B. Go away otherwise you will lose....
> I'm telling you all your livestock is going to vanish like dew during sunrise. If you listen to that dead living man Z, if the land is under black Z will be the victim of all Mdubuzweni people due to his evil deeds. He has treated his people like animals. He has dehumanised all of them threatening to practice his magic over them Mr L, not because they are afraid of him. He is under your armpits just because he is your spy.
> We as the youth of people who were evicted from there from 1879 are united to achieve one goal. Remember Mr L, Z is the most wanted criminal in S.A. who if he might be caught shall be sentenced to life imprisonment.... We want you Mr L to move away from this area. We hope you know that now our chief has been fooled by the government and you (Boers). That land will end up being under black rule like it or not sir we gonna fight sir. I mean underground warfare to destroy everything of farmers who make Mr B benefit from our land....
> Mr B is a fool. Go—Go Boers Go.[396]

---

of farm houses.

[396] Extract from an anonymous letter to a farmer, published in *Briefing* 12, (Johannesburg: Helen Suzman Foundation, September 1998).

Even where no conspiracy is seen, the rise in violent crime against farm owners is linked by organized agriculture to the government's land reform policies: "There is no way that you can look at the issue of the murder of farmers without also looking at the whole process of land reform and the expectations created. The statements of senior government officials are not helpful.... We don't say there must not be reform and there must not be legislation, but we also don't know if there is not intimidation in the farm attacks."[397] Senior police officers also believe that comments by politicians relating to land rights, evictions, and assaults against farmworkers may reinforce the view among farm owners that violent crime is political.[398] Agri-SA has protested "hate speech" against farm owners by politicians.[399] Mike de Lange, formerly head of the KwaZulu-Natal Agricultural Union (KWANALU) security desk, who still monitors crime against commercial farms closely commented that, "I don't believe that there is an organized plan to drive farmers off the land; but I do believe that the government knows what is happening and is doing nothing about it. The threats to farmers are being ignored. There is a perception that farmers mistreat their labor and pay too little, so they don't care too much."[400]

From the perspective of many black South Africans the interpretation of violent crime against farm owners is equally clear, but opposite, tending to attribute the "farm attacks" to longstanding ill treatment of farm labor.[401] As one employee of the Department of Land Affairs commented: "The attacks are not politically motivated, in the sense of being organized, but many arise from a culture of barbarism. The taking of the land was done by the gun, and some of the farmers still enjoy today making people suffer just to show their supremacy. Then if something small happens it can lead to brutality in revenge."[402] A union worker put

---

[397] Human Rights Watch interview with Jack Loggenberg, Transvaal Agricultural Union, April 17, 2000.

[398] Human Rights Watch interviews with representatives of the SAPS, April 10, 2000.

[399] SAPA, June 22, 2000, quoting Agri-SA President Pieter Erasmus.

[400] Human Rights Watch interview with Mike de Lange, formerly KWANALU security desk, September 14, 2000.

[401] This perception reflects a general division of opinion between blacks and whites in South Africa on the origins of the current crime problems: "by nearly a 3-to-1 margin, 65 to 23 percent, whites say that today's crime is not rooted in the apartheid period. In contrast, a strong plurality of blacks, 47 to 23 percent, disagree." *People on War Country Report: South Africa*, Report by Greenberg Research, Inc. for the International Committee of the Red Cross (Geneva: ICRC, November 1999).

[402] Human Rights Watch interview with Mpumalanga Department of Land Affairs staff, April 12, 2000.

it similarly: "You can't divorce the farm attacks from our history and the fact that farmers refuse to take steps to transform life on farms; they still take it that they are the owners of the universe."[403] A black policeman agreed: "The treatment on farms is not human.... That's why you find attacks on farmers; the attitude of white farmers against black workers causes blacks to retaliate. They still have the attitude that you have no rights."[404] Commenting on reports of a farm owner who forced his workers to share accommodation with pigs, the ANC issued a statement that "it is an open secret that some of the brutal attacks on farmers are revenge attacks by farmworkers who have been brutalized by their employers. It is unfortunate that sometimes it is innocent farmers who pay the price for the actions of their racist colleagues."[405] However, no systematic study has been undertaken that draws any direct correlation between brutality towards farmworkers or evictions of farm residents and attacks on farm owners.

Just as some farm owners and their representatives are convinced that violent attacks against whites living on farms are part of a conspiracy, so farm residents often believe that attempts to organize private security or commando protection for farms are throw-backs to the "third force" of the 1980s and early 1990s, covert action by the previous government to promote violence among black communities and assassinate black leaders. This view is reinforced by the fact that in some areas, among those employed as private security are ex-members of South Africa's more notorious apartheid security units, including the 32 and Koevoet ("Crowbar") battalions deployed in Namibia and Angola.[406]

Contrary to these beliefs, those few more-or-less systematic studies that have been carried out into violent crime against farm owners have found that in the majority of cases violence was used to achieve another purpose rather than for its own sake: "To the extent that the attacks were violent, the violence generally appeared to be tactical and instrumental, rather than gratuitous. While the culprits appeared to have few qualms about injuring or even killing their victims, violence was deployed in the cases studied either to access safes, to leave the victim

---

[403] Human Rights Watch interview with Howard Mbana, SAAPAWU, March 24, 2000.

[404] Human Rights Watch interview with police inspector, Northern Province, March 28, 2000.

[405] "ANC Statement on Workers Sharing Accommodation with Pigs," May 12, 2000.

[406] See, for example, Johnson and Schlemmer, *Farmers and Farmworkers in KwaZulu-Natal*, p.7; interview with Graham McIntosh, (then) president of the KwaZulu-Natal Agricultural Union, published in *Briefing* 12, (Johannesburg: Helen Suzman Foundation, September 1998); Ann Eveleth, "Now Koevoet soldiers guard farmers," *Mail and Guardian*, December 13, 1996.

incapable of signaling for help, or to overpower the victim."[407]   There is no substantive evidence for a coordinated campaign of intimidation to drive whites off the land. Moreover, though the majority of victims are white, reflecting property ownership in South Africa, there is clearly no hesitation in killing people of other ethnic groups. Studies carried out or commissioned by the SAPS have repeatedly concluded that the main motive for these crimes is criminal, especially the theft of firearms, cash, and vehicles.[408] Human Rights Watch interviewed one smallholder, a university professor, just east of Johannesburg who had been the victim of a burglary:

> I came home after class at about 8:30 pm. I phoned my wife when I was about five minutes away to say I was almost home, and she opened the door and waited for me. When I stopped and got out of the vehicle I was attacked by three people and my wife was attacked by another two. They forced us into the bedroom, tied our hands behind our back with flex from the bedroom lights. One guy held a rifle against my wife's head, another held a pistol against my head and they asked us where are the keys of the safe, and where are our firearms. I told them where the keys were and where a pistol was that I had. Then they started ransacking the house looking for money... they took R250,000 (U.S.$33,000) worth of goods, but they were very selective and didn't take things that could identify them; they were very professional. They took the bakkie [pick up truck] and my car and left at around midnight, leaving us tied together on the bathroom floor.[409]

Some have pointed out the links between different types of crime: for example, in KwaZulu-Natal crime against farm owners can often be related to violence in surrounding areas of the former KwaZulu homeland, where organized political violence between the ANC and the Inkatha Freedom Party (IFP) since the 1980s has continued, or diversified into simple gangsterism or the struggles

---

[407] Martin Schönteich and Jonny Steinberg, *Attacks on Farms and Smallholdings: An evaluation of the rural protection plan* (Pretoria, Institute of Security Studies, 2000), p.85.
[408] See for example, *Attacks on Farms and Smallholdings No.2 of 1998* and *Attacks on Farms and Smallholdings, No.1 of 1999*; Schönteich and Steinberg, *Attacks on Farms and Smallholdings*.
[409] Human Rights Watch interview, Bapsfontein, Gauteng, September 19, 2000.

between neighboring political leaders or clans known as "faction violence."[410] As one police officer commented: "There are a number of cases where attacks are just to steal firearms. Many farmers have nine or ten firearms and the information goes out to the perpetrators that the weapons are there. The farm attacks are also linked to faction violence, since the factions need to arm themselves and know that there are a large number of firearms available. Stock theft also increases with faction violence because you can exchange cattle for guns; and there is theft of cash too."[411] Others have noted strong links between violent crime in rural areas and criminal networks in the big cities, where the proceeds of a robbery can be more easily disposed of.[412] Finally, close monitoring of violent crime against white farms in some areas has revealed a seasonal variation: crime increases in July and August, the "hungry months," when food stocks from subsistence farming in the former homeland areas are running low at the end of winter.[413]

Considering the widespread fear of violent crime in South Africa, where no population group has been invulnerable and people typically purchase the maximum amount of personal protection that they can afford, some farm owners also appear to be surprisingly casual about the threat that violent crime poses to them. Reports by the SAPS have noted the absence at farmsteads of precautions of the type that South Africa's urban population now regards as normal.[414] Again, few attempts are made to screen temporary labor for reliability, and often commercial farms will simply send a truck during harvest season to the nearest "tribal" area, and pick up whoever is first in line to take the work. "Farmers will hire someone from the street, without vetting them at all, and then they work for one or two months and are laid off again. Some of these could get involved in attacks. They know the place but they are not long term residents with a

---

[410] For example, "Some of the attacks on white farmers, such as that carried out on 60-year-old Mrs Norris-Jones in Colenso, take place in areas where it is known that well armed bands are terrorising black residents. In some violence-wracked areas, the alleged actions of farmers themselves and/or traditional leaders are exacerbating tensions and open hostilities, as illustrated by events in Vryheid and Msinga." *Natal Violence Monitor*, June to September 1999, compiled by Mary de Haas of the University of Natal, Durban, available at <www.violence.co.za>, accessed October 6, 2000.

[411] Human Rights Watch interview with Capt. Moodley, acting station commissioner, Greytown police station, April 3, 2000.

[412] Schönteich and Steinberg, *Attacks on Farms and Smallholdings*, pp.45, 53.

[413] Human Rights Watch interview with Mike de Lange, formerly KWANALU security desk, Eshowe, September 14, 2000.

[414] *Attacks on Farms and Smallholdings, No.1 of 1999* and *Attacks on Farms and Smallholdings No.2 of 1998*.

relationship with the farmer. "If there's a group of four or five involved in an attack you often find that one of them has been on the farm, the others from elsewhere."[415] One paralegal advising farmworkers and labor tenants believed that outsiders must be responsible, those hired to work from outside the area; even the security being hired by the farmers themselves.[416]

In accordance with this line of thinking, a police analysis of "attacks on farms and smallholdings" carried out in the first five months of 1998 based on "thorough interrogation" of suspects concluded that "irrefutable evidence exists that the motive for approximately 99 percent of the attacks on farms and smallholdings is common criminality, with robbery being the prime incentive ... at this stage no evidence is available to suggest that any sinister forces are responsible for the attacks. However, there have been a few incidents where racial tension, dismissals and conflict between employer and employee played a contributing role in the attacks."[417] Another study considering "attacks on farms and smallholdings" reported during the first six months of 1998, concluded that the "vast majority of attacks are committed by strangers who are unknown to the victims," based on information that in less than 10 percent of cases was one or more of the suspects an employee, former employee or relative of an employee of the victims.[418] These conclusions were described as "preposterous" by an academic supporting the theory that farm killings are driven by hatred of the Afrikaner and the delays in land redistribution.[419]

However, the most comprehensive and in depth study of the motives for violent crime against farm owners, carried out by Technikon SA, also found that criminal motives were dominant in the vast majority of cases, with a small number motivated by personal grudges against the victim or his or her family.[420] None had

---

[415] Human Rights Watch interview with Dion Pelser, Director of Support Services, Northern Province Department of Safety and Security, Pietersburg, March 29, 2000.

[416] Human Rights Watch interview with Philip Shabalala, paralegal, Christo Loots Attorneys, Vryheid, April 6, 2000.

[417] K.J. Britz and M.E. Seyisi, *Attacks on farms and smallholdings* (Pretoria: SAPS, August 1998), as discussed in Schönteich and Steinberg, *Attacks on Farms and Smallholdings*, p.34.

[418] In 4.5 percent of the incidents analyzed one of more of the suspects was employed by the victims at the time of the attack, 2.2 percent had previously been employed by them, and in 1 percent suspects were relatives of their victims' employees. *Attacks on Farms and Smallholdings No.2 of 1998.*

[419] Moolman, "An investigation into farm attacks in South Africa," section 5.2.

[420] Human Rights Watch interview with Duxita Mistry and Jabu Dhlamini, Technikon SA, Johannesburg, September 6, 2000; Duxita Mistry and Jabu Dhlamini, *Perpetrators of Farm Attacks: An Offender Profile* (Johannesburg: Institute for Human Rights and Criminal

a political motivation. The robberies were carefully planned, but the offenders had no special military training, and the planning of the crime was what might be expected for a crime rather than anything more elaborate. Information about the farm was gained from current or former employees; though it was not clear whether such information was gathered by deception or with knowledge of what it would be used for. The offenders were split half-and-half between those who had some connection with a farm themselves and those who did not. Some were experienced criminals, and half had previous convictions; for others it was their first offence. In one case where the motive for murder was a grudge against the farm owner, a farmer's wife was murdered by a farmworker when the farm owner and his wife intervened in a domestic dispute between the farmworker and his wife. The farm owner offered the worker's wife a room outside the main house and told the worker he could not see her; the worker killed the farmer's wife in anger.[421]

There is some supporting evidence that revenge for real or perceived previous wrongs by a farm owner is a motive in some cases. Although the conclusions of police studies of motive are questionable, being based on the off-the-cuff opinions of the station commissioners who fill out the questionnaires circulated by SAPS headquarters, rather than interviews with perpetrators or in-depth studies of particular cases, they can be suggestive. One study found that in 18 percent of 284 "attacks on farms and smallholdings" reported between November 1998 and March 15, 1999, the main motive seemed to be revenge, mainly to do with past labor disputes. In 76 percent of the incidents, at least one of the attackers was known to his victims; in 20 percent of the incidents all the attackers were known to their victims.[422] In June 2000, a spokesperson for the SANDF Regional Joint Task Force North stated to the press that a study of the forty most recent "attacks on farms and smallholdings" in Northern Province and Mpumalanga revealed that as many as 22.5 percent were motivated by revenge; though the majority were perpetrated for criminal motives (40 percent robbery; 27.5 percent petty crimes). According to the statement, which gave no indidcation of the basis for these distinctions, 7.2 percent were motivated by racism, and 5

Justice Studies, Technikon SA, March 2001). The study was based on in depth interviews in prison with forty-eight individuals in five provinces convicted of crimes ranging from robbery to murder against farm owners.

[421] Ibid., "Free State: Case Study Two."

[422] Brig.-Gen. J.F. Lusse, *Research Report: Attacks on farms and smallholdings November 1998 to 15 March 1999* (Pretoria: Chief of the South African National Defense Force (Joint Operations), March 1999), as discussed in Schönteich and Steinberg, *Attacks on Farms and Smallholdings*, pp.28-29.

percent by land claims.[423] In individual cases, the victims identify revenge as a motive: "There is no doubt they came to kill.... We believe they were hired by a farmworker who sought revenge after a disagreement with his employer."[424] In other cases, individuals with knowledge of a case will report that there had been confrontations between the farm owner and a farmworker, and then one of the workers had been involved in the killing.[425] In one April 1998 case in the Piet Retief area, a white visitor to a farm was shot and killed with an AK-47 rifle at the entrance to the farm he was visiting. Nothing was stolen. The police subsequently learned that the murder had been carried out in planned revenge for eviction of several families from the farm, but that the perpetrators had mistaken the identity of their victim.[426] Sometimes, killings appear to be related to a farm owner's sexual involvement with black women resident on the farm.[427] Even when the principal motive for a crime is acknowledged to be for theft, some victims identify aspects of the incident that seems to have racial aspects, such as gratuitous violence. But as the author of many of the police reports on farm attacks noted to Human Rights Watch, "If a farm is attacked and property is stolen and the farm owner murdered, how do we know if murder or robbery is the motive?"[428]

Part of the problem in determining possible motives lies in the definition of the "attacks" which rolls the figures for "farms" and "smallholdings" together. Even the 1998 study that concluded that "irrefutable evidence" existed that the motives for "attacks" were criminal drew a distinction in this regard between commercial farms and smallholdings: a large proportion of the perpetrators of incidents recorded at commercial farms lived or had friends or relatives who lived on or near the farm; in the case of smallholdings, many lived rather in informal

---

[423] Col. Hester Boshoff, quoted in "Robbery main reason for attacks in Nprov, Mpuma," SAPA, June 7, 2000. (The figures as quoted did not add up to 100 percent.) Six of those killed were members of the commandos, police reservists, or the commercial agricultural unions.

[424] "Eight involved in farm attack on couple were on murder mission, claims family," *Cape Argus*/SAPA, July 8, 1998, quoting a family member of Willie and Elizabeth Kuhn, killed on their farm near Makwassie, North West Province.

[425] Human Rights Watch interview with Theo van Rooyen, farmer, member of KWANALU executive committee and of the local committee coordinating the rural protection plan, who knew of three or four such cases. Utrecht, September 15, 2000.

[426] Schönteich and Steinberg, *Attacks on Farms and Smallholdings*, p. 53, note 3.

[427] Human Rights Watch interview with Mike de Lange, formerly KWANALU security desk, Eshowe, September 14, 2000.

[428] Human Rights Watch interview with J.C. Strauss, SAPS Crime Information Analysis Centre, Pretoria, April 10, 2000.

settlements nearby and had no specific connection with the site of the crime.[429] Given the difficulty of gaining access to a commercial farm in a remote area without detection, and the fact that many of the incidents in which farm owners had been subject to violent crime or burglary have been based on local knowledge, it makes sense that current or former employees or residents might have some connection with the crime. Police officers in farming areas interviewed by Human Rights Watch about farm attacks agreed that employees or former employees or people who knew the area well were involved in a number of attacks. But though the evidence from the large commercial farms is somewhat ambiguous, it does seem to be clear that in virtually all violent crime committed on smallholdings, the perpetrators are strangers.[430] There seems little reason to distinguish in terms of motive between smallholdings and crime committed in neighboring suburbs; especially since gratuitous violence is a feature of much South African crime, wherever committed.

Those convicted in these cases share similar profiles.[431] They belong to a frustrated generation of un- or underemployed young people, with more education than their parents and less tendency to accept their lot, but without marketable skills. They have seen democracy come to South Africa, but have little to show for it themselves—though they see the privileged status of white farm owners apparently unaltered by the new order. These frustrations are no excuse for crime, but can provide some explanation for why the property of others can seem less than sacrosanct, and taking guns, cattle and money from the commercial farms, even killing in the course of taking them, justified. Among young men from farms interviewed by Human Rights Watch, anger was widespread at the lack of transformation in relationships in the countryside since the new government took power.

Despite the SAPS findings that the motives for violent crime against farm owners are largely criminal, the police and the army continue to use the terminology of "farm attacks," reinforcing, through the use of the word "attack," the idea that there is a military or terrorist basis for the crimes, rather than a

---

[429] Britz and Seyisi, *Attacks on farms and smallholdings*, as discussed in Schönteich and Steinberg, *Attacks on Farms and Smallholdings*, p.34.

[430] Schönteich and Steinberg, *Attacks on Farms and Smallholdings*, pp.69-77, a study of Wierdabrug, near Pretoria.

[431] The Technikon SA study found that, in common with most crime, the typical offender was a young, unemployed, black male from a dysfunctional family background—rather than, for example, an ex-member of the armed wings of the liberation movements. Mistry and Dhlamini, *Perpetrators of Farm Attacks*, executive summary.

criminal one. As an official working for the Northern Province Department of Safety and Security noted, "The idea of 'attacks' has support from conservative whites and the media, but I don't agree with that. It sounds as if you're talking of an organized military force or crime syndicates or a terrorist war; I prefer to call it rather violent crime on farms and smallholdings, since we have no evidence that it is organized in any way.... We have been saying to the farmers who say there is an organized campaign 'bring us the evidence,' but since 1996 we have found nothing."[432] Use of the language of "farm attacks" tends to cloud analysis of possible solutions to the violence.[433]

---

[432] Human Rights Watch interview with Dion Pelser, Director of Support Services, Northern Province Department of Safety and Security, Pietersburg, March 29, 2000.

[433] In January 2001, Minister for Safety and Security Steve Tshwete promised to commission further independent research into the motives behind murders of farm owners, and later appointed a seven-member committee to carry out the research. "Govt to probe reasons for farm attacks," ZA Now, January 18, 2001.

THE STATE RESPONSE TO VIOLENCE ON FARMS

Constitutional and International Law Obligations

A fundamental concept in the South African bill of rights is the right to human dignity: "Everyone has inherent dignity and the right to have their dignity respected and protected."[434] The importance of this right in the South African context flows out of South Africa's particular history, in which the apartheid state daily violated the dignity of the majority black population through segregation, arbitrary detention, and various forms of abusive policies based on racial discrimination.[435] The right to freedom and security of the person is also protected by the bill of rights, in particular the right "to be free from all forms of violence from both public and private sources," the right "not to be tortured in any way," and the right "not to be treated or punished in a cruel, inhuman or degrading way."[436] The constitution also prohibits unfair discrimination against anyone directly or indirectly on the basis of race, gender, sex, pregnancy, marital status, and other grounds.[437] Although the right to family life is not explicitly mentioned in the constitution, the Constitutional Court has ruled that it is nevertheless constitutionally protected.[438] These provisions clearly place limitations on the manner in which all persons are to be treated by the various agencies involved in the criminal justice system. In addition, the right "to be free from violence from both public and private sources" places a positive obligation on the security forces to take all possible steps to protect all persons from assaults by private individuals, including vigilante violence, and can be argued to place a positive obligation on private actors to refrain from violence.

---

[434] Constitution of the Republic of South Africa, 1996, Section 10.

[435] "The history of systematic discrimination in South Africa, from segregation through apartheid, was premised on gross invasions of human dignity. The denial of this human right, protected in many international human rights instruments, most notably the Universal Declaration of Human Rights (art. 1) and the African Charter on Human and Peoples' Rights (art. 5), was so pervasive that its inclusion [in the bill of rights], immediately after the rights to equality and life, was entirely uncontroversial." Lourens Du Plessis and Hugh Corder, *Understanding South Africa's Transitional Bill of Rights* (Cape Town: Juta, 1994), p. 149.

[436] Constitution (1996), Section 12(1).

[437] Ibid., Section 9 (3) provides, "The state may not discriminate directly or indirectly against anyone on one or more grounds, including race, gender, sex, pregnancy, marital status, ethnic or social origin, colour, sexual orientation, age, disability, religion, conscience, belief, culture, language and birth."

[438] *Dawood and another vs. Minister of Home Affairs and others*, CCT 35/99, judgment handed down June 7, 2000.

158

Under international law, governments have a duty to guarantee equal protection of the law to all persons without discrimination, and to prosecute serious violations of physical integrity, including cases in which the perpetrator is a private citizen.[439] The Human Rights Committee, which monitors compliance with the International Covenant on Civil and Political Rights (ICCPR, ratified by South Africa in 1998), has made it clear that human rights protections apply regardless of nationality or statelessness, and that states have a responsibility to guarantee basic human rights equally for both citizens and aliens (including for example, migrant workers from other countries).[440] The International Convention on the Elimination of All Forms of Racial Discrimination (CERD), also ratified by South Africa in 1998, calls on national governments to take steps to eliminate racial discrimination and to prohibit discrimination under the law as well as to guard against discrimination arising as a result of the law. CERD defines discrimination as conduct that has the "purpose or effect" of restricting the enjoyment of rights on the basis of race. The same international law principle of non-discrimination was strengthened in relation to women by the Convention on the Elimination of All Forms of Discrimination against Women (CEDAW), which South Africa ratified in 1995. CEDAW reaffirms women's right to enjoy all human rights, and details states' obligation to ensure non-discrimination on the basis of gender and to ensure equal protection of the law for women.[441] States' obligations in relation to violence against women in particular were clarified by the 1993 Declaration on the Elimination of Violence Against Women, which provides that states must "exercise due diligence to prevent, investigate, and, in accordance with national legislation,

---

[439] Article 26 of the International Covenant on Civil and Political Rights (ICCPR) guarantees: "All persons are equal before the law and are entitled without discrimination to the equal protection of the law. In this respect, the law shall prohibit any discrimination and guarantee to all persons equal and effective protection against discrimination on any ground such as race, colour, sex, language, religion, political or other opinion, national or social origin, property, birth or other status." The U.N. Human Rights Committee has further held that the state not only has a duty to protect its citizens from such violations, but also to investigate violations when they occur and to bring the perpetrators to justice.

[440] Human Rights Committee, General Comment 15, "The position of aliens under the covenant" (Twenty-seventh session, 1986).

[441] Article 2 of both CERD and CEDAW provide that states parties shall condemn discrimination and "undertake to pursue by all appropriate means and without delay a policy of eliminating racial discrimination/discrimination against women" including specific programs of legislative reform and other steps.

punish acts of violence against women whether those acts are perpetrated by the states or other private persons."[442]

South Africa's constitution also provides protections for a wide range of social and economic rights, including the right to education, housing, and health, as well as protection for property rights and certain rights in respect of land (see above, under "Land Reform since 1994"). Section 26 of the constitution provides that "Everyone has the right to have access to adequate housing," that "the state must take reasonable legislative and other measures, within its available resources, to achieve the progressive realisation of this right," and that "No one may be evicted from their home, or have their home demolished, without an order of court made after considering all the relevant circumstances." A groundbreaking decision of the South African Constitutional Court handed down in 2000, concerning an application brought by a group of people evicted after they illegally occupied land, ruled that the South African government has an obligation to provide relief for people who have no access to land, no roof over their heads, and who are living in intolerable conditions or crisis situations.[443]

The U.N. Commission on Human Rights has declared that "the practice of forced eviction constitutes a gross violation of human rights, in particular the right to adequate housing" and urged governments to undertake immediate measures aimed at eliminating the practice, as well as to "confer legal security of tenure on all persons currently threatened with forced eviction and to adopt all necessary measures giving full protection against forced eviction, based upon effective participation, consultation and negotiation with affected persons or groups."[444] The Office of the U.N. High Commissioner for Human Rights notes

---

[442] U.N. General Assembly, *Declaration on the Elimination of Violence Against Women*, U.N. General Assembly Resolution 48/104 (A/RES/48/104) Art.4(c).

[443] *Government of RSA and others vs. Grootboom and others*, CCT11/00 (October 4, 2000). Judgment available on the Constitutional Court website <www.concourt.gov.za>, accessed October 4, 2000.

[444] Commission on Human Rights, Resolution on Forced Evictions 1993/77. Commenting on this resolution the Office of the U.N. High Commissioner for Human Rights (OHCHR) noted that "to be persistently threatened or actually victimized by the act of forced eviction from one's home or land is surely one of the most supreme injustices any individual, family, household or community can face." *Fact Sheet No.25, Forced Evictions and Human Rights* (Geneva: Office of the High Commissioner for Human Rights, 1996). In a general comment on the right to housing, the Committee on Economic, Social and Cultural Rights, which monitors compliance with the International Covenant on Economic, Social and Cultural Rights (ICESCR), stated that "instances of forced eviction are *prima facie* incompatible with the requirements of the [ICESCR] and can only be justified in the most exceptional

that many other rights may be violated by forced evictions in addition to the right to adequate housing: "the right to security of the person ... means little when evictions are carried out with violence, bulldozers and intimidation. Direct governmental harassment, arrests or even killings of community leaders opposing forced evictions are common and violate the rights to life, to freedom of expression and to join organizations of one's choice. In the majority of eviction cases, crucial rights to information and popular participation are also denied."[445]

The South African Criminal Justice System

Violent crime on South Africa's farms must be seen partly in the context of the fact that South Africa is in general a very violent country. Although the murder rate, which escalated sharply during the years leading up to the 1994 elections, has reduced somewhat since its worst levels, at least 23,823 people were murdered in 1999 among South Africa's population of about forty-two million, one of the highest rates in the world; 51,249 cases of rape were reported in the same year, and figures for other violent crimes are also very high.[446] Moreover, contrary to what might be expected, crime rates in South Africa are similar in rural and urban areas. According to the results of South Africa's first national victim survey, carried out by the national statistical office, Stats SA, and published in 1998, 29.9 percent of those living in urban environments experienced at least one crime during the period 1993 to 1997, and 6.6 percent experienced at least one violent crime; of those living in rural areas, 26.1 percent had experienced at least one crime, and 6.4 percent at least one violent crime over the same period. As many as 4.7 percent of

---

circumstances and in accordance with the relevant principles of international law." General Comment No.4 (1991) of the Committee on Economic, Social and Cultural Rights on the right to adequate housing (art. 11(1) of the Covenant), paragraph 18. South Africa signed the ICESCR in 1994, but has not yet ratified it.

[445] *Fact Sheet No.25, Forced Evictions and Human Rights* (Geneva: Office of the High Commissioner for Human Rights, 1996).

[446] According to police statistics, 26,832 murders were reported in 1994, and 23,823 in 1999; this was a decline from 69.5 murders per 100,000 population to 55.3 per 100,000. Tables supplied to Human Rights Watch by SAPS by email, August 3, 2000. In July 2000, Minister for Safety and Security Steve Tshwete ordered a moratorium on the publication of crime statistics, due to concerns over their accuracy, while the police conducted a review of the way in which they were collected and trained officers in new methods. The government has stated that publication of the statistics on the new basis will recommence with effect from July 20, 2001. "Media Statement by the Minister for Safety and Security Mr S.V. Tshwete, Cape Town, 2001-05-31," Department of Safety and Security, May 31, 2001.

rural respondents reported a murder in their household.[447] According to police statistics, 185 police were murdered during 2000, sixty while on duty, from a total force of approaching 130,000, and suicide rates among police are also high.[448]

In the face of this violence, and in common with other countries undergoing transition from autocratic rule, South Africa's criminal justice system is under severe strain.[449] A rise in crime has been matched by a collapse in discipline and morale among the "old guard," especially within the police who were called upon to defend the old order—many have left on "medical grounds." Despite efforts to demilitarize policing and instill a commitment to community service and human rights, the government has yet to be able to create an effective force devoted to the ideals of the new constitution.

Since taking office in 1994, the ANC-led government has engaged in a broad-based attempt to restructure and improve the criminal justice system in South Africa. As regards policing, a green paper (a policy discussion document) and draft bill published in July 1994 emphasized the importance of democratic control and community participation, and led to the passage in October 1995 of a new South African Police Service Act.[450] The act symbolically renamed the police "force" to the South African Police Service (SAPS) and established new national and provincial structures for the police (amalgamating the police forces of the ten black homelands into the national police service, and at the same time devolving a significant degree of political control to provincial level). The new law demilitarized the rank structure of the police, gave statutory backing to the community police forums created on an ad hoc basis over the previous years, and set up a national civilian secretariat for safety and security (mirrored at provincial level) to advise the minister and to monitor the implementation of policy and

---

[447] Eric Pelser, Antoinette Louw, and Sipho Ntuli, *Poor Safety: Crime and policing in South Africa's rural areas* ISS Monograph Series No. 27 (Pretoria: Institute for Security Studies, May 2000), p.5 and p.36. Statistics in relation to "rural areas" can be confusing, since the definition of rural area can change to mean only the former homelands, or to include commercial farming areas.

[448] "Farm and Police Murders: SAPS briefing," *Minutes of the Safety and Security Portfolio Committee*, April 4, 2001. In 1999, the SAPS employed 128,000 individuals, of whom 28,000 were civilians, the remainder uniformed police; *Minutes of the Joint Meeting of the Parliamentary Committees on Safety and Security and Justice*, February 19, 1999.

[449] See, for example, Mark Shaw, *Crime and Policing in Transitions: Comparative Perspectives* (Johannesburg: South African Institute of International Affairs, Research Report 17, September 2000).

[450] South African Police Service Act, No. 68 of 1995.

directions set for the police service. In line with the bill of rights in the new constitution, the police legal department prepared a human rights training programme for new recruits and existing members of the force, and affirmative action processes have been attempted in the promotion of police officers. A comprehensive National Crime Prevention Strategy (NCPS) was adopted in 1996 by the Department of Safety and Security (responsible for the SAPS) in conjunction with other government departments. The NCPS sets out a four-pillared approach to fighting crimes: (1) ensuring effective law enforcement through the criminal justice system; (2) reducing crime through environmental design; (3) ensuring public education against crimes; and (4) ensuring a transnational crime prevention approach. In 1998, the Department of Safety and Security published a white paper (a statement of government policy) on safety and security to direct the next five years.[451]   The white paper emphasized the importance of crime prevention, improving criminal investigations, improving the quality of service to victims of crime, as well as strengthening systems for civilian control of the police. In November 1998, a comprehensive police policy on the prevention of torture was published. The police have also established a number of specialized units to deal with sexual and domestic violence.[452]

The Police Act also established an Independent Complaints Directorate (ICD), to oversee investigation of criminal offenses and other misconduct committed by the police, and investigate directly all cases of deaths in police custody or otherwise as a result of police action. (The ICD does not have responsibility for investigating misconduct by members of the army when carrying out policing duties.) In practice, due largely to resource constraints, the ICD is unable to fulfil its mandate effectively, or investigate even all cases of deaths in

---

[451] Department of Safety and Security, *White Paper on Safety and Security: "In Service of Safety" 1999-2004*, September 1998 (the white paper and other government documents, including legislation, are available at the South African government website <www.gov.za>).

[452] See the section below on "The Response to Rape and other Violence Against Women on Farms" for details on the SAPS' Family Violence, Child Abuse, and Sexual Assault Units. Also see Vetten, "Paper Promises, Protests and Petitions."

police custody or as a result of police action.[453] The 1998 Domestic Violence Act expanded the ICD's duties to include monitoring of police enforcement of that act.

Despite these positive developments, the period since 1994 has also seen serious problems within the police service, perhaps inevitable in a body facing such huge changes in orientation and priorities. Racism in the force remains a serious problem. In KwaZulu-Natal and the Western Cape, where political and gang violence continue to threaten the overall maintenance of the peace, some police officers maintain links to those organizing the violence that were developed during the apartheid years. In Gauteng Province and elsewhere, police officers have been involved in car-hijacking rings and other high visibility crimes. Brutality and corruption remain depressingly common among police officers. The ICD reported 681 deaths in custody or as a result of police action during the year to March 2000 (a slight decrease on the previous year).[454] As of August 2000, there were 1,165 police members in court facing charges of corruption, and 2,551 dockets (files) opened by the SAPS anti-corruption units against 2,061 members to investigate corruption.[455] Moreover, the police have severe resource constraints. A three-year moratorium on police recruitment was lifted in May 1997, but in April 2000, Minister for Safety and Security Steve Tshwete stated that the SAPS still had a shortage of 7,000 personnel and 371 vehicles; additional recruitment was planned to address the shortage over the next four to five years.[456] A high percentage of police are illiterate or barely literate, many of them formerly members of the homeland police forces, who were integrated into the new SAPS.

Government efforts at improving police response have largely been devoted to urban areas, where the demands have been most pressing. The NCPS does not specifically address the needs of rural people, including farm workers. Though the White Paper on Safety and Security did consider rural areas, it focused

---

[453] See Bronwen Manby, "The South African Independent Complaints Directorate", in Andrew Goldsmith and Colleen Lewis (eds.), *Civilian Oversight of Policing: Governance, Democracy and Human Rights* (Oxford: Hart Publishing, 2000). The interim constitution of 1993 made explicit provision for the ICD; the final constitution of 1996 excludes it from the list of "State Institutions Supporting Constitutional Democracy" in chapter 9.

[454] Address by Minister for Safety and Security Steve Tshwete to the National Assembly during the budget vote on the ICD, May 18, 2000. Available on the ICD website <www.icd.gov.za>, accessed August 11, 2000.

[455] ICD presentation to the Parliamentary Portfolio Committee on Safety and Security, October 11, 2000, available on the ICD website, accessed December 8, 2000.

[456] Barry Streek, "7,000 police still needed," *Mail and Guardian*, April 14, 2000.

on the former homelands. Neither the NCPS nor the White Paper looked explicitly at the needs of people working or living in commercial farming areas.

There have also been significant initiatives to improve the delivery of criminal justice, starting from the development of a comprehensive five-year-plan known as "Justice Vision 2000," formally launched in September 1997. Under this plan and in line with the constitution, the government states that its aim is to "provide fair and equal access to justice for all South Africans, regardless of their race, gender, marital status, ethnic or social origin, sexual orientation, age, economic status, disability, religion, belief, culture, language, or any other attribute."[457] One of the most important pieces of legislation adopted since 1994 to improve the justice system is the National Prosecuting Authority Act (No. 32 of 1998), which establishes a new prosecution system in South Africa, headed by a National Director of Public Prosecutions (NDPP). As for the police, the transition to a new order has been difficult for the court system, and delays in the criminal justice process have vastly increased the backlog of cases awaiting trial, while there are a disturbing number of cases in which dockets (case files) go "missing," apparently as a result of corruption among police or court officials. The NDPP has appointed task groups to clear the backlog in some rural magistrates courts. Among both police and court officials, continuing racism is a huge problem, with hostility or lack of understanding between white and black police or court staff remaining prevalent—though not universal.

With regard to women, the Department of Justice adopted a Gender Policy Statement recognizing the historical discrimination suffered by South African women, especially black South African women, and aiming to implement the values underpinning Justice Vision 2000, including gender equity.[458] The NCPS highlights the need to prioritize gender-based violence in national strategies to combat crime in South Africa, and the Department of Safety and Security has expanded its policy initiatives to include violence against women.[459] However, rather than applying all the strategies proposed by the NCPS in the case of other crimes to combating violence against women, the NCPS limits strategies to end

---

[457] *Justice Vision 2000,* Executive Summary, available at <www.doj.gov.za>, accessed March 4, 2001.

[458] *Department of Justice Gender Policy Statement,* Second Edition, May 1999, available at <www.doj.gov.za/docs/policy/gender01.html>, accessed March 3, 2001.

[459] Vetten, "Paper Promises, Protests and Petitions," in Park et al, *Reclaiming Women's Spaces,* p.94.

violence against women to classifying them under a single section on "victim empowerment and support."[460]

Despite efforts at reform, it is clear that the criminal justice system is not delivering the service it is mandated to carry out—there is a low probability generally of reported crimes resulting in a conviction. A study on sentencing policy in the criminal justice system carried out by the South African Law Commission, for example, found that "a mere 5.4% of more than 30,000 randomly sampled cases reported to the police resulted in a conviction."[461] Once a prosecution is launched, however, three quarters of prosecutions for "more serious offenses" result in convictions.[462] A survey of attitudes to policing in rural areas (mostly the former homelands) carried out in 1998 found that more than a third of those questioned felt that policing had declined in quality in the previous few years; more than 40 percent believed the police were ineffective in curbing crime in their area.[463]

Many see the response to all violent crime—including that on commercial farms—as inadequate. In this context, vigilante violence has assumed a high profile, with groups such as Mapogo a Mathamaga (discussed above) or People Against Gangsterism and Drugs (PAGAD), a largely urban Western Cape group, rapidly becoming as much of a problem to society as the criminals which they originally targeted.

---

[460] Ibid.

[461] South African Law Commission, *Sentencing (A New Sentencing Framework)*, Discussion Paper 91, Project 82 (Pretoria: South African Law Commission, 2000). It should be noted, however, that "attrition rates" in clearing up crimes are high everywhere. In the U.K., for example, statistics collected by the police compared with the number of offenses measured by crime surveys indicate that of every one hundred offenses committed, 45.2 will be reported, 24.3 will be recorded, 5.5 cleared up, 3 result in a caution or conviction, 2.2 result in a conviction, and 0.3 in a custodial sentence. That is, 9 percent of offenses recorded by the police result in a conviction. Gordon C. Barclay and Cynthia Tavares, *Digest 4—Information on the Criminal Justice System* (London: Home Office Research, Development and Statistics Directorate, October 1999), available at <www.homeoffice.gov.uk/rds/digest4/chapter4.pdf>, accessed May 3, 2001.

[462] "Crimes: Prosecutions and convictions with regard to certain serious offences 1995/96," press release by the South African government Central Statistical Services (now Stats SA), March 26, 1998. Of 291,774 prosecutions for more serious offenses recorded by the police during 1995/96, 218,394, or 74.9 percent, resulted in convictions; 72,781, or 24.9 percent, were discharged.

[463] Pelser, Louw, and Ntuli, *Poor safety*, p.60.

The Rural Protection Plan

The new vulnerability of a group previously shielded from violent crime, as well as the perceived political basis for "attacks on farms and smallholdings," has given the issue of violent crime on farms a high media profile—murders on farms (of owners, or of workers by owners) are given an individual attention that many other killings are not—and a high level of political focus. In particular, protests from organized agriculture about "farm attacks" led first to the implementation of a "rural protection plan" in October 1997, after consultation with a variety of interested parties by a security force task team, and then to a "rural safety summit" in October 1998 called by then President Nelson Mandela.[464] The aim of the summit was to "bring all role players together to find a common strategy to step up the fight against crime, especially violent crime in all farming communities."[465] Participants included representatives of the government departments for safety and security, defense, and agriculture and land affairs, as well as the office of the president and deputy president; organized agriculture, trades unions, NGOs, and the Business Against Crime initiative. The summit adopted a set of resolutions condemning criminal activity affecting rural communities, recognizing that the causes of such crime are complex, accepting that "the Rural Protection Plan should be utilized as the operational strategy to combat and prevent violent crimes against farming and rural communities," but calling for a comprehensive policy framework to be developed "to ensure long term safety in rural and farming communities."[466]

The rural protection plan uses the nationwide structures that coordinate the activities of the police and army, seeking to ensure effective cooperation among all relevant parties, but in particular the SAPS, SANDF and organized agriculture. These structures are headed by the National Operational Coordinating Committee

---

[464] In some cases there were initiatives earlier than this. In the Northern Province, for example, there were several murders or serious assaults of farm owners in late 1996. As a consequence, a regular bi-monthly meeting was established among relevant players—including the police, army, agricultural unions, justice, correctional services, home affairs—at which violent crime on farms and smallholdings are discussed. Human Rights Watch interview with Dion Pelser, Director of Support Services, Northern Province Department of Safety and Security, Pietersburg, March 29, 2000.

[465] "Summit on Rural Safety and Security," press release issued by the Ministry for Safety and Security, October 7, 1998.

[466] "Summit on Rural Safety and Security: 10 October 1998," press release issued by South African government Communication Information Service; also reprinted in Schönteich and Steinberg, *Attacks on Farms and Smallholdings*, pp.23-24.

(NOCOC) based in Pretoria. Each province has a Provincial Operational Coordinating Committee (POCOC); and within   provinces there are Area Operational Coordinating Committees (AOCOCs) and Groundlevel Operational Coordinating Committees (GOCOCs) headed by SAPS station commissioners and SANDF commando commanders. Each of the committees has its own priority committees on different types of violence; priority committees on rural protection were added to these in October 1998, after the rural safety summit.[467] At police station level, the GOCOCs usually meet once a month.

The summit established a Rural Safety Task Team made up from the groups that had participated. The task team in turn had three working groups, on communication, information and research; on operational interventions (effectively consisting of those role players involved in rural protection under the NOCOC); and on rural safety policy (developing long term strategies). These working groups have now been wrapped into the NOCOC priority committee on rural protection: in February 2000, representatives of Agri-SA met with President Mbeki over the issue of violent crime against farm owners, and the president committed the government to a re-activation of the rural safety task team, which would in the future function within rather than outside police structures.[468]

Police

Under the rural protection plan, police are supposed to visit commercial farms on a regular basis. Resource constraints mean that this is not an effective strategy in practice: understaffing and lack of vehicles are a significant problem in most rural police stations. A detective at the Mid-Illovo police station in the KwaZulu-Natal Midlands identified the key problem facing the police station as lack of manpower "Nineteen or twenty people work out of these premises, of which five are detectives, with four vehicles. We are responsible for a huge area with more than 200 farms and smallholdings, though no former KwaZulu areas. When we visit farms we go to the farm owner or manager and then the induna [headman].... About once a week to each farm is the best we can do.... Farm owners usually phone us when there is a problem in their workers' compounds, because we do not have the manpower to talk to everybody on the farm."[469] At Levubu police station in Northern Province, Human Rights Watch found in April 2000 that there were only seventy-two police officers responsible for policing

---

[467] Schönteich and Steinberg, *Attacks on Farms and Smallholdings*, p.20.

[468] "Rural safety task team to be reactivated: Mbeki's office," SAPA, February 22, 2000.

[469] Human Rights Watch interview, Insp. Stuart Brodie, Mid-Illovo police station, April 4, 2000.

approximately 45,000 people.[470] This police station used to be responsible for policing a small geographical area occupied by white farm owners under the former government, but with the new government in 1994, its geographical jurisdiction was increased, although this was not also matched with a meaningful increase in staffing and vehicles. At Louis Trichardt police station each farm out of 400 in the area might only be visited once a month, due to lack of better resources. The farm owner, or person in charge—many owners live in the cities and have a manager to run it on a day to day basis—must sign a register and note any remarks in it. "We are visiting them and giving them hints; the farmers themselves make their own plans, but we advise them."[471] Similarly, Pietersburg police station was responsible for more than 100 farms, with only two men and one vehicle available for the visits.[472] The small Ingogo police station, near Newcastle, in northern KwaZulu-Natal, has thirteen officers serving an area of 576 square kilometers, about 250 farms, with three vehicles, which means they are able to visit about fifteen farms a day.[473] Because of the infrequency of the visits, many farmers see this system as more or less useless.

Farmwatch Cells

In practice, due to resource constraints and other weaknesses, of more importance than the police initiatives in most cases is the system, set up both under the rural protection plan and independently, of joining farmers together in "security cells" of geographically close farmhouses, linked by radio, often known as the "farmwatch" system. "We must protect ourselves. There is no way that the SAPS or SANDF can protect us. They are the legal force of the government, and we must make use of them, but we can't expect them to protect us: they don't have the

---

[470] Human Rights Watch interview, community relations officer, Levubu police station, April 2, 2000.

[471] In Northern Province the system is that if there is a violent crime on a farm against the farm owner the uniformed police are involved in the initial interventions, but later a police evaluation team will go to the farm and see what went wrong, for example, with the security provisions there. Human Rights Watch interview with Capt. Vollgraaff, Louis Trichardt police station, March 29, 2000; Human Rights Watch interview with Dion Pelser, Director of Support Services, Northern Province Department of Safety and Security, Pietersburg, March 29, 2000.

[472] Human Rights Watch interview with Snr. Supt. Shingange, station commissioner, Pietersburg police station, March 31, 2000.

[473] Human Rights Watch interview with Insp. De Klerk, station commissioner, Ingogo police station, April 7, 2000.

capacity, the knowhow, or in some cases the will."[474] Accordingly, in many farming areas, farm owners living along one road or within easy reach of each other will form a committee and if something untoward happens will call a neighbor for assistance. "In some areas you find Farmwatch is operating as a virtual police force, insisting that everybody carries ID all the time, because no one else will. The farmworkers feel safe and cooperate."[475] Informal patrols take place to deter strangers: "though there have been no farm attacks here, when they hear of a murder the farmers are getting together and discussing what they must do. The young men drive around in bakkies [pick-up trucks] and make sure that there is nobody on the farm who must not be there, and so it stops."[476]

At national level, farmers' representatives have sought to strengthen such self-protection. In August 1999, Agri-SA launched the Agri-Securitas Trust Fund with the aim of "generating funds to protect farming communities throughout South Africa and reverse the growing trend of rural crime." The commercial farmers union stated that the fund would directly benefit the "85,000 commercial and small scale farmers, their families and their workers," and indirectly benefit the whole country "by assisting to manage the high incidence of farm-related attacks."[477] The fund was co-sponsored by Mercedes Benz Commercial Vehicles and Nortel Dasa, a provider of satellite network technology, both companies within the DaimlerChrysler Group.

---

[474] Human Rights Watch interview with Pieter Basson, farmer, Bapsfontein, Gauteng, September 19, 2000.

[475] Interview with Graham McIntosh, (then) president of the KwaZulu-Natal Agricultural Union, published in *Briefing* 12, (Johannesburg: Helen Suzman Foundation, September 1998).

[476] Human Rights Watch interview, private security company executive, Northern Province, March 28, 2000.

[477] "Farmers' union raising money for rural security," *ZA Now*, August 11, 1999. The Agri Securitas project was originally announced in October 1998, following the rural safety summit. "Rural safety project launched," transcript of transmission on Radio Sonder Grense, October 29, 1998, available on <www.agriinfo.co.za/>, accessed October 6, 2000. Elsewhere, commercial agriculture is quoted as stating that there are 40,000 commercial farmers and 32,000 small scale farmers. "MPs express concern about SA farm attacks," SAPA, May 10, 2000.

Commandos

These initiatives are closely linked to the commandos, a system of army reserve units which has its origins in the nineteenth century, when Afrikaner commandos fought against the British in the South African War of 1899-1901 (the Boer War).[478] Drawing on this history, the National Party government continued to use the commandos during the apartheid era, especially for border defense. Until the early 1990s, all white men in South Africa were required to do compulsory national service in the army, and many farmers therefore have military training, making the organization of a military security outfit at local level a relatively easy task. In many areas of the country, commandos are no longer very active, but they remain strong along the borders with Zimbabwe, Swaziland, and Lesotho. Many of their members are farmers—though the percentage participating varies widely[479]—and some commando units have been revived specifically for policing duties in response to current concerns about security in the commercial farming areas. Many farmers involved in farmwatch initiatives are also commando members. The level of activity of the different commandos and of their subunits, however, varies considerably, according among other things to the motivation of the individuals in charge of them. In the most active areas, there will be several vehicle patrols a night, roadblocks once or twice a week, and checkpoints looking for illegal weapons even more frequently. There are also systematic efforts to obtain information about illegal weapons and stock theft through the use of informers. In other areas, a commando subunit can exist in name, but in practice carry out very few activities; the same is true of the private farmwatch systems. Several farmers involved in the farmwatches or commandos commented to Human Rights Watch that, despite fear of violent crime, it was difficult to get their neighbors to participate in these organizations.

---

[478] See Fransjohan Pretorius, *Life on Commando During the Anglo-Boer War 1899-1902* (Cape Town: Human and Rousseau, 1999; originally published in Afrikaans); Sandra Swart, "'A Boer and his Gun and his Wife are Three Things Always Together': Republican Masculinity and the 1914 Rebellion," *Journal of Southern African Studies*, vol. 24, no. 4, December 1998, pp.737-751; and Jeremy Krikler "The Commandos: the Army of White Labour in South Africa," *Past and Present* vol. 63, May 1999 (for a discussion of the role of the commando movement in the widespread strikes of white mine workers during 1922).
[479] In KwaZulu-Natal, for example, participation by farmers who are members of KWANALU in the commandos varied from 30 to 90 percent in 1995. Fax from KWANALU to Human Rights Watch, August 7, 2000.

Today, there are 186 commando units in South Africa, with a total of about 82,000 members.[480] Membership has declined since 1994; many white members who did not want to work for a black government left the system when the ANC came to power. The commandos are governed by the Defence Act, and members are subject to disciplinary control in the same way as the regular army when on active duty.[481] In each province they fall under the overall command of the relevant SANDF group headquarters (of which there are two in each province, except for Gauteng, which has nine, and KwaZulu-Natal, which has three). In practice they operate quite autonomously. While there are procedures under the Defence Act for allotting individuals to the commandos in some circumstances, members today are volunteers. Volunteers must serve up to twelve days in any calendar year, as called upon, though they can serve for longer if they wish. Volunteers are entitled to receive an annual allocation of free ammunition for target practice, and may be allowed the temporary use of a government firearm while carrying out target practice, and temporary use of other items of military clothing or equipment. They may also buy military rifles from the government at cost price, or obtain one on loan, subject to conditions such as payment of a cash deposit.

The army divides up the commando system into different types. There are "area-bound reaction force commandos," who can be called up in an emergency and are paid for the hours they work; "home and hearth protection reaction force commandos," staffed by farmers and smallholders and their workers, who go into action only if an attack has occurred, until the area-bound reaction force commando arrives and takes over from them; and "house and hearth protection commandos," similarly staffed, who are only responsible for protecting their own farm or smallholding and themselves.[482] The commandos vary in size, but each generally has several hundred members. When deployed on SANDF business, members of commandos are supposed to be clearly identifiable as such. If they do not have time to dress in full uniform, they should put on a jacket that is issued to them that clearly identifies them as members of the army, with their name and rank. They are not allowed to wear military uniform unless they are officially on commando duty.

The commandos operate theoretically under the control of the police when they carry out patrols and are supposed to have a member of the police with them at all times, either a full time officer or a reservist, who is responsible for arresting suspects and carrying out policing duties. The commandos themselves do not have

---

[480] Schönteich and Steinberg, *Attacks on Farms and Smallholdings*, p.20.

[481] Defence Act (Act No.44 of 1957), as amended. Chapter V relates to the commandos. The act is currently under review.

[482] Schönteich and Steinberg, *Attacks on Farms and Smallholdings*, p.21.

powers to arrest suspects, or to search vehicles or people. "The police are playing mostly a prosecution type of role, they are not so much involved in prevention. The whole operation involves mostly the military and the commandos, working with the farmers, though the police are pulled in to make the official arrest.[483] In practice, the commandos often operate independently, simply keeping the police informed as to their movements: "They inform us in advance if they will conduct farm patrols or other operations."[484] If the police do patrol with the commandos it is usually in a subordinate role, and often a reservist rather than a full time officer. "They always come to the charge office and let us know they are in our area, and as far as possible they will then work with a reservist or permanent force member."[485] Some commando members are themselves also police reservists.

The South African government's 1996 White Paper on Defence recognized problems with the deployment of military units to undertake policing duties, though it stated that such deployment was necessary in the short term because of the high level of crime and the shortage of police.[486] The 1999 draft

---

[483] Human Rights Watch interview with Lourie Bosman, Mpumalanga Agricultural Union, Ermelo, April 12, 2000.

[484] Human Rights Watch interview with Capt. B.A. Mchunu, branch commander, Estcourt police station, April 5, 2000.

[485] Human Rights Watch interview with Insp. De Klerk, station commissioner, Ingogo police station, April 7, 2000.

[486] Chapter 4 of the white paper states that "[T]he history of South Africa and many other countries suggests that it is inappropriate to utilise armed forces in a policing role on a permanent or semi-permanent basis. This perspective is based on the following considerations:

P   Armed forces are not trained, orientated or equipped for deployment against
         civilians. They are typically geared to employ maximum force against an external
         military aggressor.

P   On-going employment in a law and order function invariably leads to the defence
         force becoming increasingly involved in non-military activities.

P   Such employment may also undermine the image and legitimacy of the defence
         force amongst sections of the population.

P   Efforts to apply military solutions to political problems are inherently limited and
         invariably lead to acts of repression.

In light of these considerations, the policy goal of the government is to build the capacity of the police to deal with public violence on their own while political solutions are being sought or have failed. The SANDF would then only be deployed in the most exceptional circumstances, such as a complete breakdown of public order beyond the capacity of the SAPS, or a state of national defence."

Defence Bill accepted that the SANDF should be deployed in cooperation with the SAPS, and provided for soldiers to have "all the powers" that are conferred by law on police officers in similar circumstances, though this provision was reportedly amended following parliamentary hearings on the bill.[487]

There is no system for independent investigation of civilian complaints against the commandos. The Independent Complaints Directorate, set up to monitor and investigate complaints against the police, has no jurisdiction over members of other branches of the security services, even when they are carrying out policing duties. If there is a complaint, then the army legal department is supposed to inform the member accused, investigate the complaint, and then hold a disciplinary board of inquiry. If the internal inquiry finds that there is a case of assault, the case is then handed to police for follow up, and from moment of arrest is handled as a civilian matter.

Private Security

South African farmers—like South Africans generally—have increasingly turned to commercial private security companies to safeguard their property and personal safety. There are, for example, as many as forty private security companies operating in the KwaZulu-Natal midlands area alone.[488] In 1995, those employed in the private security industry were estimated to outnumber the total number of police by about five to one, and the industry has seen continuing growth since then.[489] In 1996, there were 240,000 registered security guards, of whom 100,000 were active within the 3,000 registered companies; by the beginning of 1999, there were 350,000 registered guards, of whom 147,000 were active in more than 5,300 companies, and another 60,000 security guards were estimated to be

---

[487] Submissions to and minutes of the hearings of the National Assembly Defence Portfolio Committee on "Police powers for the SANDF when in support of the SAPS," May 9, 2000. Following the hearings, the committee recommended that the army not have policing powers, and the bill was reportedly amended accordingly. A new version of the bill had not yet been published as of June 2001. Email from Laurie Nathan, Centre for Conflict Resolution, to Human Rights Watch, June 12, 2001.

[488] Schönteich and Steinberg, *Attacks on Farms and Smallholdings*, p.62.

[489] Mark Shaw, *"Partners in Crime"? Crime, political transition and changing forms of policing control*, (Johannesburg: Centre for Policy Studies, 1995), p.69. This ratio is double that in countries such as the UK—though estimates of the ratio vary.

working "in house" and not registered.[490] Many of those working in the private security industry are former members of the South African security forces or, especially in urban areas, of the armed wings of the liberation movements—tending to reinforce a militarization of the industry already developed in the course of a close collaboration between private security companies and the state under the National Party government.[491]

The private security industry is currently governed by legislation dating from 1987, amended in 1997, which provides only a weak regulatory framework.[492] In practice, private security companies can operate virtually as vigilante groups. Although private security companies must be registered with and can be deregistered by the Security Officers' Board, a self-regulatory body formed of industry representatives, none had ever been deregistered by 1996, despite investigation of numerous disciplinary charges and widespread reports of abuse.[493] The Security Officers' Board also oversees training of security officers, who are graded according to the level of training they have received; most receive only the most basic level. The training requirements have been heavily criticized. For example, a minimum of five hours of firearm training is required for guards to be allowed to carry firearms while on duty, but licenses are provided to security

---

[490] Sara Blecher, *Safety in Security? A report on the private security industry and its involvement in violence*, (Durban: Network of Independent Monitors, 1996), p.5; Jenni Irish, *Policing for Profit: The future of South Africa's private security industry* (Pretoria: Institute for Security Studies, 1999), introduction (available at <www.iss.co.za>, accessed January 30, 2001).

[491] There are serious concerns surrounding the involvement of private security companies in political violence and organized crime, as well as abusive methods of work generally. See Blecher, *Safety in Security?*; Irish, *Policing for Profit*.

[492] Under the current system, the Security Officers Interim Board (reconstituted in 1997), appointed by the minister for safety and security in consultation with the security industry and the parliamentary Portfolio Committee on Safety and Security, is charged with the duty "to exercise control over the occupation of security officer, and to maintain, promote and protect the status of that occupation, and *to ensure that the industry acts in the public interest and to submit reports from time to time to the Minister on the regulation of the security officer industry*." Security Officers Amendment Act, No. 104 of 1997, section 2(1) (which added the phrase in italics to the existing legislation). The Interim Board is also charged to advise the minister on the establishment of a new permanent board, the drawing up of an enforceable code of conduct, and the promotion of accountability in the security industry. The amendment act requires the minister to introduce new legislation within eighteen months of its own coming into effect.

[493] Blecher, *Safety in Security?*, p.5.

companies, not to individuals, and the company itself is reponsible for ensuring that the training is effective.[494] There is no requirement for the police or courts to notify the Security Officers' Board if a case is opened against a private security company; though, as one court official put it to Human Rights Watch, "the Security Officers' Board is free to ask us if we have heard of any problems."[495]

In February 2001, the government published the Security Industry Regulation Bill, which will greatly strengthen the system for regulating "security service providers," requiring them to obtain accreditation from and to allow inspection by an independent Security Industry Regulatory Authority. The authority will be appointed by the minister for safety and security, and will not include representatives of security companies.[496] The bill sets out criteria for the registration of security service providers, including training requirements, a clean criminal record, and compliance with a legally binding code of conduct to be prescribed by the minister. It provides that accreditation of a security service provider may be suspended or withdrawn in the event of a criminal conviction or of improper conduct, though this will not be mandatory. It does not provide for the police to report to the regulatory authority alleged offenses involving security service providers. Human Rights Watch believes that the bill should be amended to require the police to notify the regulatory authority where they have information concerning alleged criminal behavior by a security service provider.

At national level, the police recognize that private security companies have a role to play, where they are properly regulated and trained and working within the framework of the law, though they are concerned that companies can spring up overnight with no intention of following the rules. "These people would not be there if there was not a need."[497] Locally, too, overstretched police stations often rely on the private security companies for assistance. "We have good relations with the Farm Protection Unit [a private security company]. Many times we are in a fix with manpower and vehicles and they have assisted us, for example, by attending complaints like assaults where they are contracted to the farm. They go to the scene and if someone needs an ambulance they can arrange for that, and

[494] Irish, *Policing for Profit*, section on "Problems in the Industry."

[495] Human Rights Watch interview with control prosecutor, Louis Trichardt district magistrates court, March 29, 2000.

[496] Security Industry Regulation Bill, No. 12 of 2001, available at <www.gov.za/bills>, accessed March 12, 2001.

[497] Human Rights Watch interview with Commissioner Johann Burger, SAPS, Pretoria, April 10, 2000.

if the suspect is there they can bring him to us with witnesses and then we can handle the matter."[498]

Despite this reliance, there can also be conflict between the police and private security companies where the private companies take over police responsibilities. In Greytown, for example, there have been problems relating to the control of the crime scene in cases of violent crime against farm owners; such as cases where the private security have followed a trail with their dogs, meaning that the police have not been able to find the same evidence later.[499] According to Dave Carol, a commando unit commander and the coordinator of the Greytown 911 Centre (described in the next section), "Those guys in the private security companies have no more rights than any private citizen, but they see themselves as a pseudo police force, or above the law. They can be called in by the farmer and beat the hell out of the laborer, no questions asked; and the laborer is too nervous to do anything because it's a guy in uniform, so it must be official. We have good security companies and, shall we say, not so good security companies. We have good relationships with the good companies, and not so good relationships with the others."[500] In Greytown, as elsewhere, the burgeoning number of private security companies have also been brought into the rural protection plan, to resolve potential points of conflict or misunderstanding as they arise. Private security companies are usually invited to attend the GOCOC meetings at which rural safety issues are discussed; at Greytown, the first such meeting involving private security companies was held in March 2000, and was due to be held monthly thereafter.[501] At Estcourt police station, also in the KwaZulu-Natal midlands, the police meet at least once a week, and sometimes more often, with the two private security companies operating locally. The police, private security and commandos cooperate in, for example, conducting joint raids searching for stolen livestock.[502]

---

[498] Human Rights Watch interview, Insp. Stuart Brodie, Mid-Illovo police station, April 4, 2000.

[499] Human Rights Watch interview with Capt. Moodley, acting station commissioner, Greytown police station, April 4, 2000.

[500] Human Rights Watch interview with Dave Carol, Greytown 911 Center, September 13, 2000.

[501] Human Rights Watch interview with Capt. Moodley, acting station commissioner, Greytown police station, April 4, 2000.

[502] Human Rights Watch interview with Capt. A. Reddy, head of crime prevention, Estcourt police station, April 5, 2000.

The Rural Protection Plan in Practice

The mix of different security systems mobilized for rural safety varies across South Africa for reasons of historical tradition (farmers in the areas bordering South Africa's neighbors have always been more militarized) and for reasons of economics and geography. In wealthier areas, for example, the KwaZulu-Natal coastal belt where sugar cane is grown and the farms are relatively small, farmers tend to employ private security. In remote areas, where rainfall is low, farms very large, and profit margins small, private security is prohibitively expensive, and the commando system is used instead. In yet other areas, for example in Gauteng, where commando units tend to be less under the control of farm owners and to have more black members, farmers tend to rely more on private farmwatch initiatives, integrated into the rural protection plan through the GOCOCs: "Without the cell group there would be a vacuum. The police and the commandos can't cope. The cell group fills a big gap, and is there first when anyone is attacked.... The commando will give you a uniform and a rifle, and a vehicle for patrols, but then the vehicle must be kept secure in a garage all the time, rifles must be signed for and kept at a police station, and so you must go there to get the vehicle and the rifle. It makes it more difficult. It's better just to use your own vehicle and your own gun. The commando is a good system, but it can't meet the need. They are better as a support system, to do an organized raid for illegal immigrants or for illegal weapons."[503]

The GOCOCs established under the rural protection plan join other structures at police station level designed to increase public participation and confidence in policing, including the Community Police Forums (CPFs) which began to be developed in the early 1990s and are provided for in the 1995 South African Police Service Act.[504] The aims of the CPFs, which are to be "broadly representative of the community," as well as including police representatives, are to promote communication and cooperation between the police and the community regarding policing and to improve the rendering of police services.[505] The CPFs

---

[503] Human Rights Watch interview with Gert van Wyk, Farmwatch member, Bapsfontein, September 19, 2000. As another smallholder in the same area put it, commenting on the preference of farm owners to engage in self-help, rather than making use of the Benoni or Kempton Park commandos, both with substantially black membership: "The people wouldn't like black ones coming along in the middle of the night because we are all so nervous now." Human Rights Watch interview, September 19, 2000.

[504] South African Police Service Act, No. 68 of 1995. Chapter 7 deals with the Community Police Forums.

[505] South African Police Service Act, sections 18 and 19.

have had some successes in improving police-community cooperation, especially in urban areas, but have had limited success overall. In particular, there has been a conflict between community attempts to gain influence over police decision-making through the CPFs, and the police vision of the CPFs as purely a source of information and support for their operations.[506] Many officers in police stations visited by Human Rights Watch identified lack of community interest in these structures as a problem. Police often find themselves outnumbering civilians both at the CPFs and at the GOCOC meetings for the rural protection plan. Community leaders interviewed by Human Rights Watch, on the other hand, stated that they had ceased attending CPF meetings simply because they felt that there was no response from the police to their efforts at support or demands for action; and, indeed, that the police were themselves involved in crime. More systematic studies suggest that CPFs have also been ineffective in former homeland areas.[507]

In many areas, it seems that there is an effective racial division between the GOCOCs and the CPFs: the GOCOC structures are perceived as being focused on the needs of white farmers, the CPFs directed at the black community. This perception is partially recognized by some police: "Unfortunately the rural protection plan committee is not very representative; just the farmers and some indunas [headmen], but not enough to make it really worth while, since many of the black people don't come. Some have said they have difficulty with transport, and though we can try to help we can't promise to bring them."[508] In some areas, the GOCOCs are entirely white, and farmers have objected to any attempt to broaden membership to include, for example, chiefs from the tribal areas adjoining commercial farmland, on the basis that to include any blacks (other than members

---

[506] See Wilfried Schärf, "Community Justice and Community Policing in Post-Apartheid South Africa: How Appropriate are the Justice Systems of Africa?" paper presented at the International Workshop on the Rule of Law and Development: Citizen Security, Rights and Life Choices in Low and Middle Income Countries, Institute for Development Studies, University of Sussex, June 2000; Diana R. Gordon, "Democratic Consolidation and Community Policing: Conflicting Imperatives in South Africa," *Policing and Society* (forthcoming, 2001).

[507] Pelser, Louw, and Ntuli, *Poor safety*, pp.65-67. These problems have led NGOs to develop the idea of Community Safety Forums, run by local government and involving not just the police but also other government departments, currently being piloted in the Western Cape. See Schärf, "Community Justice and Community Policing."

[508] Human Rights Watch interview, Insp. Stuart Brodie, Mid-Illovo police station, April 4, 2000.

of the security forces) would constitute a security risk.[509] In other areas, chiefs from the former homelands have been involved in the GOCOCs, but this involvement is often focused on obtaining cooperation with efforts to prevent or punish crime on the white farms, rather than issues which might cross the borders of land tenure.

A declaration following the October 1998 Rural Safety Summit recognized that "all initiatives to ensure greater safety and security, in particular the rural protection plan, need to be more inclusive of all people in the farming and rural communities by *inter alia* strengthening and expanding the commandos and police reservists so that they become more accessible to the whole rural community."[510] Moreover, there is widespread recognition that it is in the interests of farm owners to bring farmworkers and residents into crime-fighting activities. As noted by a senior SANDF officer involved in the rural protection plan, "Any farmer not involving his workers in security is dumb; if they are well trained, they can be his first line of defense."[511] But, in practice, it seems that few, if any, blacks are involved in security structures on an equal footing with whites.   One coordinator of a local farmwatch system noted to Human Rights Watch that, though there had been talk of involving farmworkers in the nightly patrols, it was not practical since most could not drive, "and you can't trust all the people working for you. Sometimes they are involved and also they are intimidated very easily."[512] The farmwatch cell had begun to include some black people in the system, including a local school principal who had asked for help after several break-ins, but noted the need for trust to be established. "You must be careful not to take in someone not truly committed to preventing crime, or all the inside information on how the cell group works could be exposed."[513]

Similarly, there is only one commando unit in the country that has a black commanding officer; this unit is in the Eastern Cape, in the former homeland area of Transkei.[514] Elsewhere, whites, usually commercial farmers, are very firmly in

---

[509] Human Rights Watch interview with Theo van Rooyen, farmer, member of KWANALU executive committee and of local the GOCOC, Utrecht, September 15, 2000.

[510] "Summit on Rural Safety and Security: 10 October 1998," press release issued by South African government Communication Information Service; also reprinted in Schönteich and Steinberg, *Attacks on Farms and Smallholdings*, pp.23-24.

[511] Human Rights Watch interview, Lt-Col H.J. Boshoff, March 23, 2000.

[512] Human Rights Watch interview with Pieter Basson, farm owner and farmwatch coordinator, Bapsfontein, Gauteng, September 19, 2000.

[513] Ibid.

[514] Human Rights Watch interview, Lt-Col H.J. Boshoff, March 23, 2000.

control of the commando system. Some commandos, for example those in Piet Retief, Mpumalanga, and (rural) Ixopo, KwaZulu-Natal, have only white members. Although others have substantial black membership, for example the Umvoti commando in the KwaZulu-Natal midlands, which has one-third black membership, mostly unemployed young men, the inclusion of black members need not in itself create the common crime fighting agenda that is hoped for. Most commandos with substantial black membership are in urban areas, and their patrols restricted to towns or townships. Although some commando units claim to have made genuine efforts to widen the commando membership to include farmworkers, and to send black members away for training to enable them to be promoted into officer positions, black members of the commandos are often not from the local community, being recruited from far afield, or if they are local they may be coerced into participation. In the case of the Wakkerstroom commando, for example, black members are usually farmworkers and they are very firmly subordinated to the commanding officers, often the owners of the farms where they work or live. In some cases, refusal to serve in a commando can result in victimization by those who are members: young men who were former farm residents from Driefontein near Piet Retief in Mpumalanga spoke to Human Rights Watch about assaults by the Wakkerstroom commando, which they believed were provoked by the fact that they had refused to sign documents saying they would join the commando.[515] A representative for one of the farmworkers' unions noted more generally: "There may be farmworkers participating, but they are not at the core of the structure; they are just footsoldiers who are sent out if there is a problem, they are just following orders."[516] In other cases, the black members of the commandos are not local people; many farm residents told Human Rights Watch that those wearing military uniform did not speak the local language.[517]

There are some attempts to break down these barriers. At Levubu police station, Northern Province, for example, which is responsible for policing areas of commercial farmland and the former homeland of Venda, the GOCOC involves both farmers and chiefs in the implementation of the rural protection plan. While, as in other locations, the primary focus of the rural protection plan appears to be visiting farmers, an inspector at the police station responsible for the Community Police Forum informed Human Rights Watch that chiefs also attended the GOCOC

---

[515] Human Rights Watch interviews, Johannesburg, March 26, 2000.

[516] Human Rights Watch interview with Howard Mbana, SAAPAWU, March 24, 2000.

[517] For example, Human Rights Watch interviews, Vryheid and Ingogo, KwaZulu-Natal, April 2000.

meetings and passed on information to the police regarding crime in their areas.[518] Similarly, in Paulpietersburg, the army reservist in charge of the local commando subunit (part of the Northern Natal commando), while acknowledging that "usually the commandos are seen negatively," explained that "here we are trying to help. We get calls to assist with problems in the tribal areas, where people don't trust the police either; in fact we do more in the tribal areas than in the commercial farming areas."[519] The white farmers and commando members have bought a house, which they intend to turn into a twenty-four hour operations center, also functioning as a community center, and as a base from which the white farmers can offer assistance to black farmers trying to break into commercial farming. In the Umfolozi policing area, the farmwatch system has supplied radios to the rural areas as well, linking them into the rural protection plan, even though in practice there have been problems with ensuring that there is effective cooperation.[520] Nevertheless, in general, the commandos and farmwatch cells operate only in the commercial farming areas, not attempting to engage with any homeland areas, except for the purpose of conducting raids for illegal weapons or in "hot pursuit" of a suspect. "If there is a serious problem in the tribal areas we do go, but not generally. The police cover all areas, but the private farmwatches don't."[521] Yet, in several places, Human Rights Watch heard of black farmers approaching the white officers of the local commando unit to assist them to counter stock theft, which affects farm owners, labor tenants, and subsistence farmers in the tribal areas, and is often carried out by organized gangs operating from outside the district: to a large extent frustration with the police exists across all racial groups.

In at least one district, the rural protection plan has become highly organized, bringing farmers, police, and commandos together in a very structured fashion, and also making efforts to reach out beyond the white community. In Greytown, a formerly "white" town with associated commercial farmland surrounded by impoverished and historically highly militarized chieftaincies of the former KwaZulu homeland, all security structures are linked to a "911 center," a control room in the center of the town. The system grew out of the local Umvoti

[518] Human Rights Watch interview with Inspector Risimati Robert Maluleke, Levubu Police Station, March 28, 2000.
[519] Human Rights Watch interview with Arno Engelbrecht, farmer and commando member, Paulpietersburg, September 14, 2000.
[520] Human Rights Watch interview with Mike de Lange, formerly KWANALU security desk, Eshowe, September 14, 2000.
[521] Human Rights Watch interview with Mike de Lange, formerly KWANALU security desk, Eshowe, September 14, 2000.

commando, but was based on a recognition by its prime movers that the different security services were competing rather than cooperating, especially as white suspicion of the police grew after 1994.[522] The center, still supported primarily by SANDF resources and personnel, is in daily radio contact with 200 farms, and is also linked to relevant police units and emergency services, to the SANDF Group 9 headquarters in Pietermaritzburg, and to the Umvoti commando. The control room has the capacity to reroute incoming phone calls to any one of its linked services, and indeed functions as the police station switchboard. It has a ten-person rapid reaction force from the commando at its disposal, twenty-four hours a day, and a twenty-person unit that conducts regular patrols.[523] Among the primary roles of the commando is to conduct raids for illegal weapons. Notably, those running the 911 center have made efforts to reach out to other sectors of the community than simply the white farm and business owners, though it is the farmers who are the principal funders of the effort; in particular, chiefs from the surrounding tribal areas have been approached, and the center will provide security for events taking place in the black areas where it can.[524] Community leaders in the area note that, while in the past the commando had regularly harassed or assaulted community leaders and farm residents, including assisting in illegal evictions, and had failed to curb the abusive actions of private security companies, the situation had significantly improved in recent years.[525] The police station itself has sixty-three uniformed officers, eleven detectives, and a total of twenty-one vehicles; with which it covers more than 320 farms, an area of about 1,500 square kilometers. Each one is visited every week or two weeks.[526]

The Response to Violent Crime Against Farmworkers

The government has made the laws, the constitution is there, but to implement them is the problem. The farmers don't want to accept the changes, and there is no one to force them. Most

---

[522] Human Rights Watch interview with Dave Carol, Greytown 911 Center, September 13, 2000.

[523] Schönteich and Steinberg, *Attacks on Farms and Smallholdings*, p.61-63.

[524] Human Rights Watch interview with Dave Carol, Greytown 911 Center, September 13, 2000.

[525] Human Rights Watch interview with Jotham Myaka, Zibambeleni, September 13, 2000.

[526] Human Rights Watch interview with Capt Moodley, acting station commissioner, Greytown police station, April 3, 2000.

things that are happening here, it doesn't show that it is the
new South Africa.[527]

Although presented as a broad-based initiative on rural crime, the Rural Safety Summit was seen by groups representing farm workers and residents, including the agricultural workers' unions and the National Land Committee and its affiliates, as dominated by farm owners and the security force hierarchy, who have shown little concern for the violence facing the groups they represent.[528] These groups and many ordinary black farm residents believe that violence against farm workers and residents has not received the same priority from the government as "farm attacks." According to one community leader, "The farmers are under threat from criminals, but they don't organize to protect all who live on the farm, just themselves. If it were inclusive it would be OK, but it seems just to be for the white farmers. As a result the criminals have an easy time, because the workers say we don't care, and if someone is killed no one on the farm will come forward."[529] Even though laws have been adopted to improve the lot of farm residents, there is a frustration at the failure to implement them forcefully.

In particular, many advocates for farm residents are concerned that illegal, and often violent, evictions are continuing apace despite legislation to prevent this practice. Even officials within the Department of Land Affairs complain that it is difficult to enforce the legislation:

> These cases are not properly investigated, we struggle to get the police to open a docket. If we send people to the police, they tell them to go back to Land Affairs, but Section 23 of ESTA makes clear that it is a criminal offense.... Speaking to the people on the front desk is a waste of time, you have to go to the station commissioner and get him to give instructions; I have had experiences where people on the front desk have even run away.... Many of the people we are helping are illiterate, and the police are very intimidating, asking aggressive questions, when their duty is to take a statement, investigate, and let the prosecutor do the work. There was a case here a man had been

---

[527] Human Rights Watch interview with member of the Ingogo Crisis Committee, Ingogo, KwaZulu-Natal, April 7, 2000.

[528] Human Rights Watch interviews SAAPAWU and NLC, March 23 and 24, 2000.

[529] Human Rights Watch interview with Jotham Myaka, Zibambeleni, New Hanover, September 13, 2000.

to the police three times to say that he was being intimidated to leave his home, but he was still threatened. Eventually we went with him to the police station and asked for the station commissioner. They eventually opened a charge and we got a police escort to his place, where we found everything upside down: he had been chased away and they had taken his belongings, and then apparently the police had told the farmer we were coming and they had replaced them, but everything was in chaos.[530]

The Legal Resources Centre in Pretoria, which handles many cases of illegal evictions, stated to Human Rights Watch that despite approaching police and prosecutors to charge those carrying out evictions with an offense under the act, they have been repeatedly turned down.[531] The police themselves often continue to talk of farm residents using the terminology of apartheid era legislation which referred to "illegal squatting," even when claiming to enforce the new laws: "We have a very good relationship with the farmers. They usually ask us to attend to their squatter problems; but there is very little we can do, we tell them they have to follow the procedure. They used to phone often to tell us they want squatters removed, but now most of them know the procedures."[532] There have been virtually no prosecutions under section 23 ESTA, which criminalizes illegal evictions: "Originally, I did affidavits for my clients to take to the police to open a case, but it was never successful, so I gave up. I don't believe the police even

---

[530] Human Rights Watch interview with Mpumalanga Department of Land Affairs officials, April 12, 2000. Section 23 of the Extension of Security of Tenure Act provides that:

> (1) No person shall evict an occupier except on the authority of an order of a competent court.
> (2) No person shall wilfully obstruct or interfere with an official in the employ of the State or a mediator in the performance of his or her duties under this Act.
> (3) Any person who contravenes a provision of subsection (1) or (2) shall be guilty of an offence and liable on conviction to a fine, or to imprisonment for a period not exceeding two years, or to both such fine and such imprisonment.
> (4) Any person whose rights or interests have been prejudiced by a contravention of subsection (1) shall have the right to institute a private prosecution of the alleged offender.

[531] Human Rights Watch interview with Oupa Maake and Charles Pillai, Legal Resources Centre, Pretoria, April 10, 2000.

[532] Human Rights Watch interview with Capt Moodley, acting station commissioner, Greytown police station, April 3, 2000.

know about the law."[533]   Human Rights Watch heard of no more than two prosecutions under this power in the country.

The Police

Similarly, advocates for farm residents are concerned that violent crimes against those living or working on commercial farms are not properly handled by the police: "The great majority of eviction cases we handle are accompanied with violence and intimidation, threats with guns and other types of harassment, and when poor occupiers of land try to lay charges, the police refuse to do anything; sometimes we have to force them to open a case."[534]   Again, officials working for the Department of Land Affairs also find themselves unable to ensure a proper response: "Cases of assaults are reported to the authorities, including to our offices, but we are not the police and can only refer them.   Then the attitude of the police is that they don't want to record cases; if they are recorded it is often through the intervention of our offices, but even then you find there is strong resistance and we have to talk to the station commissioner."[535]   One paralegal working with farm residents told Human Rights Watch, "There are a lot of cases that are not followed up. I don't know of any cases where the police have investigated and someone has been prosecuted.   Not one.   But I have heard of up to twenty or more cases of assault in the past year.   Of these about five were reported to the police, and then the prosecutor says the witnesses are not sufficient and the case is closed down."[536] Often particular police stations are problematic, while their neighbors may be more responsive: a union worker based in Randburg, for example, noted that the Muldersdrift police station consistently failed to respond satisfactorily to complaints.[537]

Women farm residents interviewed by Human Rights Watch near Naboomspruit, Northern Province, told of a case involving a farmworker on the neighboring farm who had been reported to the police by the farm owner following

---

[533] Human Rights Watch interview with Christo Loots, Pietermaritzburg, September 11, 2000.

[534] Human Rights Watch interview with Oupa Maake and Charles Pillai, Legal Resources Centre, Pretoria, April 10, 2000.

[535] Human Rights Watch interview with Mpumalanga Department of Land Affairs officials, April 12, 2000.

[536] Human Rights Watch interview with Philip Shabalala, paralegal, Christo Loots Attorneys, Vryheid, April 6, 2000.

[537] Human Rights Watch interview with Farayi Moyo, South Africa Effective Union Brokers, Randburg, September 5, 2000.

a difference over his wages. He was allegedly tortured by police at the police station, and arrested on several other occasions: "A white policeman said, 'so long as the farmer calls us there is nothing you can do; when the farmer says we must come and arrest you we must do so. You must complain to your boss and not to us about your arrest.' They were harassing him to leave the farm."[538]

In some cases, the police themselves confess to difficulties in investigating cases against powerful local interests. As one black detective noted to Human Rights Watch: "It's difficult to investigate cases involving the commandos. Before we are allowed to speak to them we have to have permission from SANDF Group 12 at Camden. Then most members of the commandos are not giving us statements; they come with a legal adviser but refuse to say anything. They are not accepting that they have to change. Then the prosecutor always declines to prosecute, none of the cases have gone to court, though there have been some arrests. There have been no convictions since 1998 when I joined the detective branch. Most of the time they come to people in the night, so it is hard for the victims to identify their attackers."[539] A policeman based at the Ixopo police station, who is involved in investigating cases against soldiers, said he was struggling to get information from SANDF members. He had attempted to find out which soldiers were based in Ixopo at any particular time, to find out which might have been involved in assaults, but the army had refused to provide the patrol report which contains a list of people deployed.[540] In one case in which members of the Umkomaas commando based at Ixopo had been charged with murder and attempted murder, the SAPS alleged that they initially received no cooperation from the legal adviser representing the SANDF members, who registered cases of

---

[538] Human Rights Watch interview with farm resident, near Naboomspruit, Northern Province, March 30, 2000. Translated from Pedi. The farmworker, the brother of the woman interviewed, had allegedly complained to the farm owner about his wage of R200 a month after deductions, and asked for a raise. When the farmer refused, the worker, Koos, said that he would resign, and the farmer said that he should therefore leave the farm. The farmer reported the case to the police, saying that Koos was aggressive and had threatened to attack him. He was taken to the Seiplaas police station and allegedly beaten, as well as tortured by having a rubber bag put over his head till he became unconscious. He was kept three days at the police station. When he was released he went home, but was taken back to the police station three or more times, once from the store at the neighboring farm where his sister lives, when the police made this comment.

[539] Human Rights Watch interview with detective inspector, SAPS, southern Mpumalanga, April 13, 2000.

[540] Telephone interview by Cheryl Goodenough with policeman from Ixopo Police Station, November 13, 2000.

unlawful arrest at Ixopo police station instead of talking to the investigating officer.[541] In some cases, farmers lock the gates of their farms to deny police access, refuse to speak to police officers, or deny their employees permission to speak with the police—all in violation of the law. One farmer in an assault case from a farm in Citrusdal, Western Cape, refused to speak to junior police officers and wanted to speak to the station commissioner only.[542]

At police stations visited by Human Rights Watch during research for this report, station commissioners and others we spoke to could often refer to all recent cases of "farm attacks" by the name of the victims, but were unaware of similarly serious cases of assault or murder of black people on the same farms. At every police station visited, we were told that when visiting farms police visited either the farmer or someone designated by him, and occasionally also the headman of the workers; in no case did the police consult with workers on the farm as to their concerns. While "the farm owner may also involve workers in gathering information," the police did not consult farmworkers separately.[543] A police inspector at Levubu police station near Louis Trichardt told Human Rights Watch, "We [the police] trust farm owners. If they say there are no problems on the farm, then it means the situation is okay."[544] At Ingogo police station, near Newcastle in KwaZulu-Natal, for example, the station commissioner could name half a dozen cases where farm owners had been assaulted, burgled or killed in the four years he had been at the police station. He was unable to name any cases of assaults against farmworkers or residents, although Human Rights Watch had spoken to a large number of people who had been assaulted by farm owners or security, often in the course of an eviction. There had also been one case of murder, in which a farmworker responsible for looking after cattle had gone to work one morning and not returned; his body was found on the farm some days later with a bullet wound. The wife of the victim had been informed of the death of her husband by the

---

[541] Letter dated August 1, 2000, from Assistant Commissioner P.F. Holloway, Office of the Area Commissioner, Umzimkulu, to Mary de Haas. See further below on the situation in Ixopo.
[542] Human Rights Watch interview station commissioner, Citrusdal police station, Western Cape, April 11, 2000.
[543] Human Rights Watch interview with Capt. Vollgraaff, Louis Trichardt police station, March 29, 2000.
[544] Human Rights Watch interview, police inspector, Levubu police station, Northern Province, April 2, 2000.

police.[545]   Often, police officers reported that assaults on farm workers were unknown in their area: "We don't get cases where white farmers are assaulting their employees; they are too important to him."[546]

The police note that reported assaults by farm residents against each other are far more common than reported assaults by farm owners. But even though common assault is often the most common offense reported to the police, property crimes among the more affluent are usually targeted as the priority for police response.[547] Understaffing is another obstacle. A police officer will often handle tens of cases at the same time. "At the end one would have to 'prioritize' which case to attend to because you can't deal with them all."[548] Although prioritization may be a necessity, given resource constraints, the message sent is that crime among farm residents, even quite serious crime, is not important. "When a person was stabbed on the farm and seriously injured when they had been drinking, the police didn't do anything. They said they would come back for statements from witnesses but they never did. The man who did it ran away and we haven't seen him again."[549] The Vryheid-based Farm Eviction and Development Committee (also known as Isikhalo se Africa, the Cry of Africa) wrote to the KwaZulu-Natal deputy director of public prosecutions in July 2000 to complain of a series of cases that had not been properly followed up by police, several of them relating not to evictions or assaults by farmworkers, but to general assaults in the community.[550] A station commissioner in the Western Cape noted that, in cases of common assaults reported from the farms "the prosecutor often declines to prosecute all of them because they are not serious cases."[551] A white farm owner in Gauteng also noted to Human Rights Watch that farmworkers reporting crimes to the police—for

---

[545] Human Rights Watch interview with farm resident, Ingogo, April 7, 2000. Translated from Zulu.

[546] Human Rights Watch interview with control prosecutor, Louis Trichardt district magistrates court, March 29, 2000.

[547] At Estcourt police station, the top crimes were identified to Human Rights Watch as burglary, theft of a vehicle and theft from a vehicle; while a chart on the wall showed assault as the most common crime by far. Human Rights Watch interviews, Estcourt police station, April 5, 2000.

[548] Human Rights Watch interview, station commissioner, Citrusdal police station, Western Cape, April 11, 2000.

[549] Human Rights Watch interview near Nylstroom, Northern Province, March 30, 2000.

[550] Letter dated July 5, 2000, from Isikhalo se Africa to KwaZulu-Natal deputy director of public prosecutions.

[551] Human Rights Watch interview, station commissioner, Citrusdal police station, Western Cape, April 11, 2000.

which they would usually use the telephone in the farmhouse—got very poor service: "they come and take statements and then nothing happens. The police are trying to look after us because of our structures, but I don't think the black worker on the farm is getting any response."[552]

The police assert that they are wholly impartial in handling complaints by farm owners or residents. At Estcourt police station, in the KwaZulu-Natal Midlands, Human Rights Watch was told that "Every docket that comes in is personally taken by the branch commissioner who makes a note of what should be done and given to the investigating officer. There would be nothing shelved in this area; we treat people equally. Even if a case was reported against Graham McIntosh [then the Democratic Party spokesperson on land and agricultural issues and former president of KWANALU, who owns a farm near Estcourt] we would charge him."[553] Yet Estcourt is the police station responsible for the area including a farm where multiple assaults were reported to Human Rights Watch, some of which are described above, and had also been reported to the police but not taken forward.

Where farm owners and their representatives see an inadequate police response to their concerns over "attacks on farms and smallholdings," farm workers and residents often see a hostile force: "We are the victims of the farmers and the police; the farmers and the police are working together."[554] The assessment of police response does vary significantly by individual police station, or according to the officer currently in charge: "We were having OK relations with the police for some time; we would take people to the police station and ask the police to call the farmers to a meeting to negotiate. But then Breytenbach came as station commissioner in 1998, and said he would not work under those conditions. When we tried to talk to him if someone was evicted, he refused because he said we want him to work the way we want not the way he wants. The big evictions started then. In one case he was even directing the traffic so that the farmer who was evicting someone could have free use of the road. Then they removed him at the end of 1999.... The current commissioner, we do at least communicate."[555]

---

[552] Human Rights Watch interview with Gert van Wyk, Bapsfontein, Gauteng, September 19, 2000.

[553] Human Rights Watch interview with Capt. A. Reddy, head of crime prevention, Estcourt police station, April 5, 2000.

[554] Human Rights Watch interview with member of the Ingogo Crisis Committee, Ingogo, KwaZulu-Natal, April 7, 2000.

[555] Ibid.

Often, police insist that the victim must be able to identify the assailant positively, for a docket to be opened. This causes problems not only in murder cases, where the victim is dead (see, for example, the case described above of Jabulani Simelane, allegedly killed by members of the Wakkerstroom commando), but also if he or she is incapacitated, or if an assault took place in the dark so that identification is difficult.

> We have lived on the same farm since 1951. In 1998, my husband said to the farmer that he was old and too tired to work any more and that his son should work instead. The farmer said he was not interested, and the next day he wrote a letter saying we must leave. We disregarded the letter, and after some time he called my husband to the farmhouse, where he met three of the family, who asked him why he was not leaving. My husband said he wanted his son to take over the work, and then the younger brother beat him up. He told me they were using their fists and they kicked him on his eye. He was badly affected; one week later he had a stroke and since then to today he has not been able to speak and his hand on one side is not working and he can't walk. They took away our six cows on that day also. We reported the case to the police, and they gave us a case number, but there has been no progress. They took a statement from my husband before his stroke, and they wanted a doctor's letter. I came back with a doctor's letter, but then they said they needed the victim himself if they were going to go further with the case. They came to visit him, and finding he could not speak, they said they would wait for him to be able to speak, so that's the end of the story.[556]

Alternatively, police may insist on an official medical report confirming an assault, even though this is not a formal requirement to open a docket. An elderly man told Human Rights Watch of an incident in which his son-in-law had been assaulted by a farmer, and later badly beaten by private security personnel who came to his house alleging that he was keeping stolen goods there. He was then taken to the local police station, where he was kept in the cells for two months and refused permission to see a doctor for his injuries. He was charged with theft and

---

[556] Human Rights Watch interview with farm resident, Ingogo, April 7, 2000. Translated from Zulu.

eventually released on bail. When asked if his son-in-law had laid a charge of assault against the individuals working for the private security company, the man told Human Rights Watch, "We tried to open a case, but the station commissioner said 'where have you been beaten, we can't accept that kind of case; it is better you have a doctor's letter.' My son-in-law said, 'how can I have a doctor's letter, since I was in the cells.' There is a strong connection between the security and the police, there is no point reporting anything."[557]

In some cases, parallel offenses are held to cancel each other out. A farm owner may lay a charge against a farm worker or resident who has brought a charge of assault against him, in order to obtain this result. A woman living on a farm near Estcourt told Human Rights Watch: "During 1998, [the farmer] was burning the grass for a fire break and the fire jumped to my house and burnt the roof. He didn't allow us to repair the house with more thatching; he said he didn't want people to build houses on the farm. We started arguing because I was insisting I wanted to rebuild it, and he pulled me out of my hut, pushing me up against the fence and assaulting me until he tried to throw a stone at me but I ran away. He was hitting me with a big coil of wire for fencing, he was kicking me, and he pulled my hair. I went to the doctor and to the police station; the doctor gave the police a letter, but the matter was not investigated. Some time later the police came to arrest me for cutting grass on the farm to thatch my hut and they took me to the police station in Estcourt. At the police station the investigating officer said that 'you have assaulted him and he also assaulted you, so we are not going to investigate.' They kept me overnight. I don't know if any charge was opened against me. After this incident he fired my daughter who was working on the farm."[558]

As a consequence of poor police work in cases of assaults against farmworkers, even very serious charges can take years to come to court, if they reach trial at all. Newspaper reports pick up on some of these cases. For example, farmworker Jantjie Sebako was reportedly shot in 1993 by two white men, believed to be part of a police stock theft unit, who came to his house after he asked for money that had been deducted over many years from his salary as savings by his employer, a farmer near Groot Marico, North West Province. He was paralyzed by

---

[557] Human Rights Watch interview with farm resident, Vryheid, April 6, 2000. Translated from Zulu.
[558] Human Rights Watch interview with farm resident, near Estcourt, KwaZulu-Natal, April 5, 2000. Translated from Zulu.

the shooting. Five years later, no one had been brought to court for the shooting.[559] Sometimes, low amounts for bail are set for individuals accused of murder. For example, three men, Johann Potgieter, Christo Coetzee, and Joost Heystek, appeared in the Potgietersrus magistrates court in 1997 after Joyce Mbedzi, a forty-five year old woman farmworker, was kicked and beaten to death on a Northern Province farm. The three, who had been hunting, allegedly attacked a group of farmworkers returning from a neighboring farm. They were released on R2000 (U.S.$264) bail each.[560]

Human Rights Watch was shown numerous letters addressed to local station commissioners, provincial commissioners, or those in charge of prosecutions complaining of failures to investigate or prosecute cases against farm owners. For example, on January 13, 1999, members of the Farm Eviction and Development Committee (Fedco), a support group, met with the SAPS area commissioner in Vryheid to express concern at delays in investigating cases of assaults against farmworkers. A written list of fourteen cases, including two murders and several assaults, was handed over, and followed up by letter some months later, when no feedback had been received. The police responded on July 7, 1999: in six of the cases referred by the police to the magistrates court, the prosecutor had declined to prosecute, one case had been closed as "undetected" because there were no known suspects, and in only two was a trial due to take place.[561] In July 2000, Fedco wrote to the KwaZulu-Natal deputy director of public prosecutions listing many of the same cases, and requesting that the DPP look into the failure to investigate the cases reported.[562] In some cases, it seems that the same farm owner can commit repeated assaults, which are never followed up by the police.[563]

---

[559] Abbey Makoe, "Death draws near and justice is not yet done," *Sunday Independent* (Johannesburg), May 17, 1998.

[560] "Three in court over death of farmworker," *Star*, July 10, 1997.

[561] Letter from Farm Eviction and Development Committee (Fedco), Isikhalo se Africa, to Area Commissioner, SAPS, Ulundi, (undated); response from Area Commissioner SAPS, Ulundi, to Fedco, July 7, 1999.

[562] Letter dated July 5, 2000, from Fedco to KwaZulu-Natal deputy director of public prosecutions, Pietermaritzburg.

[563] For example, Human Rights Watch was given a letter addressed to the Transvaal director of public prosecutions in Pretoria from an advice worker in the Machadodorp area, Gauteng. The letter listed three cases of assault, illegal eviction, and intimidation opened against the same farmer, in 1997, 1999, and 2000. None of them had been followed up, and those inquiring about the case had themselves reportedly been threatened with arrest. Letter dated February 8, 2000, from J.N. Nkosi to director of public prosecutions, Pretoria.

The Courts: Prosecutors and Magistrates

Like the police, many prosecutors are unaware of cases of assault against farmworkers in their area: "For the last year or two there have been no reports of assaults by farm owners against their workers in the Louis Trichardt area itself."[564] Sometimes this is the case even when when there have been prosecutions in such cases; assaults on white farm owners simply make a deeper impression. The control prosecutor at Vryheid magistrates court, an area where Human Rights Watch received numerous reports of assaults against farmworkers, including a murder the previous month in which the security guards responsible had been charged with murder and several others that had been reported to the police and charges laid, stated that she did not know of any cases of assaults against farmworkers being reported to the court. She was aware, however, of a few cases of farm owners being attacked and killed.[565] Similarly, the control prosecutor at Piet Retief magistrates court, the heart of the area where most brutality against farmworkers by the commandos was reported, could recall only one case of assault against a farmworker during the three years she had been at the court, though she was aware of several attacks against farm owners. She did know, however, of one charge pending against a private security company for an alleged assault on a black farm resident.[566]

A prosecutor at New Hanover district magistrates court, KwaZulu-Natal, when asked by Human Rights Watch about how the court handles cases of assault against farmworkers even appeared dismissive of such reports, "You mean a white man assaulting his employees, it is very difficult to prove these cases. Farm workers also exaggerate some of these cases. A person may allege that he had been assaulted with an iron bar and sustained serious injuries, but the person just has minor bruises. When the medical affidavit does not state that the victim sustained serious injuries, we decline to prosecute the case."[567] The prosecutor added that in some cases where farmers assault their farm workers this was, in his view, an "assault perpetrated under the auspices of an interrogation or discipline."[568] The

---

[564] Human Rights Watch interview with Capt. Vollgraaff, Louis Trichardt police station, March 29, 2000.
[565] Human Rights Watch interview with Mrs Lloyd, control prosecutor, Vryheid magistrates court, April 6, 2000.
[566] Human Rights Watch interview with control prosecutor, Piet Retief magistrates court, April 13, 2000.
[567] Human Rights Watch interview, prosecutor, New Hanover district court, KwaZulu-Natal province, April 5, 2000.
[568] Ibid.

magistrate at the same court, however, recognized that the power imbalance between farmers and farmworkers had a significant impact: "farm workers easily accept that when the 'baas' beats you, it's OK. They are so caged and solely dependent on the farm owner. Moreover, when they come to court with cases against their employers, they are easily 'grilled' by the defense lawyers and left to appear like liars before the court."[569] The court officials at New Hanover also told Human Rights Watch that some cases of violence against farm workers could not be successfully prosecuted at court because of intimidation or threats of eviction by farm owners: "Witnesses are subjected to serious intimidation by the farm owners prior to the court date. In some cases, even when witnesses appear in court, they change their testimonies because they have been threatened with eviction from the farm, if they testify against the farm owner."[570]

Where convictions are obtained, the sentences handed down have sometimes appeared grossly inadequate. In the past, suspended sentences or fines were common, even where convictions for homicide were obtained.[571] Admission of guilt fines are still common in lesser assault cases, for example at Louis Trichardt magistrates court, where they usually amount to a few hundred rands.[572] In 1997, a Free State farmer, Wessel Wessels, was convicted of kidnapping and assault for severely beating his employee, Samuel Mohapi, and chaining him to a workshop table, the previous year. He was sentenced only to a R3,000 (U.S.$395) fine (R2,500 for the kidnapping, and R500 for the assault).[573] In March 1999, a

---

[569] Human Rights Watch interview, magistrate, New Hanover district court, KwaZulu-Natal province, April 5, 2000.

[570] Ibid.

[571] For example: In 1988, a farmer who had killed his worker by tying him to a tree and whipping him over two days, for allegedly killing a dog, was convicted of culpable homicide and given a suspended sentence of five years and a fine of R3,000. He was also ordered to pay the widow R130 a month for five years. In 1989, two farmers who had assaulted a farm worker who later died of a brain hemorrhage were convicted of assault and sentenced to a fine of R1,200 or four months' imprisonment, with a further six months' imprisonment suspended for five years. Aninka Claassens, "Rural Land Struggles in the Transvaal in the 1980s," in Murray and O'Regan (eds.), *No Place to Rest*, note 25.

[572] Human Rights Watch interview with Inspector Risimati Robert Maluleke, Levubu Police Station, March 28, 2000. By contrast, he noted that if an assault case between two black people came before the magistrates at Vuyani (former Venda) then, if convicted, they could be sentenced to a fine of several thousand rands or one year in prison.

[573] Ann Eveleth, "'Sadist' grins at light fine," *Mail and Guardian*, November 7 to 13, 1997; see Eugene Roelofse, "Of Serfs and Lords," *Sidelines* (Johannesburg), Winter 1998, pp.25 to 28, for a fuller account of this case.

judge imposed only a suspended sentence on smallholder Nicholas Steyn after he was convicted of culpable homicide. He had shot dead a baby, Angelina Zwane, while she was being carried in her elder sister's arms across his land near Johannesburg. The judge in the case, which was heard amidst considerable media attention, found that the killing had been an accident and that the farmer had fired over the heads of the children and the baby had been killed by a ricochet.[574] The Independent Complaints Directorate (ICD), charged with investigating police misconduct, looked into police handling of the case, and recommended that disciplinary proceedings be instituted against the officers involved for failing to arrest Steyn promptly.[575] In another case, a farmer was convicted of culpable homicide in a case where he shot dead a woman walking near his farm on the West Rand near Johannesburg, and given only a suspended sentence.[576] In February 2000, Mpumalanga farmer Frederick de Beer was found guilty of assault with intent to do grievous bodily harm for painting a farmworker silver, from top to toe, for allegedly trespassing on his farm near Balfour the previous year. He was sentenced to eighteen months in prison, suspended for four years, and a fine of R3,200 (U.S.$422); his employee and accomplice, Andries Majola, was sentenced to eight months and was suspended for four years.[577]

Recently, there have been reports that some more appropriate sentences have been handed down. In August 1999, Pieter van Heerden Henning and Johann Potgieter were sentenced to prison terms of sixty-three years and twenty years,

---

[574] He was given a five year sentence, suspended for three years. The case was extensively reported. See, for example, Anso Thom, "Farmer who shot baby charged with murder," *Star* (Johannesburg), April 16, 1998; Mike Masipa, "Bigwigs descend on grieving family's shack," *Star*, April 17, 1998; "The day an innocent baby died," *Saturday Argus*, May 8, 1998; "Political slogans and threats greet baby Zwane's killer," SAPA, March 23, 1999; Chris McGreal, "The hate that won't go away," *Guardian* (London), July 26, 1999.

[575] Tangeni Amupadhi, "Police procedure questioned in Steyn murder case," *Mail and Guardian*, April 17-23, 1998; "Highlights and Achievements," in Report of the Independent Complaints Directorate to the Parliamentary Portfolio Committee on Safety and Security, March 2, 1999. According to the ICD, disciplinary proceedings were in fact instituted, as well as other recommendations relating to the training of officers. It is very rare for the ICD itself to investigate a case where complaints have been made about police investigation of another crime; usually, such cases would be delegated to an internal police complaints investigation unit.

[576] Jovial Rantao, "Judicial system puts itself on trial," *Star* (Johannesburg), May 15, 1999.

[577] "Two appear in court after painting of farmworker," SAPA, July 14, 1999; Justin Arenstein, "Silver paint farmer in court," *ZA Now*, July 14, 1999; Selby Bokaba, "Outrage over sentence for painting worker silver," *Star* (Johannesburg), February 23, 2000.

respectively, for the murder of Sibusiso Sibisi, Sipho Mkhize, and Mandlenkosi Ernest Mabaso in 1996. Mkhize was killed for calling his employer "Piet" instead of "baas" at a barbecue held on the farm; Mabaso after he tried to run away when he was shown the body of his co-worker. This trial followed a reported reign of terror by the Henning family on their farm near Dundee in northern KwaZulu-Natal, in which repeated deaths had gone uninvestigated and those believed to be responsible uncharged.[578] In September 2000, Henning's father, Cooks Henning, was found guilty of attempting to hire a hitman to kill Potgieter, who had testified against his son. In November, Pieter Henning's brother Eiker was sentenced to twenty-five years imprisonment for the murder of farmworker Ndelwa Kepisi Mgaga in January 1997 after he allegedly stole some farm tools.[579]

However, these stiffer sentences are still not the rule. In February 2001, Parys farmer Chris van Zyl was found guilty of assault and fined R19,000 (U.S.$2,500) for brutally assaulting two workers for Eskom, the state electricity parastatal, whom he tied to a motorbike and dragged around naked saying "I will show you how I killed kaffirs." The (white) magistrate refused to declare van Zyl unfit to hold a firearm, saying that it would amount to a passport for those who wished to enter the farmer's property with criminal intent.[580] Racial solidarity appears still in some cases to trump the state's obligation to provide impartial justice and protect its citizens.

The Response to Sexual Violence Against Women on Farms

It is difficult for women farm workers and residents to access other state mechanisms for assistance. Programs and services to provide support for victims of gender-related violence are limited and mostly concentrated in urban areas.[581]

---

[578] Ajith Bridgraj, "Braai, booze and deadly baaskap," *Sunday World* (Johannesburg), June 20, 1999; Darran Morgan and Jason Venter, "Shifting the balance of justice," *Mail and Guardian*, August 20, 1999.

[579] Craig Bishop, "Henning's father guilty of hiring hitman," *Natal Witness* (Pietermaritzburg), September 27, 2000; "The Week that Was," *Mail and Guardian*, November 17, 2000.

[580] Glenda Daniels, "Farmer fined for trying to 'kill kaffirs,'" *Mail and Guardian*, February 9, 2001.

[581] For details on developments in the government's policy and programs to address violence against women in South Africa since 1994, see Human Rights Watch, "South Africa: Violence Against Women and the Medico-Legal System," *A Human Rights Watch Short Report* (New York: Human Rights Watch, August 1997), vol.9, No. 4 (A), pp.8-13; Human Rights Watch, *Scared at School: Sexual Violence Against Girls in South African Schools* (New York: Human Rights Watch, March 2001); and Vetten, "Paper Promises, Protests and

In cases in which measures have been taken to bring some of these services to rural areas, the programs are ad hoc and ineffective. For example, while the police have introduced specialized units to handle crimes committed against women and children, known as Family Violence, Child Protection, and Sexual Offenses (FCS) units, these units are more established in urban than in rural areas.[582] As of September 2000, there were thirteen FCS units, thirty Child Protection Units (awaiting transformation into FCS units) and two Indecent Crimes Units (also to become FCS units) nationwide, situated in the main urban centers. Specialized individuals attached to the detective service were in charge of policing crimes against children in another 156 smaller towns.[583] FCS units based in more rurally located towns visited by Human Rights Watch were mostly fragmented, uncoordinated, ad hoc, and therefore also ineffective. The senior superintendent responsible for overseeing all FCS units told Human Rights Watch that because of a lack of resources, there were no plans to open more FCS units in rural police stations, much as she would like to be able to do so. She told Human Rights Watch, however, that plans were underway to improve existing FCS units and train more police on how to investigate cases of violence against women.[584]

The rural protection plan initiated by the SAPS in response to rising rates of crime on farms was not initiated with female farmworkers and residents in mind. A police commissioner in KwaZulu-Natal told Human Rights Watch how police find out if there are problems of rape of women on farms: "The farm owner has to phone us; if he doesn't, then tough luck."[585] In most cases, police will remain unaware of crimes committed against farm residents, especially women

---

Petitions" in Park et al, *Reclaiming Women's Spaces*.

[582] Human Rights Watch interview, Senior Superintendent Anneke Pienaar, national commander, Family Violence, Child Protection and Sexual Offences Unit, Pretoria, September 18, 2000. SAPS approved and launched the Family Violence, Child Protection, and Sexual Offences (FCS) unit in 1995. The objectives of "FCS" units are to prevent and combat crimes against women and children and to render sensitive services to victims of these crimes. For details on these units, see Human Rights Watch, "South Africa: Violence Against Women and the Medico-Legal System, pp. 12-13.

[583] *Family Violence, Child Protection and Sexual Offences Unit*, (Pretoria: SAPS September 2000).

[584] Human Rights Watch interview, Senior Superintendent Anneke Pienaar, national commander, Family Violence, Child Protection and Sexual Offences Unit, Pretoria, September 18, 2000.

[585] Human Rights watch interview, police commissioner, Mid-Illovo police station, Pietermaritzburg, April 6, 2000.

farmworkers and residents, unless they take measures to speak directly with the women and hear their perspectives about the security situation on farms.

The Police and Courts

Human Rights Watch found that many police did not recognize the problem of rape of women farmworkers by farm owners, creating a false impression that such rapes were not taking place. Some police officers interviewed by Human Rights Watch held condescending views about women farmworkers. Others readily dismissed the fact that farm owners were raping their employees. They told Human Rights Watch that "no farm owner ever raped women farmworkers."[586] This assertion was contradicted by those working with farmworkers and by women farmworkers themselves, who said they or others they knew had been raped.[587]

Women farmworkers are more likely to report to the police cases of rape by other farmworkers or residents than by farm owners. Women attempting to seek police assistance, however, complained to Human Rights Watch that in these cases too they faced bias and obstruction from officials. In some cases, police dismissed complaints, either refusing to believe the woman's allegations or failing to recognize intra-family violence as a crime. Police demonstrated a simplistic and biased understanding of the dynamics of rape, a lack of knowledge and experience as to the range of circumstances in which rapes of women occur, or a lack of sensitivity in dealing with rape victims.

Human Rights Watch found that the police in rural police stations had little understanding of the circumstances constituting rape. Police officers Human Rights Watch interviewed admitted that they had dismissed complaints after finding out or suspecting that there was a previous intimate or emotional relationship between the suspect and the complainant. For example, fifteen-year-old Busani Nsingo that alleged she was raped by a farmworker at Rosedale farm in the Estcourt area of KwaZulu-Natal. The rape occurred while Nsingo was on her way home from the same farm where she had a temporary job. She reported the case to Estcourt police in May 1999. The suspect was arrested in May 1999, but the investigating officer closed the case without any further investigation after the

---

[586] Human Rights Watch interviews station commissioner, Citrusdal police station, Western Cape, April 11, 2000; station commissioner, Piketberg police station, Western Cape, September 12, 2000; and station commissioner, Mid-Illovo police station, KwaZulu-Natal, April 5, 2000.
[587] Human Rights Watch interview, staff attorney, Lawyers for Human Rights, Pietersburg, April 2, 2000; and see other interviews above.

suspect told him that the victim was once his girlfriend.[588]   Similarly, the investigating officer who dealt with the case of Sylvia Malele closed the investigation of the case against Philip, the farmworker who allegedly raped Malele, his friend's wife. The investigating officer suspected Malele to have consented to having sex with Philip.[589]

In some areas, it seems that police routinely dismiss reported rape cases without further investigation where the complainant was allegedly under the influence of alcohol when the incident occurred. In the Citrusdal area of the Western Cape, police attributed the problem of rape and other crimes on farms almost solely to alcohol. The police commissioner at Citrusdal police station estimated that 99 percent of women on farms in Citrusdal get raped while under the influence of alcohol. He added, "If there was no drop of liquor in Citrusdal, there would be no crime. Often, the victim of rape gets herself drunk to the extent that she would not even know of the incident, unless someone else tells her about it. There is a lot of illegal sale of wine and alcohol on the farms."[590]   Similarly, the station commissioner at Piketberg police station in the Western Cape told Human Rights Watch that a lot of rapes reported at Piketberg police station "were not genuine rape cases." He added:

> Once you start the investigation you will realize that the victim
> was drunk when the incident occurred. Its only when her
> boyfriend or husband finds out about the incident that she runs
> to open a case of rape against the person whom she had sex with.
> This is not what we call rape.[591]

In the case of Kasy Mwale, reported above, the investigating officer dismissed the cases simply because he believed the word of the suspect over that of the complainant. Thirteen-year-old Mwale alleged she was raped by a man she identified as a farmworker from Thomson farm in the KwaZulu-Natal province. She reported the case to police and her assailant was arrested. The police took

---

[588] Human Rights Watch interview, social worker, Victim Support Centre, Estcourt, KwaZulu-Natal, April 4, 2000.

[589] Case recorded in the file of cases of violence against women kept by the Victim Support Centre, Estcourt, KwaZulu-Natal, April 4, 2000.

[590] Human Rights Watch interview, station commissioner, Citrusdal police station, Western Cape, April 11, 2000.

[591] Human Rights Watch interview, station commissioner, Piketberg police station, Western Cape, September 12, 2000.

Mwale to the government medical officer in Dalton for a medical examination. The results of the medical examination confirmed that she had been raped. The investigating officer however, released the alleged rapist, when he denied during questioning that he raped Mwale.[592]

Women farm workers also complained about the harsh and unfriendly attitudes of some police officers when they attempted to open cases of rape or sexual abuse. In some cases, victims of rape and other crimes said they just were sent away by police without their cases being recorded.[593] In others, victims were required to give their statements in public under circumstances which compromised their privacy and confidentiality.[594] For example, a staff attorney with Lawyers for Human Rights told Human Rights Watch that some police officers tended to "interrogate victims of rape in the reception area of the police station while talking loudly so that others waiting for attention can hear what is going on."[595]

Like the police, many prosecutors and magistrates Human Rights Watch interviewed were dismissive of cases of rape of farmworkers in their areas. As one commented:

> We get a lot of cases of rape from the farmworkers, but most of them are reported by prostitutes who don't get their money. They come to court without a single injury recorded on their J88 form [used by the district surgeon to record injuries for use in the court case]. How can a woman be raped without even a scratch on her body? I would never say it is rape, I believe very few of these women.[596]

---

[592] Human Rights Watch interview, Kasy Mwale, New Hanover, KwaZulu-Natal, April 5, 2000.

[593] Human Rights Watch interview, group of farmworkers at the advice office, Piketberg, Western Cape, September 12, 2000.

[594] Human Rights Watch interviews, Nkuzi Development Project field workers, Pietersburg, April 2, 2000.

[595] Human Rights Watch interview, staff attorney, Lawyers for Human Rights, Stellenbosch, April 10, 2000.

[596] Human Rights Watch interview with control prosecutor, Louis Trichardt district magistrates' court, March 29, 2000.

Medico-Legal Evidence

Another obstacle is a lack of easy access to medical services for women farm workers. Medico-legal evidence is especially important in cases of sexual assault to corroborate the evidence given by the victim in court.[597] In South Africa, medico-legal services are provided free to the public. Although medico-legal services are therefore accessible in terms of cost, the distances to reach government medical officers or other medico-legal facilities still preclude women farmworkers from undergoing medical examinations. In addition to the problem of transportation and the critical shortage of accessible medico-legal services in rural areas, some women farmworkers are denied permission by farm owners or managers to visit medical facilities when they experience rape.[598] The victims' failure to undergo medical examinations seriously compromises the outcome of their cases in court.[599]

Obtaining accurate information about the extent of medico-legal services provisions country-wide is difficult, since they are provided on a provincial basis, and different methods are used to calculate the services provided. However, in most cases doctors providing medico-legal services (known as district surgeons) are based in towns. Mobile clinics of the type that visit farms do not have staff capable of carrying out a medico-legal examination. Victims of rape in rural areas and farms often take a long time before reaching a government medical officer who is qualified to examine them.[600] A timely examination of a victim can yield significant evidence in rape or other sexual or domestic violence cases. Such evidence is lost if it is not recorded within a short period of time after the attack.[601]

---

[597] See Human Rights Watch, "South Africa: Violence Against Women and the Medico-Legal System."

[598] Human Rights Watch interviews, group of women farmworkers, Northern Province, April 2, 2000, and group of women farmworkers, East Rand, April 15, 2000.

[599] Human Rights Watch interview, prosecutor, New Hanover district magistrates' court, KwaZulu-Natal, April 5, 2000.

[600] Human Rights Watch interview, district surgeon, KwaZulu-Natal, April 4, 2000.

[601] During its 1997 research on performance of district surgeons (now government medical officers) in the provision of medico-legal services where a woman has allegedly been raped, Human Rights Watch interviewed officers of the Pretoria Medico-Legal clinic who stated that a woman who has been raped should be seen within four hours to ensure that each minor physical abrasion—which may be crucial to the woman's claim that sexual intercourse took place without consent—may be detected. Other district surgeons also noted to Human Rights Watch that, if a woman is seen soon enough there is in the majority of cases—even if a woman has had several children—physical evidence suggesting forced penetration. For details, *see* Human Rights Watch, "South Africa: Violence Against Women

Another problem relates to the handling of specimens collected during the medical examinations. While police are supposed to collect all specimens from the government medical officers and pass them on to forensic medical laboratories for further analysis, police often do not actually send these specimens to the forensic laboratories. A government medical officer complained to Human Rights Watch that many specimens "sit in police stations" for months and never reach the forensic laboratories for analysis. In many rape cases, the suspect is not convicted because the medical evidence is incomplete, even if government medical officers "have done their part, only to be let down in the process by police."[602]

Victims of rape often need support when they visit medico-legal facilities for examinations. While police often accompany victims to the government medical offices, police often "dump" victims without informing them about why they need to undergo a medical examination.[603] In some cases, government medical officers also carry out the medical examination without explaining the process to the victim and obtaining her consent to an examination for legal purposes. Programs to assist traumatized rape or assault victims with counseling and other support services before and after undergoing medical examinations are not available to most women farmworkers.

Insufficient Resources

Lack of resources and trained police officers also severely limits the effective investigation and prosecution of rape and other crimes against farmworkers. Mercy Ndhlela, a fourteen-year-old girl living with her mother on Mdotsheni farm in KwaZulu-Natal, was raped by an unidentified person who broke into their house while she was sleeping at night. Her mother reported the case to police but the police failed to follow-up the case due to lack of transportation.[604]

In other cases, police could not cope with the level of crime in their area. Many police station commissioners interviewed by Human Rights Watch complained that they lacked sufficient and trained officers to respond to crime in general and in particular rape and other crimes against women.[605] For example, the Citrusdal police commisioner told Human Rights Watch that police officers had to

---

And The Medico-Legal System," p.24.

[602] Human Rights Watch interview, district surgeon, KwaZulu-Natal, April 4, 2000.

[603] Ibid.

[604] Human Rights Watch interview, social worker, Victim Support Centre, Estcourt, KwaZulu-Natal, April 4, 2000.

[605] Human Rights Watch interview, head of detectives, Citrusdal police station, Western Cape, April 11, 2000.

handle large numbers of cases at the same time.[606] In April 2000, the station had twenty-three police officers, including detectives responsible for conducting investigations, to cover an area of approximately 1300 square kilometers, including about 150 farms. Seventy percent of the crimes handled at this police station occurred on the farms.[607] Only one police officer at Citrusdal had attended a course on investigating rape cases, for one week only.[608] Similarly, when Human Rights Watch visited Piketberg police in September 2000, there was only one female detective trained to investigate cases of rape.[609]

The Response to Violent Crime Against Farm Owners

> *If you took the farmwatch and the reservists out of the system, there'd be nothing left. There are some good police out there, but there are no vehicles. The private farmwatches are vital. We have an arrest rate of 90 percent in KwaZulu-Natal for farm murders, and though we can't say how many of those result in convictions, we've had a couple of good results recently. Everything is in chaos, the police, the justice system. Dockets are going missing, and there is corruption everywhere. Some guys are doing the best they can working in a system that is bloody difficult.[610]*

The rural protection plan has ensured that the arrest rate in cases of violent crime against farm owners or managers is very high by comparison with crime in South Africa generally. According to police information, 40.6 percent of the "farm attacks" reported during the first six months of 1998 had already led to arrests by July of that year.[611] For "attacks" on farms rather than smallholdings, the arrest rate

---

[606] Human Rights Watch interview, station commissioner, Citrusdal police station, Western Cape, April 11, 2000.

[607] Human Rights Watch interview, head of detectives, Citrusdal police station, Western Cape, April 11, 2000.

[608] Ibid.

[609] Human Rights Watch interview, station commissioner, Piketberg police station, Western Cape, September 12, 2000.

[610] Human Rights Watch interview with Mike de Lange, formerly KWANALU security desk, Eshowe, September 14, 2000.

[611] *Attacks on Farms and Smallholdings: Report by the Crime Information Analysis Centre, No.2 of 1998.*

is higher, estimated at up to 80 or 90 percent.[612] Key to this success, at least in some areas, is the rapid response time of the farmwatch and commando system: "Cell members invariably arrive on the scene long before the security forces."[613] Part of this speed of response is due to regular patrols: in one case in August 2000, for example, burglars broke into a house one Sunday morning, apparently believing it was empty, and attacked an elderly woman, chopping off four of her fingers and breaking her pelvis and her arm. Even so, she was able to hit the alarm. Within a few minutes, members of the farmwatch were on the scene. One of the perpetrators was caught in the house, one in the getaway vehicle, and one an hour later; two more were arrested a few weeks later.[614] Speed is crucial to the chances of apprehending a suspect. As a study by the Institute for Security Studies noted, "Senior police management in the area [Piet Retief] openly acknowledge that, when a suspect is not apprehended within a couple of hours of the attack, the chances of making an arrest are close to zero."[615] However, where local police detective units are effective in following leads, especially outside their area, it can also make an important difference. In Greytown, where 74 percent of "farm attacks" result in arrests, the rapid reaction unit operating from the "911 center" is responsible for the arrests in only 35 percent of cases; the remainder result from standard police detection work.[616] In the Utrecht area, northern KwaZulu-Natal, the police, rather than farmwatch or commando units, have arrested suspects after the few murders of farmers that have happened in the district.[617]

There is some acknowledgment of government attempts to improve the response to the threat of violence against farm owners from organized agriculture. One farmer, formerly responsible for monitoring security issues for the KwaZulu-Natal Agricultural Union (KWANALU), noted that "The rural protection plan isn't perfect, but it has gone a long way."[618] Another representative of KWANALU commented to Human Rights Watch that "the rural safety plan has been successful

---

[612] Human Rights Watch interview with Col. H.J. Boshoff, SANDF, Pretoria, March 22, 2000.

[613] Schönteich and Steinberg, *Attacks on Farms and Smallholdings*, p.48.

[614] Human Rights Watch interview with Arno Engelbrecht, farmer and commando member, Paulpietersburg, September 14, 2000.

[615] Schönteich and Steinberg, *Attacks on Farms and Smallholdings*, p.48.

[616] Ibid., p.63.

[617] Human Rights Watch interview with Theo van Rooyen, farmer, member of KWANALU executive committee and of local GOCOC, Utrecht, September 15, 2000.

[618] Human Rights Watch interview with Mike de Lange, formerly KWANALU security desk, Eshowe, September 14, 2000.

in terms of building relationships with the police."[619] He added, however, that "the main beneficiaries have been those farming areas that have of their own accord achieved a high level of organizational capacity around crime containment," which excluded the areas where the union's small scale members predominate (that is, the former homelands).[620] Lourie Bosman of the Mpumalanga Agricultural Union, though critical of the government on this issue, in particular of the slowness of police response to many cases of violent crime against farm owners, acknowledged that "Where farm attacks take place it is one of the areas, funnily enough, where police are doing their utmost to solve those cases. I don't have examples where they have not been followed up."[621]

Generally, white farmers' representatives consider the government response to be inadequate: "The government response has been zero, a little bit of lip service but nothing happened after that. The rural safety plan is just an academic exercise, a coordinating mechanism, but there are no proactive plans. The feeling is that it is not a priority for the government. You can see that if there is a human rights problem where a laborer is involved the minister is there, but if a farmer is killed there is no response. The whole story creates mistrust. Our message to the farmers is that if you don't protect yourself then no one else is going to do it for you."[622] The Transvaal Agricultural Union has called for farmers "to behave as if a national state of emergency is in place," accusing the government of "a lack of will ... to look after the safety of farmers."[623] Others call for equal protection of the law, in accordance with their rights under the constitution: "The point is that farmers should not be seen differently from any other section of the community; all of us deserve the protection of the rule of law and that is what we are demanding."[624] From the police side, there is frustration at the harsh response of organized agriculture to the best efforts of the service: "The farmers have unrealistic expectations of what the security forces can do; they would like to see

---

[619] Human Rights Watch interview, Peter Southey, KWANALU, Pietermaritzburg , April 4, 2000.

[620] Email from KWANALU to Human Rights Watch, August 7, 2000.

[621] Human Rights Watch interview with Lourie Bosman, Mpumalanga Agricultural Union, Ermelo, April 12, 2000.

[622] Human Rights Watch interview with Jack Loggenberg, Transvaal Agricultural Union, Pretoria, April 17, 2000.

[623] "Act as if in a state of emergency, TLU tells farmers," SAPA, November 22, 2000.

[624] Interview with Graham McIntosh, (then) president of the KwaZulu-Natal Agricultural Union, published in *Briefing* 12, (Johannesburg: Helen Suzman Foundation, September 1998).

a member of the police permanently stationed at each farm, which is impossible. We have a problem of resources."[625]

Many white farmers feel that the police service has deteriorated since 1994.[626] Commercial farmers are used to privileged treatment, and—perhaps inevitably as the police have taken on duties to the wider community, while farm owners have faced a real threat of violent crime for the first time—farmers perceive that their problems now receive less attention: "The quality of police services have gone down tremendously. That is why questions are being asked. There are many incidents where dockets are removed, people are not prosecuted, or the police don't even have the facilities to come to the crime scene."[627] Others are more explicitly racist: "Affirmative action is the biggest problem. You take a tea girl and give her a rank. We don't want to lower our standards, and you are putting people in place who can't write a statement."[628] Dave Carol, the driving force behind the Greytown 911 center, noted frankly that "there is a lack of confidence in the police. People feel that the police force has become more black than it was—and in South Africa we have reservations when dealing with the other race color. Though I think it will break down, if we can build more trust."[629] Indeed, in one case, a white farm owner and commando member noted that his relationship was better with the new black station commissioner than with his Afrikaans-speaking predecessors.[630]

The most common complaint is of poor police response time. According to a representative of a private security company benefiting from this frustration,

---

[625] Human Rights Watch interview with Commissioner Johann Burger, SAPS, Pretoria, April 10, 2000.

[626] As do many of those living in the former homelands. A survey carried out in 1998 found that more than a third felt that policing had declined in quality in the last few years; more than 40 percent believed the police were ineffective in curbing crime in their area. Pelser, Louw, and Ntuli, *Poor safety*, p.60.

[627] Human Rights Watch interview with Lourie Bosman, Mpumalanga Agricultural Union, Ermelo, April 12, 2000.

[628] Human Rights Watch interview with members of the Northern Natal commando, Vryheid, September 14, 2000. As noted above, functional illiteracy in the police service is a serious problem; however, qualifications required to enter the police have risen significantly in recent years, and those members who are illiterate were largely employed by the former government, especially in the former homelands.

[629] Human Rights Watch interview with Dave Carol, Greytown 911 Center, September 13, 2000.

[630] Human Rights Watch interview with Arno Engelbrecht, farmer and commando member, Paulpietersburg, September 14, 2000.

in one case the police had arrived a day after a burglary happened: "The farmers have a lot of complaints about the police; they are not answering the phone at night, and then you can't get through during the day, or they say they have no vehicle. So most farmers are phoning us first; though we also contact the police to let them know what we are doing."[631] Farmers belonging to the Northern Natal commando based in Vryheid commented to Human Rights Watch, "There aren't any police in South Africa. When you phone them, it takes two, three, four hours, a week, to respond. Their excuse is no vehicles, but some are drunk on duty, or they don't answer the phone. And if you speak a little hard to these people you are accused of racism.... We don't see anything from the rural protection plan. We pay ourselves to protect ourselves against criminals."[632]

And yet the same group of people, when asked to tell of particular cases where the police had been slow in responding, were unable to do so. Of seven "farm attacks" since the beginning of the year, at least four had resulted in arrests. One farmer, who had been the victim of a violent burglary, stated that he "couldn't fault" the police in their response:

> We were attacked by persons unknown. They waited for us to drive off the farm and then held us up on the road and forced us to drive back to the house and open the doors. We opened the safe and everything, and then they tied us with wire. They were dressed military style; one in brown, another in uniform. When we got free we radioed a neighbor. The neighbor came over and alerted other neighbors, the police, commandos, everyone. But by that time they had got away, and nobody was caught. The neighbor was there in five minutes, the police dog unit in about half an hour, and the last police about two hours later.[633]

Even where there is recognition of policing efforts among white farmers, there is a strong sense that the criminal justice system generally is failing: "The police and the commandos are overwhelmed, they try their best and we are grateful, but then if a suspect is caught he does a short period and then is out again. There may be arrests, but there are too few convictions, and they stay there too

---

[631] Human Rights Watch interview with Sannet Haasbroek, Beaufort Vallei Sekuriteit, Northern Province, March 28, 2000.
[632] Human Rights Watch interview with members of the Northern Natal commando, Vryheid, September 14, 2000.
[633] Ibid.

little time."[634] In other cases, victims of violent crime commented that the police responded professionally enough in the first case, but then little was done to find the perpetrators if they were not caught at the scene:

> It took us about half an hour to untie ourselves. The phone lines had been cut. They hadn't been able to start my wife's car, so I took it and phoned the police from a neighbor. They were here very quickly, within half an hour. They were very professional, I must say, we were well handled. I guess because we are high profile people around here. They took a lot of statements. But we've heard nothing since then. I've phoned a couple of times, but they say they are still investigating, and the firearms have not been recovered.... They never even spoke to my workers. I have the feeling that they felt that they'd done their duty when they came and took the statements. The initial response was good, but then there was no follow up; they didn't even take up the offer of my wife, who is an artist with a very good visual memory, to draw up an ID kit.[635]

The high arrest rate in cases of violence against farm owners is seen as little comfort: "What concerns us about the farm attacks is the justice system. In over 90 percent of cases the perpetrators get caught, but then what is worrying are the escapes and the cases not being followed through. The absence of a deterrent factor of being caught and punished is worrying."[636]

In this context, many feel it is understandable if farmers take direct action outside the structures of the criminal justice system. Responding to a survey of commercial farmers conducted on behalf of Agri-SA in early 2001, 65 percent "agreed" or "wholeheartedly agreed" with the statement that "famers will take the law into their own hands if farm murders are not curbed."[637] Graham McIntosh, when president of KWANALU, commented in an interview that, "What is needed is not just that the government should provide greater security and the rule of law in the countryside but that it should provide leadership and education.... It is simply irresponsible for them to say nothing or to half justify what is going on. You can't

---

[634] Human Rights Watch interview with Jack Loggenberg, TAU, Pretoria, April 17, 2000.

[635] Human Rights Watch interview, Bapsfontein, Gauteng, September 19, 2000.

[636] Human Rights Watch interview with Peter Southey, KWANALU, April 4, 2000.

[637] Summary of March 2001 Markinor survey commissioned by *Landbouweekblad*, the magazine of Agri-SA, among 405 randomly selected readers of the magazine.

be surprised if farmers take the law into their own hands in such circumstances."[638] Though deploring such responses, McIntosh said he could understand why "many people will simply shoot first and ask questions afterwards," adding that "farmers can get away with this now if they simply say that the man was attacking them. The police will lay charges, of course, but on the charge sheet they will put down self-defense and nothing much will happen."[639] Individual farmers have been even more forthright: "We must run after them because next time they will come back and kill us.... Let me tell you, if there is someone to be caught I will help to catch him, and if he is running away I will shoot him."[640] Several farm owners stated that cases alleging assault against farm owners seemed to be more enthusiastically prosecuted than those against the person assaulted, accused of committing a crime: "There was a case where poachers were caught redhanded. They were assaulted, which is wrong. But then the poaching case was dropped, and the assault case continued."[641] One Vryheid farmer seemed genuinely bemused that he had been charged with assault when, after some "gentle persuasion," a young man resident on the farm that he said was known to be a thief confessed to stealing from the farm shop but complained to police about his treatment. Another asked, "What is an assault? If we discipline our children, is that assault? If we discipline our laborers, is that assault?"[642]

Others feel that the bill of rights in South Africa's constitution gives too many protections to those suspected of perpetrating crime: "You can protect yourself only if your life is threatened, if there is no other way but to shoot, and in the South African situation with isolated farmhouses it is very difficult to abide by the law.... The law is in favor of the criminal, not the ordinary citizen."[643] In one case, two people had been caught after they broke into a farmhouse. Both of them escaped out of prison and within a month went back to the same place and robbed

---

[638] Interview with Graham McIntosh, (then) president of the KwaZulu-Natal Agricultural Union, published in *Briefing* 12, (Johannesburg: Helen Suzman Foundation, September 1998).

[639] Ibid.

[640] Farm owner Willie Kuhn, Groot Marico, North West Province, quoted in Tangeni Amupadhi, "No defence like self-defence," *Mail and Guardian* July 17-23, 1998.

[641] Human Rights Watch interview with Mike de Lange, formerly KWANALU security desk, Eshowe, September 14, 2000.

[642] Human Rights Watch interview with members of the Northern Natal commando, Vryheid, September 14, 2000.

[643] Human Rights Watch interview with Pieter Basson, farmer and farmwatch coordinator, Bapsfontein, September 19, 2000.

it again, taking the safe while the owners were away. Only one was rearrested. "The criminals see that whatever they do they will pretty much get away with it."[644] This belief, shared by many South Africans, has led to the rise of vigilante groups such as Mapogo a Mathamaga. In October 1998, as part of a nationwide week of protest, KWANALU handed a petition to the KwaZulu-Natal secretary for safety and security, calling for a state of emergency or proclamation of martial law, and arguing that criminals enjoyed unprecedented rights in terms of the constitution, while victims' rights were ignored.[645]

Perhaps the deepest concern of farm owners is a sense that, despite the Rural Safety Summit and other assurances from the government, they have effectively been abandoned by the new non-racial democracy. White farmers interviewed by Human Rights Watch repeatedly complained that the government paid more attention to "isolated" assaults on farmworkers rather than ongoing white deaths:

> There is a perception of racism in the government's response to farm attacks. Even for minor incidents on farms where the victim is black the minister will go and visit, but there have been 924 white farmers murdered since 1991 and the minister has never visited.   Not responding to these attacks means a condonation of what is happening.... We launched a campaign to 'stop farm attacks' earlier this year and asked the government to condemn farm murders, but there have done nothing since the October 1998 plan of action, which is just a piece of paper.... If they do have the opportunity they say it is wrong, but then they also say farm owners must stop torturing laborers, and we think it is just a predetermined piece of propaganda. The government is now in power and must be there for all its citizens, but we see they are there for their supporters only.[646]

---

[644] Human Rights Watch interview with members of the Northern Natal commando, Vryheid, September 14, 2000.

[645] Transcript of transmission on Radio Sonder Grense, October 1, 1998, available on <www.agriinfo.co.za/>, accessed October 6, 2000.

[646] Human Rights Watch interview with Jack Loggenberg and Boela Niemann, TAU, Pretoria, September 19, 2000. The figure of 924 murders is based on a combination of police and agricultural union statistics, and is problematic, as noted above.

In February 2001, labor minister Membathisi Mdladlana was strongly criticized by opposition parties for warning farmers in a comment shown on television to "adapt or die," which they asserted could be interpreted as hate speech, against the background of violent crime against farm owners. The Democratic Alliance said that "under the circumstances, Minister Mdladlana's statement can only be seen as an instigation for farm killings."[647]

Yet the ANC has issued statements condemning violent crime against farm owners. The October 1998 Rural Safety Summit was a more high profile response to "farm attacks" than any similar initiative focusing on black farm residents. Although government officials have condemned assaults on farm residents, they have also continued to speak out on violent crime against farm owners. In September 2000, for example, the Western Cape ANC stated, following the killing of a farmer in Klapmuts, that the party was "deeply shocked at yet another killing and robbery of a farmer in our province." After calling on the community to assist in finding the killers, the statement went on "The ANC is deeply concerned at attacks on farmers in our province. The whole issue of security for our people on the platteland needs urgent attention. We need to join hands with those in the landbou [agricultural] sector and develop new ways of creating a safe environment. The decisions taken at the national summit on farm security must be actively implemented."[648] Similarly, in October 2000, Minister of Agriculture and Land Affairs Thoko Didiza addressed the Agri-SA annual congress and called on landowners to work with the government to create sustainable rural communities and end arbitrary evictions. "Let us with equal vigour denounce the continuing farm killings that are overtaking our country. Farm murders and evictions show a lack of recognition of another's dignity and humanity."[649] Deputy President Jacob Zuma stated in response to an October 2000 parliamentary question that the government continued to take very seriously the issue of violent crime against farm owners, and condemned racist and inflammatory statements by any politician.[650] In November 2000, safety and security minister Steve Tshwete stated, in response to allegations that the government gave higher priority to white police brutality against blacks than to the murder of commercial farmers, that "we are deeply worried about this wave of

---

[647] "Minister slammed for 'inciting farm killings,'" AFP, February 7, 2001.
[648] "ANC calls on Klapmuts community to find farm killers," Statement issued by ANC Western Cape, September 25, 2000.
[649] "Release affordable, quality land, Didiza asks farmers," SAPA, October 5, 2000.
[650] "Farm attacks still high on agenda: Zuma," SAPA October 4, 2000.

farm murders. We want to warn the perpetrators that we are going to pursue them vigorously, wherever they want to hide."[651]

In January 2001, Tshwete agreed to commission further independent research into the motives behind crime against farm owners, and in April 2001 a former attorney-general of the Northern Cape was appointed to chair a seven-person committee investigating such crime.[652] While this announcement was welcomed by Agri-SA, the Transvaal Agricultural Union threatened again that farmers would take "drastic action" to protect themselves if the government did not stop murders of farm owners.[653] In February 2001, Tshwete announced to parliament that the government would purchase four new helicopters to fight rural crime, and expand the capacity of the commandos. The announcement was welcomed by Agri-SA, though TAU said that only security forces on the ground could stop murders being committed.[654]

The Legal Aid Board Crisis

Many farm residents have been unable to benefit from the laws intended to protect them from eviction and give them other rights because they cannot afford or otherwise obtain legal assistance. South Africa has a legal aid system, administered by the Legal Aid Board, an independent statutory body established under the Legal Aid Act (No. 22 of 1969). In recent years, the system has virtually collapsed, though efforts to revive it are just beginning to be put into effect.

Before 1994, the expenditure of the Legal Aid Board was, like other government expenditure, mostly directed to white recipients. After 1994, the demands on the system increased substantially, as South Africans invoked constitutional rights to legal representation at state expense, when they are in detention or accused of a crime, "if substantial injustice would otherwise result." In most cases, the board paid private legal practitioners to represent individuals on a case by case basis (known as the "judicare" system); though there have also been experiments with a public defender system, and support to legal aid clinics at universities. By 1998, the Legal Aid Board was in crisis, weighed down by increasing demands on legal aid funds and suffering administrative collapse. In

---

[651] "Government remains worried about farm killings: Tshwete," SAPA, November 11, 2000.

[652] "Tshwete agrees to farm attack probe," SAPA, January 17, 2001; "Former A-G to head farm attacks probe," SAPA, April 5, 2001.

[653] "Farmers threaten vigilante action," SAPA, January 30, 2001.

[654] Allan Seccombe, "Police put brakes on farm killings," Reuters, February 15, 2001; "Helicopters for rural crime: Agri-SA happy, TAU not," SAPA, February 14, 2001.

January 1998, a "national legal aid transformation forum" convened by the minister of justice recommended the appointment of a "legal aid transformation team" to propose long term reform. In the meantime, the forum recommended that the amount spent on legal aid through the judicare system be substantially reduced, and that a national infrastructure of legal aid centers be established as soon as possible to replace the expensive and inefficient judicare process. The transformation team subsequently endorsed these recommendations. As a crisis measure the Legal Aid Board decided in November 1999 to make severe cuts in the rates paid for legal aid work, to a level most lawyers considered uneconomic. Other accounts submitted by lawyers were simply not paid.

In late 2000, the government finally approved the appointment of a new chief executive officer and other management positions at the board. The new officers, who started work in February 2001, have the brief to establish the proposed national system of legal assistance for the poor through one-stop "justice centers."[655] The first of these centers opened in Benoni, Gauteng, in February 2001; the first in a rural area in Phuthaditjhaba in the eastern Free State in April 2001.[656] However, the justice centers will handle mainly criminal matters, and a ceiling of 15 percent has been placed on the amount of civil work (including eviction cases) that each center is authorized to handle.[657]

The virtual collapse in the legal aid system has severely affected farm residents faced with eviction, as many lawyers have not been prepared to take cases under the Extension of Security of Tenure Act and the Labour Tenants Act. Those organizations that are still able to offer some assistance since they have other sources of funding, such as the Legal Resources Centre, an NGO, are swamped.[658] Officials working for the Department of Land Affairs have also come under pressure. "The legal aid crisis has had a huge impact. The inability to act once people have been informed of their rights by DLA campaigns has meant that a far heavier burden has fallen on DLA officials; we have acquired a paralegal function in adjudicating cases, for lack of any other alternative. People start distrusting government because we can't do anything to protect their rights in practice. We

---

[655] Khadija Magardie, "Board's days as a cash cow are over," *Mail and Guardian*, February 2, 2001.

[656] "Govt-funded justice centre to serve poverty-stricken people," SAPA, February 7, 2001; "Justice centre launched in Phuthaditjhaba," SAPA, April 3, 2001.

[657] "Legal Aid Board: Annual Report," *Minutes of the Justice and Constitutional Development Portfolio Committee*, June 4, 2001.

[658] Human Rights Watch interview with Oupa Maake and Charles Pillai, Legal Resources Centre, Pretoria, April 10, 2000.

have set up training for lawyers on the land legislation, a legal roster; everything is in place. But we are constrained by finance."[659] According to those supporting farm residents facing eviction, farm owners have taken advantage of the collapse of the legal aid system to carry out illegal evictions: "Since the farmers have seen that the Legal Aid is no longer helping the workers they have been pushing to evict people. Innocent people with no homes are driven out."[660]

The South African Human Rights Commission and the Commission on Gender Equality

During the negotiations that led to South Africa's first elections on the basis of universal suffrage in April 1994 and the transition from a minority regime to a democratically elected government, much emphasis was placed on the need for new constitutional arrangements to ensure that the human rights abuses of South Africa's past could not be repeated. The interim constitution, which was adopted in December 1993 and came into force following the elections, accordingly provided for the establishment of a range of bodies to monitor government compliance with human rights standards. Chapter 9 of the final constitution, which was drafted by the parliament elected in 1994 sitting as a constitutional assembly and came into force in February 1997, confirmed the position of the South African Human Rights Commission (SAHRC) as one of the "state institutions supporting constitutional democracy," along with the Commission on Gender Equality, and other bodies.[661]

The Human Rights Commission Act, No. 54 of 1994, came into force in September 1995 and the commission held its inaugural meeting in October 1995.[662]

---

[659] Human Rights Watch interview with Domini Lewis, KwaZulu-Natal Department of Land Affairs, April 7, 2000.

[660] Human Rights Watch interview with member of the Ingogo Crisis Committee, Ingogo, KwaZulu-Natal, April 7, 2000.

[661] See the chapter on South Africa in Human Rights Watch, *Protectors or Pretenders? Government Human Rights Commission in Africa* (New York: Human Rights Watch, 2001).

[662] Article 184 of the Constitution of the Republic of South Africa 1996 states that the Human Rights Commission must: "(a) promote respect for human rights and a culture of human rights; (b) promote the protection, development and attainment of human rights; and (c) monitor and assess the observance of human rights in the Republic." It must also each year "require relevant organs of state to provide the Commission with information on the measures that they have taken towards the realisation of the rights in the Bill of Rights concerning housing, health care, food, water, social security, education and the environment." In fulfilment of its mandate to promote and monitor respect for human rights, the commission may investigate abuses, take steps to secure redress, including bringing

The Commission on Gender Equality (CGE) was formally established on April 1, 1997.[663] In accordance with their constitutional independence, both the SAHRC and the CGE report their findings directly to parliament. Most other government-funded local and provincial women's programs, for example, report rather to the Office on the Status of Women (OSW) in the office of the president.[664]

Among other issues, the SAHRC has examined the failure of the criminal justice system to protect the rights of particularly vulnerable groups of people in South Africa, including farmworkers. In an initiative led by the South African National NGO Coalition (Sangoco), the SAHRC and the Commission on Gender Equality held hearings on poverty throughout the country in early 1998. Following on from the poverty hearings, the SAHRC held hearings in August and November 1998 in the Messina area of Northern Province about abuse of farm workers in the region. In February 1999, it released a report in which it referred several cases to the provincial director of public prosecutions for further action.[665] The report was, however, criticized by NGOs for being too legalistic, rather than examining the

---

court cases, and carry out human rights education. It may subpoena witnesses, and has called cabinet ministers before it; it also has powers of search and seizure, though these have not yet been used. On pain of criminal penalty, all organs of state at all levels are obliged to render such reasonable assistance to the commission as it may require in order to carry out its tasks. However, it has no power to enforce its recommendations, or even to require a response.

[663] Article 187 of the Constitution of the Republic of South Africa 1996, states that its functions are: "(1) to monitor and evaluate policies and practices of government, the private sector, and other organizations to ensure that they protect and promote gender equality; (2) to engage in disseminating information and education on gender equality; (3) to commission research and make recommendations to parliament or other bodies on policies and laws affecting women; and (4) to receive and investigate complaints on any gender related discrimination; and monitor and report on government compliance with international treaties relating to the rights of women."

[664] Unlike the CGE, the Office on the Status of Women is a government structure tasked to serve government departments. It is responsible for formulating and implementing gender policies within the government and monitoring and evaluating the impact of these policies and programmes. For details on the OSW, see South Africa's first report (1997) on its obligations under CEDAW, available at <www.polity.org.za/govdocs/ >, accessed February 7, 2001. Also, see Vetten, "Paper Promises, Protests and Petitions," in Park et al, *Reclaiming Women's Spaces*, p.93.

[665] *Investigation of Alleged Violations of Farmworkers' Rights in the Messina/Tshipise District*, Report of the South African Human Rights Commission, (Johannesburg: February 1999)

systemic issues under consideration.[666] In June 2001, the commission launched a year-long national enquiry into the human rights situation in farming communities.[667]

The CGE has produced a "Working Women's Manual," a publication that targets domestic workers and women farmworkers who are within the lowest paid sectors of formal employment.[668] In 1999, the CGE worked with the Centre for Rural Legal Studies to assess the government's compliance with CEDAW in relation to the labor rights of women farmworkers in the Western Cape, and carried out similar studies in KwaZulu-Natal and Northern Province.[669] However, the CGE was unable to complete this joint survey, due to budgetary constraints and internal difficulties within the commission.[670] In an interview with Human Rights Watch, the CGE's deputy chairperson commented that rape of women farmworkers by farm owners is "a layer of abuse that tends to be ignored," but that the commission was prevented by lack of resources from giving it the attention it deserves.[671] As of September 2001, the CGE had five provincial offices, including Gauteng. Most of the provincial offices were seriously understaffed and could not function properly in accomplishing their expected goals.[672]

---

[666] *Protectors or Pretenders?*, p.309.

[667] "SAHRC launches inquiry into human rights in farming communities on 11 June," Suoth African Human Rights Commissoin, June 6, 2001; Human Rights Watch interview with Charlotte McClain, commissioner, SAHRC, February 12, 2001.

[668] See the CGE's website at: <http://www.cge.org.za/publications/legal.html>, accessed October 12, 2000.

[669] Human Rights Watch interview, vice chairperson, Commission on Gender Equality, September 6, 2000. Angela Motsa, "Women on Farms Report: Northern Province," and "Women on Farms Report: KwaZulu-Natal Province," Commission on Gender Equality, October 1999.

[670] Human Rights Watch interview, CGE, Johannesburg, April, 2000. *See* also Lisa Vetten, "Paper Promises, Protests and Petitions," Park et al, *Reclaiming Women's Spaces*, p.93, on some of the challenges currently facing the CGE.

[671] Human Rights Watch interview, deputy chairperson, Commission on Gender Equality, September 6, 2000.

[672] Ibid.

CASE STUDY: THE GREATER IXOPO AREA

Events in the greater Ixopo area in 1999 and 2000 illustrate some of the complex connections that can exist between violent crime, a response from the security forces and farmers that appears to cater to the needs of only one section of the community, and assaults on farm residents. Ixopo is a small KwaZulu-Natal town about eighty kilometers south of Pietermaritzburg, probably most famous as the setting for Alan Paton's novel *Cry the Beloved Country*. It is home to about 15,000 residents, and some 300,000 people live in the surrounding areas of Highflats, Creighton, and Donnybrook, many of them in communities that were formerly part of the KwaZulu homeland. The greater Ixopo area experienced serious political violence during the period leading up to South Africa's first non-racial election in 1994,[673] but was relatively quiet following the elections. There is not a long history of soldiers operating in the area. Since 1999 this situation has changed.

Violent Crime Against Farm Owners

Although the Ixopo/Creighton area has not been one of the worst for violent crime against white farmers, the farming community there, as elsewhere in South Africa, feels itself under severe pressure. There are constant concerns about stock theft or land invasion, as well as theft of items such as fencing, and there are always fears that such criminal activities could lead to murders.[674]

In late 1999, two white farmers were murdered. Malcolm Macfarlane, fifty-five, was killed at his farmhouse near Ixopo in October. Two men broke in and shot Macfarlane dead, who had apparently startled them.[675] Eight days later twenty-eight-year-old Bruce Mack was ambushed on a farm road and shot twice in the back of the head. His firearm was stolen, but the killers left his wallet and

---

[673] For example, on February 18, 1994, fifteen ANC youths (twelve of them under eighteen years old) were killed in the village of Mahlele near Creighton. See Human Rights Watch, "Threats to a New Democracy: Continuing Violence in KwaZulu-Natal," *A Human Rights Watch Short Report*, May 1995.

[674] According to one farmer, six of the nine white farmers in one district have been attacked or come close to being attacked over the last few years. Among other incidents reported: a farm manager survived a stabbing and a shooting; a farmer's son narrowly missed being shot; another farm manager survived a stabbing; and a store owner aged about seventy years was shot during an attempted ambush and survived but left the area. Interview with Dave Mack conducted by Cheryl Goodenough in April 2000.

[675] Wilton Mthethwa, "Burglars murder Ixopo farmer," *Natal Witness*, October 2, 1999.

mobile phone in the vehicle.[676] Bruce Mack's father, Dave Mack, had recently bought a farm in the Highflats area and had been in dispute with the people living on the farm over the conditions on which they could continue to stay there. Dave Mack later suggested that Bruce's murder might be connected with the release on bail of a man arrested for threatening Dave four days earlier.[677]

The farmers of the Ixopo area were "furious" about the murders, according to the president of the KwaZulu-Natal Agricultural Union, Fred Visser, who commented that some were on the brink of taking the law into their own hands, and "if that happens there will be a war."[678] The farmers called a meeting of the farming community on October 20, 1999, attended by KwaZulu-Natal agriculture minister Narend Singh and provincial police commissioner Chris Serfontein. The farmers threatened to withhold regional council levies and taxes unless effective action was taken to curb killings and crime.[679] KwaZulu-Natal Minister for Safety and Security Nyanga Ngubane was also invited to attend the meeting and his failure to appear further raised the ire of farmers.[680]

Police detectives arrested suspects in both cases. Twenty-year-old Bonile Mkhize was alleged to have been one of the triggermen during the attack on Bruce Mack. The other man arrested was Mpekiswa Shezi, who allegedly gave the instructions for the murder to be carried out and took the firearms afterwards.[681] The two men were kept in custody for several months, but were later released for lack of evidence, after police shot dead a third suspect in May 2000.[682] Two

---

[676] Interview with Dave Mack conducted by Cheryl Goodenough in April 2000; Ingrid Oellermann, "Farmers enraged over latest murder," *Natal Mercury*, October 13, 1999.

[677] Reginald Khumalo, "Farmers' boycott threat," *Natal Witness*, October 21, 1999. Mack said that his investigations subsequent to Bruce's murder showed that there was "no tolerance for the white farmer." He was warned not to travel alone after the attack and employed an ex-soldier as his bodyguard. Interview conducted with Dave Mack by Cheryl Goodenough in April 2000.

[678] Ingrid Oellerman, "Farmers enraged over latest murder," *Natal Mercury*, October 13, 2000.

[679] Reginald Khumalo, "Farmers' boycott threat," *Natal Witness*, October 21, 1999.

[680] C.B. Lea-Cox (Colonel), managing director, Ixopo Farm Watch, "Minister lets down Ixopo farmers," *Natal Witness*, October 26, 1999.

[681] Telephone interview by Cheryl Goodenough with the original investigating officer Andre Vorster, in about May 2000.

[682] The police officers on the scene claimed that Mbaba Shezi (the son of Mpekiswa Shezi) was arrested and then said that he could show them a gun that he allegedly returned to his father after committing the murder. He could not find the gun that was alleged to be buried in the ground and then told the police that he could produce another weapon that was used

suspects were also arrested for the Macfarlane murder, but also released for lack of evidence against them.

The murders brought to a head complaints from many farmers in the Highflats/Ixopo area that the police were ineffective, complaints not followed up, and proactive policing non-existent.

The Ixopo Community/Farm Watch

Even before these murders, farmers had established the Ixopo Farm Watch, in May 1997, because of a lack of confidence in the police. As described by farmer Roger Foster in a letter published in the *Mail and Guardian*:

> The police were, at best, ineffectual—they were under-equipped, undermanned, poorly trained and totally unmotivated. There was no response to complaints, no investigation of crimes, no records of any value and normally no police vehicle—at any of the four police stations in the district. Crime was rampant and becoming worse. Theft of vehicles, livestock, crops, fences, machinery and so on had reached levels where it was becoming difficult to farm. In certain areas it was impossible to keep cattle or grow crops. The farmers of the area decided to do something to remedy the situation before it deteriorated further. Farm Watch was started to provide the police with vehicles and basic equipment, an office with a phone, a computerised database of criminal incidents and additional personnel. Finally one could phone in a complaint, get an intelligible reply and expect an immediate response. Since then, the service from the police has continued to decline, there is still significant loss from theft,

---

by Bonile Mkhize in the murder. Mkhize had been arrested in April. The police allege that after digging in the ground, Shezi threw the pick that he was using at the police and took a buried gun out of a bag, pointed it at the police, and, when he cocked the weapon, was shot and killed by the policemen. This case is being investigated by the Independent Complaints Directorate, and the original investigating officer in the Mack murder case, Andre Vorster, who was allegedly involved in the shooting, has been suspended from the police as a result of being charged in a corruption matter unrelated to this case. Telephonic interview conducted by Cheryl Goodenough in May 2000; Cheryl Goodenough, "Murder suspect shot and killed by police," *Natal Witness*, May 5, 2000.

particularly stock theft and there have been two farmers killed, but at least we are doing something about it.[683]

Later renamed the Ixopo Community Watch, to reflect its management "considered we had a role to play in the protection of the community as a whole,"[684] the organization now operates in four police districts—Ixopo, Creighton, Donnybrook, and Highflats. It has nine full-time employees, a twenty-four hour operations room, and an annual budget of some R750,000 (U.S.$99,000), largely derived from fees paid by farmers and local timber companies. The employees include several former police officers, and all operational staff are police reservists by company policy, giving them full powers as policemen while on duty.[685]

After the two murders, this response was apparently felt to be inadequate, and soldiers were also deployed in April 2000. From April 17, the thirty-man strong Umkomaas commando, based at Ixopo and responsible to SANDF Group 9, Pietermaritzburg, conducted regular patrols throughout the greater Ixopo area.[686] According to the police, the patrols were "intelligence driven" and had "remarkable success" while enjoying "the support of the communities as a whole."[687] The managing director of Ixopo Community/Farm Watch described the deployment as "highly effective in the recovery of illegal firearms and the arrests of known criminals."[688]

---

[683] Roger Foster, Stainton, Ixopo, "Two sides to every story," a letter published in the *Mail and Guardian*, September 15 to 21, 2000. The letter was written in response to the article by Cheryl Goodenough, "Vigilantes terrorise farm workers," *Mail and Guardian*, September 8 to 14, 2000.

[684] Letter dated September 13, 2000, from Col. C.B. Lea-Cox, managing director, Ixopo Community Watch, to the *Mail and Guardian*, and supplied to Human Rights Watch by the author. The letter was written in response to the article by Cheryl Goodenough, "Vigilantes terrorise farm workers," *Mail and Guardian*, September 8 to 14, 2000.

[685] Interview conducted by Cheryl Goodenough with the managing director of the Ixopo Community/Farm Watch, former army colonel Clive Lea-Cox, in approximately April 2000.

[686] Letter dated August 1, 2000, from Assistant Commissioner P.F. Holloway, Office of the Area Commissioner, Umzimkulu, to Mary de Haas.

[687] Ibid.

[688] Letter dated September 13, 2000, from Col. C.B. Lea-Cox, managing director, Ixopo Community Watch, to the *Mail and Guardian*.

Assaults on Farm Residents and Others

Although farmers may have felt more secure, the local black population was subject to increased harassment and abuse as a result of the army patrols. By the end of 2000, according to the Independent Complaints Directorate, at least sixteen cases of assault were being investigated against soldiers and police in the Ixopo area.[689] Members of the Community/Farm Watch, accompanying the soldiers in their role as police reservists, were implicated in several of the cases.[690]

These cases largely arose from raids carried out on the homes of black farm residents and dwellers in former homeland settlements in search of illegal firearms. A raid conducted on May 30, 2000, involved men in uniform who said they were police and army members but who were allegedly wearing no identification tabs, and two of whom were wearing balaclavas. They searched the home of the Zulu family at eHlani, Creighton, without a warrant, and claimed to be looking for Thabiso Zulu, a young community leader whom they described as "dangerous." They found no firearms. Independent violence monitor Mary de Haas wrote to the police:

> It is alleged that other houses were searched that night, and some people were beaten by these men and have opened cases at the local station. It is further alleged that these security force members have a list of people they are targeting, and that these people just happen to be deemed to be 'ANC' (Thabiso Zulu is not active in the ANC at present). Some security force members (some in camouflage, others in civilian clothes) returned to the area on Thursday 1 June and visited the home of the girlfriend

---

[689] According to the KwaZulu-Natal director of the Independent Complaints Directorate (ICD), Advocate S'thembiso "Stix" Mdladla, the ICD was by September 2000 following up about six cases of assault involving soldiers and four involving police members, all opened at the Creighton Police Station. Additional dockets had been opened at the Ixopo, Highflats, and Donnybrook Police Stations. An estimated six cases were being investigated by detectives based at the Ixopo Police Station. Interview by Cheryl Goodenough with the Independent Complaints Directorate in Creighton, September 6, 2000. See also, Cheryl Goodenough, "Vigilantes terrorise farm workers," *Mail and Guardian*, September 8 to 14, 2000. It is not known whether the victims were all farm workers.

[690] Since these incidents, the police management in the Umzimkulu policing area, that includes Ixopo, have issued an instruction that full-time police officers, and not only reservists must be present when soldiers go on operations. Interviews with several police officers in Ixopo and Port Shepstone conducted by Cheryl Goodenough, August and September 2000.

of Thabiso Zulu. He was not there and they allegedly said they would be returning and made veiled threats to her. I have checked with the local police station, including the station commissioner and they disclaim any knowledge of these activities.[691]

In a subsequent letter to the authorities, de Haas wrote that:

raids by members of the SANDF have continued in this area, with serious allegations being made about damage to property and a variety of human rights abuses. Cases have been opened with the local SAPS. There seems little doubt that, amongst those participating in these illegal activities are members of commando/Farmwatch units.[692]

Similar cases from around the same time were also covered in the Johannesburg *Sunday Times*. According to reported interviews with eyewitnesses, soldiers had beaten and tortured a number of people during a three-week operation in Creighton.

Mzwandile Mdladla, 47, this week told how soldiers beat on his door at 1.55 am and demanded that he hand over an AK47. 'There were about eight of them. They dragged me outside and beat me. They kicked me with their boots. My hands were tied behind my back and a rubber was put over my face ... a tyre tube,' said Mdladla. 'The soldiers said they were looking for the gun belonging to Linda Xaba, the son of the induna [headman]. I told them I knew nothing about it. But they kept on hitting me. It went on until they left at 5.20 am. But they said they were going to come back.' He said the soldiers assaulted him on three occasions. The second time they beat him and drove him around

---

[691] Letter dated June 2, 2000, from Mary de Haas to the Area Commissioner, SAPS Umzimkulu, Port Shepstone and to the Officer Commanding, Natal Command, Durban. According to De Haas, based in the Department of Social Anthropology at the University of Natal Durban, a case of malicious damage to property was opened at the Creighton Police Station (case number 01/06/2000) as a result of the search.

[692] Letter dated June 28, 2000, from Mary de Haas to the Officer Commanding, SANDF, Natal Command, Durban.

the village in a Casspir. A few days later, he alleged, they returned to his house and again beat him. 'There were 13 soldiers this time. They told me to dig holes all over my garden. I was even made to dig in the graveyard. But they found no guns.' They tied his hands behind his back and put his head into a bag filled with water. 'I couldn't breathe. They hit me again. I kept telling them that I didn't have any guns.' The soldiers then took him to the home of the induna [headman], Magesini Xaba, who is now the acting chief of the area. 'They beat him very badly and kicked him all over the place,' said Mdladla. Thabiso Zulu, the secretary of a local community-based organisation, has been documenting the midnight raids, beatings and torture. Two weeks ago, his house was also raided and soldiers stomped on his expensive camera equipment.[693]

Another victim was assaulted in Sibizane near Creighton:

The police just arrived here and asked for my younger brother. I don't know how many people there were, but there were two police vans and the NU Farm Watch bakkie [pick up truck].[694] They started to beat me with an open hand, kicking me. They said that they were looking for guns that my younger brother had. Then they just moved away. Afterwards they arrested my two brothers. They were taken to the police station. One was released on the same day. The other has been detained. I've heard they opened a case, but I'm not clear what it is about.[695]

Writing to violence monitor Mary de Haas, Assistant Area Commissioner P.F. Holloway of the Umzimkulu policing area stated that the soldiers involved in the raids carried out on May 30 were from the Eastern Cape, even though they were operating within an area that falls under the KwaZulu-Natal SANDF. Moreover,

---

[693] Ranjeni Munusamy, "SANDF soldiers tortured us, claim villagers," *Sunday Times KZN Metro*, July 2, 2000.

[694] Community/Farm Watch employee John Arkley drives a vehicle with a registration containing the letters NU before a number. It is suspected that this is the vehicle to which the victim was referring.

[695] Interview with the victim conducted by Cheryl Goodenough assisted by an interpreter, Sibizane, September 6, 2000.

"The raids conducted in the Creighton area were done without the knowledge or consent of the station Commissioner, Creighton. The presence of the SANDF members in the Creighton area was also not reported by the SANDF to the Station Commissioner, Creighton.... at no stage were the SAPS of KwaZulu-Natal involved or had any prior knowledge of the operations conducted by the SANDF in the Creighton area."[696] Eight cases of assault and damage to property were registered at the Creighton police station following the raids, which "it would appear" were prompted by "Military Intelligence information about a large number of Illegal Arms hidden in the area. No firearms were, however, handed in at the Creighton Police Station."[697] In the case of other raids carried out at around the same time it is not clear, however, as to which army unit was involved. Police involved in investigating the cases lodged against soldiers have struggled to get information from the SANDF, including copies of the reports listing the people deployed on each patrol.[698]

These raids on the areas around Ixopo by the army, police and members of the Ixopo Community/Farm Watch culminated in the death of Basil Jaca, a farm resident in his mid-thirties who reportedly worked with a building contractor. Jaca died on July 2, 2000, the day after he was allegedly sodomized with a rifle during a raid for illegal firearms carried out by the Umkomaas commando accompanied by a member of the Ixopo Community/Farm Watch. The raid occurred at his house on Flaxton Farm, about five kilometers from Ixopo on the road to Donnybrook and about one kilometer from the main road. Jaca and two others, Bhekani Hadebe and Zama Khambula, were assaulted with sticks, and it was alleged that soldiers pushed the rifle barrel up Jaca's anus and attempted to do the same with Hadebe.[699] Others were less badly assaulted. The police arrested six soldiers (five privates led by a corporal) and Community/Farm Watch employee Constable John Arkley, a police

---

[696] Letter dated August 1, 2000, from Assistant Commissioner P.F. Holloway, Office of the Area Commissioner, Umzimkulu, to Mary de Haas.

[697] Ibid.

[698] Telephonic interview by Cheryl Goodenough with policeman from Ixopo Police Station, November 13, 2000.

[699] Ibid.; Eric Ndiyane, "Residents tortured by army: seven soldiers arrested," *Daily News* (Durban), July 10, 2000.

reservist and Ixopo resident, about five days after the attack.[700] All seven were charged with murder, attempted murder, and assault.

Arkley was granted bail of R3,000 (U.S.$395) on July 6, 2000; a separate bail hearing for the soldiers was held on July 17 and 19, 2000.[701] During the bail application for the soldiers, which was not opposed by the state, police captain Bongani Sibiya said that, according to the evidence, the assault had taken place at about 6 am on a Saturday morning. The six soldiers and Arkley allegedly arrived at Flaxton farm in an army vehicle and an unmarked pick-up truck. He stated that the accused visited two groups of homes about 500 meters apart and were reported to have assaulted people at both places. He said that witnesses accused Arkley and Corporal Brandon Eldridge of observing the assaults or being present when they were carried out. In Jaca's case, one soldier allegedly kept Jaca's wife outside their house at gunpoint, while the other four soldiers took Jaca inside.

Ixopo police inspector Zibuse Gwala told the court that there was no direct evidence that the barrel of a firearm had been pushed into Jaca's anus. However, he said that tests had been conducted and that a sample of a substance believed to be feces had been found on the barrel of a gun and sent for testing. Forensic tests were also being conducted on a jacket belonging to a member of the public that was allegedly used at the scene of the crime to wipe feces off the firearm. Inspector Gwala said that Jaca's wife was called after the assault to wash her husband and found him bleeding from the mouth and anus. He said that on his first visit to speak to Jaca's wife, she was so traumatized that he could not even take a statement from her and that Jaca's family and other people living nearby were very frightened and "some are scared that the army members will come back and kill them." Platoon commander Brent Gerhardt testified that the operation on July 1,

---

[700] The soldiers were riflemen Bhekabantu Dlamini, aged twenty-seven, of Table Mountain; Mlungwana Ngcamu, twenty-four, of Glenwood; Reginald Mazibuko, twenty-six, of Sweetwaters; Sifiso Mlaba, twenty-seven, of Ashburton; Philani Ntombela, twenty-seven, of Imbali; and thirty-two-year-old Corporal Brandon Eldridge of Westville, Durban.

[701] The state did not oppose bail for Arkley or for the soldiers. However, a bail application is required under the law for such a serious offence. During the bail application for the soldiers, police captain Bongani Sibiya testified that Eldridge had a previous conviction relating to an assault that was committed in 1998. The other accused did not have previous convictions and were not facing other charges. The following account is taken from notes by Cheryl Goodenough, who attended the court proceedings at the Ixopo Magistrates' Court on July 17 and July 19, 2000. See also Bongani Mthethwa, "Soldiers linked to Ixopo killing," *Natal Witness*, July 7, 2000; Cheryl Goodenough "Ixopo residents 'scared' of soldiers," *Natal Witness*, July 18, 2000, and Cheryl Goodenough "Six Ixopo farm raid suspects refused bail," *Natal Witness*, July 20, 2000.

2000, had taken place with his knowledge, but that the army had done nothing to investigate the charges against the six soldiers.

The soldiers were refused bail by the magistrate, who stated that he was "bemused" that the state had not opposed bail despite community objections, and that was concerned that the state witnesses could be in danger because of the degree of violence implicit in the murder charge.[702] The magistrate said that he would reconsider his decision if the soldiers could be kept in the custody of the military police. When the soldiers appeared again on July 27 the magistrate granted the men R1,000 (U.S.$320) bail on condition that they were held at the military base in Pietermaritzburg. The seven have appeared in the Ixopo Magistrates' Court several times since they were granted bail, though the case has not yet been heard. Arkley was suspended from the farmwatch in January 2001 and later dismissed.

In March 2001, residents of the Creighton area were still reporting abuses during SANDF searches for illegal firearms.[703]

Community Response to Security Measures

The Basil Jaca case brought to a head discontent among residents of the greater Ixopo area at the police response to crime. Like the farmers, local black people feel that the police are ineffective in responding to criminal activity in their area. Yet the beefed up security force response has, for them, only increased insecurity. When the seven accused appeared in court on July 17, 2000, members of the community led by Ixopo mayor Themba Louis Mahlaba held a protest outside the Ixopo court building. In a memorandum handed to court officials, the community representatives stated:

> We, the residents of the town of Ixopo are complaining to the local police and Magistrate about the crime rate that has hit our area. Over the past two years there has been countless break-ins, car thefts, hijacking, rapes and all sorts of unlawful callous acts.

---

[702] When questioned about why the state had not opposed bail, police inspector Zibuse Gwala said that it was a decision taken by his superior, the head of detectives in the Umzimkulu policing area. When asked by the presiding magistrate whether he thought in hindsight that this was correct, Inspector Gwala said that he did not agree with the decision. See also, "Ixopo assault case: soldiers released on bail into military custody," *Natal Witness*, July 28, 2000.

[703] Eric Ndiyane, "Hundreds flee army's 'terror attacks' in KZN," *Daily News* (Durban), March 5, 2001.

Out of all these incidents there has been very few arrests. What are the local police doing about it? In July 1999, Mr Brian King was murdered in this town in cold blood by known criminals. The police effected an arrest but in two days after that criminals were walking free again. We demand to know as to how does the local Magistrates Court release them back into the community, criminal who are making life unbearable for the law abiding citizens of our country, residents in this town. In July 2000 a very young Sifiso Msomi was also brutally murdered. Once again their has been no arrests up to this point.[704] Again in July 2000, Mr Basil Jaca of Flaxton Farm was assaulted and sodomized with a gun until he died a very painful death by members of the SANDF who were in the company of local police. In principle we accept that the police and army have a mandate bestowed to them by the constitution to protect our people and country from its enemies including criminals. What we are opposed to is the brutality and barbarism that is employed in carrying out this noble mandate. The actions of the SANDF in this area are typical of those of a foreign army invading enemy land. The SANDF must be investigated and those who are not here to protect us must be removed and investigations must be carried out in all areas where the SANDF has been active and more assistance must be given to the police in their line of duty. We insist that the Reservist John Arkley be removed from the reservist. We demand that the local police show commitment to eradicating crime in this area and we are very serious about this. The drug problem in Ixopo was addressed to the police and this was never attended to either, as the problem is escalating, this is another very serious matter that has to be attended to.[705]

---

[704] According to Mayor Mhlaba, the same group of suspected gangsters are believed to have been behind the killing of King and Msomi. King was killed in his house and Msomi's body was found not far from his home after he disappeared during a family function. According to the police, two people were arrested for the Msomi case a month or two after the memorandum was handed to the court.

[705] Memorandum *March—Ixopo Community*, handed to court officials and read out during the court proceedings relating to the Basil Jaca case in the Ixopo Magistrates' Court on July 17, 2000. Spelling as in the original.

Mayor Mhlaba said that numerous incidents involving SANDF members had been reported to him. These included rape and theft of money. He said that many people were reporting incidents to community structures, but not to the police, who were seen to be part of the problem. The mayor said that the community wanted to work with the farmers, but that the community policing forum was non-existent.[706]

Despite the widespread reporting of the Jaca case, there have been further allegations of abuse by individuals connected to the Ixopo Community/Farm Watch.[707] Gqomoza Mbhele, said to be in his mid-20s, died in hospital on September 5, 2000, after being assaulted outside a Creighton bar on August 25. A witness to the assault, who feared being named, said that he was in the bar with Mbhele and his attacker, who was a police reservist employed by the Ixopo Community/Farm Watch:

> The suspect walked out and then I heard a commotion outside. I saw the suspect and another policeman assaulting a man. They were hitting him with a clenched fist, with an open hand and kicking him. They were trying to put him in the [police] van. Then they began to assault the deceased. They hit him with a clenched fist. He fell and they kicked him. Then they drove off. They came back after thirty minutes and took the deceased away.[708]

---

[706] Interview conducted by Cheryl Goodenough with Mayor Themba Louis Mahlaba outside the Ixopo Magistrates' Court, July 17, 2000.

[707] Writing to the police area commissioner on July 12, 2000 and on July 17, 2000, Mary de Haas stated that the pattern of abuse had continued subsequent to her earlier correspondence: "Credible local sources in the broad area in which these abuses have been occurring allege that those involved are *extremely racist* (e.g. conversations about black people not having minds have reportedly been overheard) *and virulently opposed to the government which, if they are army employees, pays their salaries.* In ways which are reminiscent of the worst excesses of apartheid, it seems that black surrogates are made use of in the infliction of harm to the numerous victims of these abuses." Letter dated July 17, 2000 from Mary de Haas to the Area Commissioner, SAPS Umzimkulu, Port Shepstone. Emphasis in the original.

[708] Interview conducted by Cheryl Goodenough, Creighton, September 6, 2000, interpreted from Zulu. See also Cheryl Goodenough, "Vigilantes terrorise farm workers," *Mail and Guardian*, September 8-14, 2000.

Advocate Mdladla, the head of the KwaZulu-Natal office of the Independent Complaints Directorate, stated that the police claimed that Mbhele and others had intervened in an attempt to prevent the arrest of a housebreaking suspect who was being put into the police vehicle. They claim that Mbhele had a fit, fell, and hit his head. Investigations into this case were continuing in November 2000.[709]

Although the creation of the Ixopo Community/Farm Watch may have increased a sense of security for farm owners, the result of the recent assaults seems to have been the further alienation of the black population in the area from the white farming community. As much as the Ixopo Community/Farm Watch states that it tries to be inclusive of the rural community, black residents do not feel included in the structures; indeed, they see themselves as the targets of the increased security measures. One community member, commenting on the assaults, said:

> The Farm Watch is behind this. They think that they have more powers than the police. They use state weapon—R4s and 9mm guns used by the state. They go to the Creighton police station and get tear gas. The Farm Watch sometimes operate with the police and sometimes on their own. They wear jackets that are labeled police. I don't know whether they are a cult. Some people from our community are also involved. There is a certain man—the Farm Watch and farmers visit him at different times. He is alleged to be involved in weapon-smuggling activities. Why are they targeting this community? ... The police take advantage of the people because they know the people are not educated. When we're being harassed by the police and Farm Watch no one cares. When it is them killing us, no one cares. When it is them being killed everyone gives out statistics. All the stories are about the number of farmers being killed. No one cares about the people who are being killed by Farm Watch.[710]

---

[709] Interview conducted by Cheryl Goodenough, Durban, November 10, 2000.
[710] Interview conducted by Cheryl Goodenough with member of the Creighton community, Creighton, September 6, 2000.

CONCLUSION

An Evaluation of the Rural Protection Plan

> *On the face of it, there is a large area of common interest between workers and farmers with regard to the prevention of crime. Farmers complain of the encroachment of predatory strangers on their land. Given high rates of stock theft, it would appear that workers also have a powerful interest in detecting and reporting the presence of strangers on farms. There can be little doubt that the recruitment of workers into the rural protection plan can significantly enhance its capacity. Its informational capacity, and in particular, the efficacy of its early warning systems, appear to suffer from lack of worker participation.*
>
> *Bringing workers into the rural protection plan, however, is fraught with difficulty. A farmer is unlikely to accept the presence in the plan of a workforce he believes is harbouring families who do not provide labour, and perhaps commit intermittent cattle theft. A working family, in turn, that believes it could face eviction at any moment, is unlikely to be a reliable source of information where the farmer's interests are at stake.*[711]

There is a clear need for a comprehensive evaluation of the rural protection plan, from the perspective not only of the commercial farming community but also of farm residents and those living in the former homeland areas that surround commercial farmland. At present, the rural protection plan does not adequately meet the needs of farmers for protection, and it has actually increased insecurity for other sectors of the population in some areas. It still shows clearly its origins as a response to demands for action by the commercial farming sector, a response which did not ensure that the plan addressed the concerns of the entire rural population, white and black, men and women, for protection against violent crime.

The "farmwatch" systems and the use of commandos and private security to protect farming communities has increased security for (mostly white) farm

---

[711] Schönteich and Steinberg, *Attacks on farms and smallholdings*, pp.50-51.

owners. Given the strains on police capacity, the participation in security systems of civilian reservists may be unavoidable. However, in too many cases, local commandos, "farmwatch" structures, or private security companies are simply acting to protect the interests of farmers and not the wider community. Abuses inevitably result, some of them very serious. Even when police officers patrol with the commandos, both state agents, there is little scope for accountability to or control by the wider community. If the police involved are reservists, there is still less control.

Many living or working in the farming communities believe that the commando system is an anachronism and a recipe for abuse, and that it should be abolished. Others, however, including many of those involved in the rural protection plan at national level, see the commandos as an essential part of the system, and the main reason for the high arrest rate in cases of violent crime against farm owners or managers, due to their rapid response capabilities. However, it is clear that at least some commando units are responsible for very serious abuses, and that training and controls are insufficient to ensure proper discipline.

In many areas, commando membership has declined in recent years. Among those who have left the state security forces are many who have set up private security companies. Others now participate in private non-profit farmwatch structures. These private farmwatch systems or private security companies are even less accountable than the commandos, reporting only to the farmwatch structures or the people paying them, who may have little commitment to disciplining those found guilty of abuse. The management of the Ixopo Community/Farm Watch, for example, took no disciplinary action against John Arkley for months, even after he was charged with murder. The regulation of private security companies is woefully inadequate. Although proposed new legislation will strengthen the regulatory regime, it could still be improved in several regards. There are currently no concrete proposals for legislation to regulate "farmwatch" or similar private non-profit initiatives.

The rural protection plan needs to be restructured to ensure that it meets the needs of all residents of the farming communities and addresses public concerns about the quality of police services. However, the answer is not to allow one powerful group to take on the role of the police and operate parallel, essentially unaccountable structures. What is needed is a protection plan that meets the needs of farm owners and far less powerful farm residents alike.

Human Rights Watch believes that in all cases other than emergencies, police and not soldiers should carry out policing duties. Accordingly, the commando units made up of army reservists should not be involved in policing. Civilians who wish to be involved in policing on a part time basis should be police reservists, and should receive training in policing skills and instruction on the laws of South Africa and respect for human rights, rather than army-style boot camp. Where soldiers are deployed for policing duties, they should not have full police powers, but only those that are required to fill a support role. For example, police should carry out duties such as house searches, even if soldiers are deployed to establish a cordon around the house. This objective should form part of the current review of the Defence Act.

There would be resistance to this idea among the commandos, for both good and bad reasons. Among the good reasons are the fact that commando members get paid a small amount which, though almost token for a commercial farmer (three to four hundred rands a month), assists to cover expenses and for black employees may form a substantial addition to income; police reservists receive no payment at all. In addition, those individuals who are both members of commandos and police reservists report that the army logistical and administrative systems are simply more efficient than those in the police service. As one commented, "I joined up to be a police reservist three years ago, and did all the courses, but I'm still waiting for my uniform today, I don't even have an ID card showing that I am a police officer. If you join the commandos, the whole system goes quicker."[712] Others note that discipline among the police is a big problem, so that many police have no pride in their job, absenteeism is rife, equipment is not maintained, and so forth, while the army has a stronger public service ethos. The bad reasons include the fact that the police service is now perceived by many white farmers as simply "too black" in its command structures.

Those in charge of implementing the rural protection plan should take urgent steps to implement a transition from military to civilian policing. Pending this transition, immediate steps should also be taken to bring part-time members of the security forces, as well as their full-time colleagues, under proper discipline and control. All those involved in policing areas must be required and trained to respond even-handedly to reported crimes, irrespective of the color or social status of the victim. Commando units carrying out policing duties should be accompanied by a full time police officer, preferably of middle or senior rank, not a reservist, who should be in command as regards all policing duties. The SANDF should urgently develop an effective internal mechanism for handling public complaints and to ensure proper disciplinary action against those who have allegedly committed abuses. In addition, the Independent Complaints Directorate (ICD), the body responsible for investigating complaints against the police, should

---

[712] Human Rights Watch interview with Arno Engelbrecht, farmer and commando member, Paulpietersburg, September 14, 2000.

be empowered to investigate or oversee the investigation of complaints against SANDF members deployed for policing purposes. The Departments of Justice and Safety and Security should take particular steps to ensure the effective prosecution of cases against individual farmers, private security operatives, or vigilante groups, for example by deploying detectives and prosecutors from outside the area, who would be less susceptible to pressure from powerful local interests, to follow these cases. There should be exemplary prosecutions where particular commando units, farmwatch schemes or private security companies have a reputation for abuse, ideally carried out by the National Directorate of Public Prosecutions (NDPP).

Stricter controls should also be enforced against private security initiatives, including farmwatch and similar private schemes, to ensure that they do not act as vigilante groups. Government should introduce legislation to regulate such schemes, and work with representatives of commercial farmers and other interested parties to develop a code of conduct for those who participate in them. Private security companies and farmwatch structures should be permitted only to carry out preventive patrols and "citizen's arrests" of persons actually found in the course of committing a crime. They should be required to hand individuals arrested to the police without delay, and they should be prohibited from taking the initiative in conducting house searches for illegal weapons or similar activities, but required rather to pass relevant information to the police. Laws regulating the private security industry should strengthen the provisions relating to the withdrawal of registration for security service providers found guilty of a violent crime or of improper conduct of a serious nature; and should require the police and courts to report to the regulatory authority alleged crimes, charges, and convictions involving security service providers.

The government should consider merging the structures of the rural protection plan—in particular the Groundlevel Operational Coordinating Committees—with the community policing forums. Under the current system, both sets of meetings are poorly attended, while the rural protection plan is often seen as being for the farmers, and the CPFs for the black community. The new structures should involve representatives of farm owners, NGOs working on land or farmworkers' rights issues, and farm owners. They should also involve women and organizations assisting women, to ensure that issues related to violence against women are addressed. Those attending these meetings need to see results, since in too many rural areas community representatives have stopped attending CPFs simply because they find there is no response from the police, or indeed it is the police themselves who are involved in crime. If the powerful lobby of the farm owners attended the same meetings and put pressure on local police stations to attend to the problems of the black communities as well as their own, substantial progress in creating a common security initiative could be achieved. In the Western Cape, a new structure known as a "community safety forum" (CSF) is being piloted in several areas. The CSFs are chaired by local government, and involve all government sectors—not only the police—in efforts to combat crime. These pilot projects may form a useful model for policing in the commercial farming areas. Trained facilitators may be needed to keep the new structures on track, in order to build trust between different participants and ensure that they actually become a route for ensuring a greater consensus in setting policing priorities.

The government should also review the collection of statistics relating to violence on farms. Currently, official statistics tend to give greater prominence to crime against farm owners and managers, whereas the real need is for accurate statistics on *all* violent crime on farms, including assaults on farm residents by other farm residents and by farm owners or managers. Specific crime codes should be established, including, for example, for murders or assaults on farm owners or managers, murders or assaults on farmworkers or residents (including sexual assaults in all cases), and for illegal evictions. A parallel effort to ensure that all reported incidents are correctly recorded by police will be necessary. Human Rights Watch also believes that it is important that the figures for "farms" and "smallholdings" be disaggregated.

Some formal proposals for a more comprehensive rural safety plan have been made. The Department of Land Affairs in the Free State developed a proposal in 1998—in advance of the national rural safety summit—for "participatory rural safety plans," which was extensively debated among interested parties, but was eventually dropped due to resistance from the Free State Agricultural Union.[713] The proposal placed "farm attacks" firmly within "the underlying socio-political context" of the apartheid past and the continuing massive inequalities of power present in farming communities today, urging farmers to work in cooperation with other rural dwellers. It argued that "the premise on which [existing] safety plans and farmwatch schemes are based is fundamentally flawed," because "emergency reactionary measures will only serve to isolate and marginalize communities." Accordingly the department recommended that:

---

[713] Ruarí Ó Conchúir, "Participatory Rural Safety Plans to Counter Farm Attacks in the Free State Province," Briefing Document for the Department of Safety and Security, Free State (undated); Human Rights Watch telephone interview with Ruarí Ó Conchúir, who is now with the NGO Farm Africa, October 11, 2000.

Farmwatch groups must constitute part of a greater Rural Safety Plan, where area based partnerships are established as joint ventures between the farmers, farmworkers, commandos, the local police and the district policing forum. They must be assisted by district based Rural Safety Networks which should include the following role players:

Dept. of Safety and Security, SA Police Service, Local Police Reserve Service, SANDF, Local Commando, DLA District Office and field staff, Local Magistrates Office, Local Municipality—TRC/TLC, District Farmers Association/Agricultural Union, Church Bodies, Farmworker Unions, NGOs, Advice Centres, Constituency Offices of all political parties.

The role of such a Rural Safety Network would be to ensure that contact between the farmers/farmworkers and the local police could be improved through training and planning.... Such area based Rural Safety Networks would be supported administratively and logistically by a Provincial Rural Safety Network Committee, with a specialised safety person located in the office of the MEC Safety and Security.[714]

Concluding that "Properly managed rural safety plans in which farm dwellers are valued and play a central role need to be developed across the country," the document proposed standard procedures to respond to "farm attacks."

Less ambitiously, Mike de Lange, a farmer who has monitored violence on farms for several years, has put forward a proposal to the KwaZulu-Natal government for a "security desk" to be established (effectively a funded and expanded version of what de Lange already operates from his farmhouse) to "gather intelligence on all crime incidents and information on pending possible conflict, of any sort, in rural KwaZulu/Natal communities (farms, tribal areas and conservation areas)."[715] The security desk would then convey that information to all appropriate authorities, including administrative structures as well as the security forces, and facilitate proper communication between those authorities as

---

[714] Ibid. TRC/TLC stands for Transitional Regional Council or Transitional Local Council, structures that have now been superseded by new municipal authorities. The MEC is the Member of the Executive Council, the provincial "minister" for policing, in this case.

[715] "The Desk," ten point summary proposal handed to Human Rights Watch, September 14, 2000.

well as the extension of the rural protection plan to those areas where it is not currently operational—that is, the "tribal areas" formerly within the KwaZulu homeland. De Lange believes that "99 percent of the black community is sick and tired of crime too. The rural protection plan won't work unless you include the tribal areas; you need structures for the rural areas to get their problems solved too."[716]

Key to the resolution of the problems surrounding law enforcement in South Africa's commercial farming areas will be the creation of a common understanding among farm owners and farm residents of the priorities in relation to violent crime and the response needed. This will, however, depend on farm owners and residents seeing themselves as having the same interests in this regard, something that will be very difficult to develop in the context of South Africa's deeply divided society. Ultimately, it will depend on a reduction in the stark economic inequalities so obvious in the South African countryside.

Class, Race, Gender, and Violence on Farms

> *The Special Rapporteur is absolutely convinced that without a complete overhauling of the [South African] criminal justice apparatus, the retraining of its members and the creation of a more representative service, violence in general, and violence against women in particular, will never be contained.*[717]

In South Africa, the heritage of apartheid and legislated segregation remain potent factors, and racial discrimination in the criminal justice system, as elsewhere in society, is a serious concern.[718] Although South Africa has a wide array of criminal laws that are today ostensibly race-neutral (by comparison with the apartheid era laws that criminalized certain activities for blacks only), de facto discriminatory law enforcement practices continue to be a chronic problem. South

---

[716] Human Rights Watch interview with Mike de Lange, formerly KWANALU security desk, Eshowe, September 14, 2000.

[717] "Report of the Special Rapporteur on violence against women, its causes and consequences, Ms. Radhika Coomaraswamy, Addendum, Report on the mission of the Special Rapporteur to South Africa on the issues of rape in the community," U.N. Document E/CN.4/1997/47/Add.3.

[718] For an overview discussion on racial discrimination and related intolerance, see Human Rights Watch, *World Report 2001* (New York: Human Rights Watch, December 2000), pp. 500-508.

Africa's criminal justice system is, as was noted in a 1997 report by the United Nations special rapporteur on violence against women, a product of the system of racial and political oppression operated by former governments. It is also a reflection of a society which, like many others, has historically treated women as second-class citizens.[719]

Consequently, while it is true that the criminal justice system is currently under severe strain due to the country's high crime rate, the state response to violent crime on farms cannot be viewed only in the context of South Africa being generally a violent country. Those living on farms in South Africa are not a homogeneous group. They are divided by their race, gender, socio-economic status, age, and other characteristics. These factors operate individually or in combination to differentiate farm owners and residents—whether workers or tenants—from one another and determine, among other things, their access or lack of access to justice when they are victims of abuse. As this report shows, the criminal justice process continues to give more favorable treatment to whites than blacks. At the same time, race and gender often converge to make black women among the most powerless in society. In such situations, rates of violence against poor black women remain particularly high and largely unremedied.[720]

Because white farm owners have historically had a close relationship to state institutions, including the police and justice system, and continue in many areas to do so, and because they are economically much more powerful than their black neighbors, they continue to have a privileged relationship to the system. White farm owners and white members of the security forces in the rural areas (sometimes the same people), socialize together and often have family links. It is unlikely, as demonstrated by this report, that those same security force members will act swiftly against one of their own, and probable that they will believe the word of another white person over that of a black farm resident. Even where black police officers have been promoted to become station commissioners, the economic reality of rural life remains much as it has always been, and acting against locally powerful figures a potentially dangerous activity. Moreover, a police officer is

---

[719] See Human Rights Watch, *Violence Against Women in South Africa* (New York: Human Rights Watch, November 1995), Human Rights Watch, "South Africa: Violence Against Women and the Medico-Legal System" (1997), and Human Rights Watch *Scared at School*, (2001).

[720] United Nations Development Fund for Women (UNIFEM) Background Paper: "Integrating Gender into the Third World Conference against Racism, Racial Discrimination, Xenophobia and Related Intolerance" (New York: UNIFEM, 2000), available at <http://www.unifem.undp.org/> accessed February 10, 2001.

likely to need the cooperation of white farmers in so many aspects of his or her work—including in some cases the loan of vehicles—that it is easier to turn a blind eye to abuse than to act against it. For the same reasons, complaints by farm owners of criminal activity affecting them usually receive priority attention.

Continuing racism, racial discrimination, and racial tension combine with gender discrimination to establish complex patterns of dominance and oppression of black women. While violence against women of all races was historically tolerated in South Africa, as in many other societies, by law and custom, violence against black women (whether committed by white or black men) was especially ignored. Under apartheid laws and practices, "Violence against women was perceived as violence against white women, implicit in that the violence was undertaken by black men. As a result, instances of black men raping white women received greater attention and were treated with severity and racist intolerance by the state. One of the consequences was that, for example, far more black men have been hanged for raping white women in South Africa, than have white men been hanged for raping black women."[721]

Even in post-apartheid South Africa, racist and sexist attitudes continue to flourish when it comes to the state's response to violence against black women. All the elements that traditionally put women at a disadvantage—poverty, poor housing, poor health services, a lack of safety and security, poor education, and lack of information—exist on the farms and often compound women's vulnerability to abuse.[722] In addition to all these risk factors, the sole gatekeepers to women's safety on farms are often their employers and male relatives, often the very people who abuse them. Women are not inclined to report such cases out of fear of retaliation from farm owners, managers, and family members. When women report these abuses, local authorities often do not take their accounts seriously.

The discrimination that black people and women face in their workplaces is directly linked to the daily violence they experience. For example, the acute power imbalance on farms between farm owners and farmworkers and men and

---

[721] Vetten, "Paper Promises, Protests and Petitions" in Park et al (eds.), *Reclaiming Women's Spaces*, p.85. For more on the debate about the intersection between race and gender, *see* Human Rights Watch, *Unequal Protection, Unequal Treatment: Domestic and Maquiladora Workers In Guatemala* (New York: Human Rights Watch, forthcoming 2001); Human Rights Watch, *World Report 2001* (New York: Human Rights Watch, December 2000), pp. 500-508; and UNIFEM, "Integrating Gender into the Third World Conference against Racism, Racial Discrimination, Xenophobia and Related Intolerance."
[722] Vetten, "Gender, Race, and Power Dynamics in the Face of Social Change," in Park et al, *Reclaiming Women's Spaces*, p.60.

women all work to the disadvantage of women. The relationships are divided on racial and patriarchal lines, with women placed near the bottom of the ladder and subjected to violence and abuse by the rest.[723] As one example of the way in which discrimination can lead to violence, some women living and working on the wine farms in the Western Cape complained to Human Rights Watch that they did not receive monetary support from their husbands, whose pay is spent on buying wine.[724] When they complain to their husbands, women are often beaten; because their housing is dependent on their husbands, they cannot leave or take any action to protect themselves.[725] When women on farms are raped, whether by farm owners or by other farm residents, they face barriers when they seek protection that are common to other farm residents but compounded by sexist attitudes within the criminal justice system. And while gender discrimination generally affects all women, white women, because of their race and economic position, fare much better in accessing justice when they become victims of violence, compared to their black counterparts.[726]

Leaving aside issues of racial or sexual prejudice, commercial farms are often remote from urban centers and from the routes covered by "black taxis," the privately-owned minibus taxis used by most black people in South Africa for transportation. Farmworkers and residents are therefore often dependent on the goodwill of the farm owner or occasional visitors for transportation. As a consequence, it is very difficult for them to access police, courts, government medical officers and other services, such as victim support programs, when they are victims of violence, since most of these services are based in towns. Lack of education, a heritage of the years of "bantu education" policies under the previous government and current confusion over the status of farm schools, is a further

---

[723] Human Rights Watch interview, Alida van der Merwe, director, Woman on Farms Project, Stellenbosch, April 13, 2000.

[724] Human Rights Watch interview, group of women farmworkers, Western Cape, April 13, 2000.

[725] Human Rights Watch interview, Rita Edwards, director, Woman on Farms Project, Stellenbosch, April 13, 2000.

[726] See Vetten, "Gender, Race, and Power Dynamics in the Face of Social Change," in Park et al, *Reclaiming Women's Spaces*, p.60. Although Human Rights Watch has carried out research on sexual violence against women of all races in South Africa in the past (see Human Rights Watch, *Violence Against Women in South Africa*, 1995; "South Africa: Violence Against Women and the Medico-Legal System," 1997; and *Scared at School*, 2001), we did not specifically examine the response of the criminal justice system to violence against white women in this report.

barrier to obtaining assistance. Often the intervention of an intermediary, such as an NGO worker, is necessary to gain entry to the system. Lack of education also means that farm residents are often unaware or only vaguely aware of their rights under South African law. Farm owners, on the other hand, almost universally own private cars, or at worst have easy access to others who would offer transportation; are comfortable demanding a response from the relevant authorities; have the literacy skills to fill out statements or take action if there is no follow-up response to their complaint; and are kept up-to-date about their rights under the law through newsletters and magazines distributed by the agricultural unions.

The ANC-led government in office since 1994 has made significant efforts to overcome the inheritance of the past as it affects commercial farming areas. New laws provide legal protections giving a measure of security of tenure to farm residents, and accord farmworkers the full range of labor rights available to other South Africans (themselves extended). But despite these legal strides, implementation of and accessibility to the rights they protect remains very difficult for farm residents in the face of the realities of farm life. Meanwhile, many farm owners feel that the labor market has become over-regulated, and do not see why, in a business context, farm residents who are not working for them should have any security of tenure or other rights to the land. Forcible eviction of farm residents continues, despite the law, while farmers have cut the number of permanently employed farmworkers and increased the use of seasonal and migrant workers, more easily exploitable groups, as a proportion of the workforce.

The consequence of the combined effect of racial and gender discrimination within the South African criminal justice system is that both male and female black farm residents are disadvantaged by comparison with white farm owners in obtaining a response to their complaints of abuse. At the same time, the additional economic resources that white farm owners have enables them to organize to compensate for the deficiencies of the criminal justice system in responding to violent crime. While some such efforts make a useful contribution to rural security, in too many cases these self-help mechanisms have become little more than vigilante groups acting on behalf of white interests only, despite the race-neutral language used to describe their activities. Though violent crime against farm owners is a serious and relatively new phenomenon, deserving of an effective state response, it should not dominate discussion of policing priorities in farming areas to the exclusion of other forms of violent crime.

By failing to ensure that police and court officials investigate, prosecute, and punish perpetrators of murder, rape and other physical assaults against black South Africans on equal terms with whites, women on equal terms with men, foreign migrants on equal terms with citizens, South Africa fails to comply with its international law obligations to provide equal protection to all under the law. The South African government is also obliged to ensure that black people and women of all races do not suffer race and gender-based discrimination in the workplace and to remedy such discrimination whenever and wherever it occurs.[727] Assuring nondiscrimination entails, at a minimum, promulgating and enforcing legislation that prohibits such discrimination. South Africa has made great progress in accomplishing this goal. But passing legislation is not enough. The laws must be enforced. Firm steps must be taken to ensure that all South Africans, regardless of race or gender, are protected from violence and other abuse.

---

[727] For a detailed discussion on governments' responsibility to remedy sex-based discrimination, see also Human Rights Watch, "A Job or Your Rights: Continued Sex Discrimination in Mexico's Maquiladora Sector," *A Human Rights Watch Short Report,* (New York: Human Rights Watch, December 1998), vol. 10, no. 1(B).